at six

PHYSICAL DEVELOPMENT

Growth proceeding more slowly; a lengthening out.

Large muscles better developed than small ones.

Eyes not yet mature; tendency toward farsightedness.

Permanent teeth begin to appear.

Heart is in period of rapid growth.

CHARACTERISTIC REACTIONS

Eager to learn, exuberant, restless, overactive and easily fatigued.

Self-assertive; aggressive; wants to be first; less cooperative than at five; keen competition and much boasting.

Whole body is involved in whatever he does.

Learns best through active participation.

Inconsistent in level of maturity evidenced —regresses when tired; often less mature at home than with outsiders.

Inept at activities using small muscles.

Relatively short periods of interest.

Has difficulty making decisions.

Group activities popular; boys' and girls' interests beginning to differ.

Much spontaneous dramatization.

SPECIAL NEEDS

Encouragement, ample praise, warmth, and great patience from adults.

Ample opportunity for activity of many kinds, especially for use of large muscles.

Wise supervision with a minimum of interference.

Concrete learning situations and active, direct participation.

Some responsibilities, though without pressure, and without his being required to make decisions and choices or achieve rigidly set standards.

at seven

PHYSICAL DEVELOPMENT

Growth slow and steady.

Losing teeth; most sevens have their six-year molars.

Better eye-hand coordination.

Better use of small muscles.

Eyes not yet ready for much near work.

CHARACTERISTIC REACTIONS

Sensitive to feelings and attitudes of both peers and adults; especially dependent on approval of adults.

Interests of boys and girls diverging; less play together.

Full of energy but easily tired; restless and fidgety; often dreamy and absorbed.

Very little abstract thinking yet; seven learns best in concrete terms and where he can be active while learning.

Cautious and self-critical; anxious to do things well; likes to use hands.

Talkative, exaggerates; may fight with words instead of blows; highly competitive.

Enjoys songs, rhythms, fairy tales, myths, nature stories, comics, radio, movies.

Able to assume some responsibility; concerned about right and wrong, though often prone to take small things.

Rudimentary understanding of time and money values.

SPECIAL NEEDS

The right combination of independence and encouraging support.

Chances for active participation in learning situations with concrete objects.

Must make adjustment to rougher ways of playground; needs adult help to do this without becoming too crude or rough.

Warm, encouraging, friendly relationship with adults.

(For age eight into adolescence, see end sheets at back)

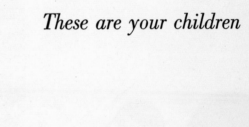

These are your children

These
are your
children

HOW THEY DEVELOP AND HOW TO GUIDE THEM

GLADYS GARDNER JENKINS, *Staff Lecturer, Association for Family Living*

HELEN SHACTER, PH.D., *Consulting Psychologist, and Lecturer in Psychology, Northwestern University*

WILLIAM W. BAUER, M.D., *Director, Bureau of Health Education, American Medical Association*

Scott, Foresman and Company

CHICAGO, ATLANTA, DALLAS, NEW YORK

Contents

Preface

THESE ARE YOUR CHILDREN. These are the actual boys and girls who are growing up and learning, adjusting well or not so well in your home, your block, your school. These are the individual youngsters who—through the guidance of all of us working together—we hope will become healthy and happy adults, for their own sakes and for the sake of a better America tomorrow.

No two of these children are alike. Basically, of course, they are all alike; all have the same fundamental needs, motivations, and drives. Yet no two children have them in the same proportion or in the same form. For each child is an individual.

As parents and teachers, present or potential, we have come more and more to realize how great must be our individual concern with the development and adjustment of these our children. And this development and adjustment, we now see, must be physical, mental, and emotional in even measures. The individual child is indeed a whole child living in a particular time and place and having to learn how to get along with other individuals.

Encouraging as our progress with children has been, a large number of them still grow up in homes that can't, or at least don't, give them proper food, love, and attention, and in schools that sometimes neglect their physical and emotional development for concern with mere subject matter. As a result, we have the sad spectacle of millions of young people unacceptable for service to their country in a time of need, and untold cases of individual unhappiness brought about by improper adjustment of one kind or another. That other millions *do* grow up to achieve reasonable health and happiness, service and fulfillment, only shows us the potential and should not blind us to the fact that as parents and teachers we should

6

be bringing a new approach and emphasis to the human beings in our charge.

These Are Your Children is designed to help point the way to this new approach and emphasis. This book offers to parent and teacher an easily understood and yet thoroughly scientific interpretation of what children really are like—their physical, mental, social, and emotional growth as it unfolds in various typical American environments. It sets no dividing line between mind and body; the child is recognized as an individual entity with many varied and sometimes troublesome relationships with other similar (but never identical) entities in his group. This interplay among children, and between children and adults, the contacts they make, the sparks they frequently strike constitute their preparation for living—education in the fullest sense.

This book provides, first of all, *descriptions of the characteristics of children of various ages*, "physical-psychological portraits" of the kindergartner, the six-year-old, the seven-year-old, the eight-year-old, the nine-year-old, and the preadolescent.

Accompanying these is a *series of carefully developed case studies* which detail the varia-tions of individual but reasonably typical children, well adjusted and poorly adjusted. Thus there is presented first the overall picture at a given age level and then how it is exemplified in particular children.

The final chapters cover *the growth of knowledge and attitudes concerning sex, suggestions for everyday relationships with children* (with special attention to the problems of teachers, but affording parents an understanding of what the school can and should be doing for children, as well as providing many suggestions equally applicable to personal relationships within the home), and finally, a *plan for action*, to help teachers and parents prepare their children for useful, happy lives.

At the end of the book are two features designed to implement its use in various situations—a guide for studying and applying the principles developed in each chapter, and materials for further investigation—an annotated list of books, pamphlets, and films to extend and enrich the text.

THREE fundamental points of view lie back of the theory and practice put forth in *These Are Your Children:*

First, *an effort has been made to show the infinite variation upon a basic sameness that is found in all our children.* Although for convenience the descriptions are tagged with age levels and applied to age groups, there is a constant reminder throughout, and particularly in the case studies, that each child is different in at least some degree in his own pattern and rate of growth, and in his reactions.

Secondly, *emphasis is placed upon the fact that growth is a continuous process.* Progress, we now know, is not made abruptly as a child passes from year to year or from one grade to another. Even the alternation of growth spurts and plateaus, while often marked and noticeable, is not abrupt, one stage usually fading almost imperceptibly into the next.

Finally, *the tremendous influence of a child's first years is stressed.* We see more and more that we cannot use the first year of school as a starting point if we are to understand a child well and guide him wisely: we must go back to the day of birth, and even beyond that into the background of the home and of the parents. We need to remember that a baby is born with certain capacities for growth. How he will use these capacities is determined by his reactions to the things which happen to him as he grows up, especially to those experiences which he has during his first five years. Personality is not static. The child will not necessarily remain within the pattern of reactions which he has developed by the age of five, but these reactions are very potent in determining within measure how he will react as he grows older.

A child will come to the schoolroom prepared to cooperate if his early growth has been within the shelter of an affectionate home environment, in which his parents have given to him consistent patterns of desirable behavior and opportunities to practice them. He will be able to take those steps away from the home which make it possible for him to adjust to the demands of the schoolroom, to relate himself to his group, and to develop normally as a member of the group. Such a child has a better chance for a good school adjustment than the child who has come from a home in which he has felt strain and anxiety, has questioned his parents' love or interest in him, or has felt rejected by his parents.

All these factors must be explored. To the busy teacher and absorbed parent it may seem to be asking too much to call for such extensive investigation and objectivity. Indeed it may not be wholly possible to achieve them. But if there is a recognition of the importance of the years of early childhood in the possible development of the boys and girls under their guidance, parents and teachers will know where to look for the beginnings of those anxieties, character traits, or patterns of behavior which are blocking the growth of an individual child.

These Are Your Children, then, is a new kind of book on child development for both teachers and parents, present and prospective. It has been designed to lend itself to systematic study, as in college courses, or to individual reading, as in the case of teachers, administrators, and parents working more or less separately. In all the uses to which it may be applied, we hope that this synthesis of the current exciting research and reports in the field of child development will be a distinct contribution—a fresh and helpful guide to everyone faced with the responsibility of guiding the physical, mental, emotional, and social development of our boys and girls at home, in school, and at play—in all of their varied relationships.

WILLIAM W. BAUER

8

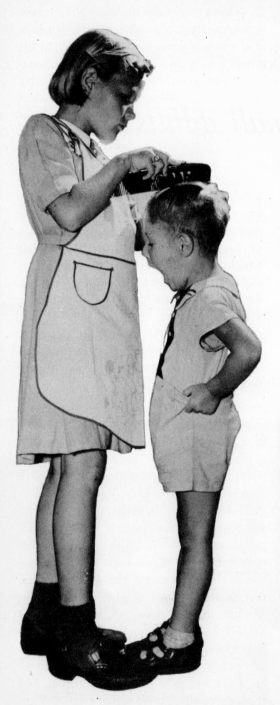

Acknowledgments

The authors and publishers wish to express appreciation for the extremely helpful cooperation of the personnel in the schools where pictures were taken especially for *These Are Your Children.*

J. C. Allen and Son, Century Photos, Inc.: 23 (lower right and upper right), 68 (upper right), 80, 81, 83 (upper right), 85, 101, 132, 133, 136

Harriet Arnold, *Pix:* 43 (upper right), 115, 165; and 45 (upper right), 63 (upper right), 119 by courtesy of *Parents' Magazine*

Baby-Craft Photographers of Chicago: 4

Thomas Bannwart: 11, 15, 16, 104, 105

E. Don Burkhart: 20. Hawthorne School, Sioux Falls, South Dakota

Chicago Park District: 46, 48, 50

Child Education Foundation: 22, 23, 30 (upper left), 145. Children's Home School, New York City

Jerry Cooke, *Pix:* 3, 44 (center right), 47, 102, 114

Devaney, Inc., N. Y.: 103, 129

Fromader Photographing Service: 147 (lower right). Jefferson School, Davenport, Iowa

Irene Elster: 2 (left), 18, 19 (upper right), 21 (lower left), 24 (upper left and lower left), 25 (lower right), 26, 27 (upper two), 29 (upper left), 30 (upper right), 62, 64 (upper left), 65 (lower left and lower right), 66, 67 (upper right), 68 (lower left), 69 (upper right), 71, 72, 82 (upper left and lower right), 83 (lower left and lower right), 84, 86, 87, 97, 100. Kindergarten pictures by Miss Elster were taken at public schools of Winnetka, Illinois

Nina Leen, *Pix:* 19 (lower left), 45 (lower left)

Life Photographer Herbert Gehr. © *Time,* Inc.: 14

Carl Mansfield, Reprinted from September, 1948, *Coronet,* © 1948 by Esquire, Inc.: 12

Judd Studios: 158, 163, 169. Columbus Avenue School, Freeport, Long Island, New York

Rae Russel, *Pix:* 13, 17, 38, 117, 148, 150, 156, 167

Gladys Relyea, *Pix:* 70, 114 (upper left), 137

Leo Rosenthal, *Pix:* 65 (upper right)

MacHenry Schafer: 25 (lower left)

Press Syndicate: 2 (right), 6, 82 (lower left), 96, 98, 99, 131, 134, 139

Herb Qualset: 25 (upper right), 30 (center right). Mark Twain School, Sioux Falls, South Dakota

Rosser Studio: 140, 141, 146 (both), 147 (all but lower right), 159. Markham School, Mount Lebanon, Pennsylvania

T. H. Rivers: 143, 144, 153, 155, 160. Sioux City Public Schools, Iowa

John Sanderson: 5, 7, 10, 21 (upper right), 27 (lower three), 28 (all but bottom), 29 (all but upper left), 30 (lower two), 39-42, 43 (lower right), 44 (upper two, lower right), 45 (center and lower right), 49, 51-54, 63 (lower left), 64 (lower left), 67 (upper left), 69 (lower right), 88, 89, 112, 113, 116, 118, 120, 121, 135, 166, 171, 174. Kindergarten pictures by Mr. Sanderson were taken at the William Beye School, Oak Park, Illinois

CHAPTER ONE

Children are not small adults

CHILDREN are not small adults. They do not think, feel, or react as grown-up people do. Physically, mentally, and emotionally each child is a growing, changing person with needs and potentialities which are his alone.

Often the child who is difficult, whose behavior is not desirable, who is labeled "naughty" or "badly behaved," is only a child who has not been understood by the adults about him. Sometimes they have pushed him too hard and expected too much from him; sometimes they have not known enough about boys and girls to realize that he is acting like other children of his age, that he is not deliberately naughty, but is having "growing pains" and trying to assert himself as a person. The first responsibility of parents and teachers who sincerely want to help a child grow to his fullest capacity is to try to understand all children's needs and patterns of growth, and particularly those of their own children.

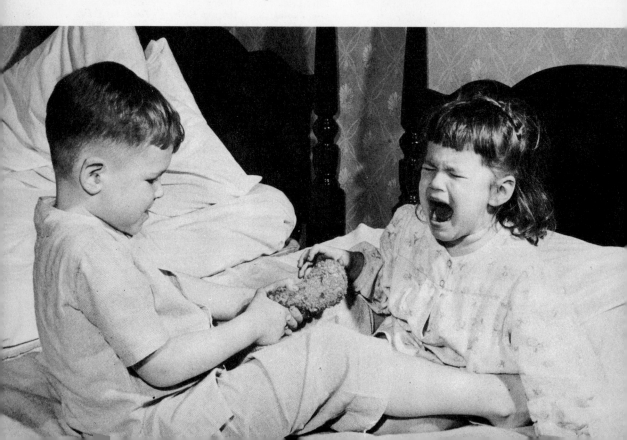

Sometimes we think of a newborn baby as a completed individual, as though all he has to do is grow up. This is not so. A baby brings with him the potentialities for completed development, but at birth even his heart, lungs, and digestive tract do not function as they will when he is older. The nerves, which are the pathways from his brain to his muscles and the contact for sense impressions from the outside world, are not yet completed in their development. The skeletal development of the child is different from that of the adult. He has to do much growing and continued developing before he becomes a "grown-up."

At each stage, the behavior of a child is directly influenced by his physical development. The active fifteen-month-old child who touches, feels, and puts in his mouth everything about him is responding to a growth need, not just being a nuisance and "in to everything." The restless six-year-old finds it difficult to sit still because of his tremendous drive toward activity.

11

The child who is passing through the growth spurt of preadolescence may be awkward and trip or drop things, not from carelessness, but because of the uneven growth of his body. We need to know the general stages of development through which our children are passing if we are to understand their behavior.

IT IS ESSENTIAL also to know the individual child, to understand his heritage, his potentialities, and his own particular pattern of growth. Although normal children are essentially similar in their sequence of growth, no two children, even in the same family, are alike in the way in which they pass through this sequence. Some meet life with eagerness, head on; others are more phlegmatic, less easily excited. Some are easily guided from birth; others seem full of an independent aggressiveness from an early age. Some have great vigor and vitality; others seem to have less stamina, less ability to meet whatever comes. It is difficult to distinguish between environmental factors and tendencies with which the child was born, but whatever their source, there are sharp individual differences in make-up which cannot be overlooked.

Within the range of "normal" some children will develop physically much more rapidly than others, some much more slowly. Yet in the total progress of growth each child will reach normal adulthood. In every

group there will be some children ahead
of the others of their age physically, mentally, and emotionally, and some who are
behind in one or all aspects of development. It is important in understanding the
√ child to know the individual rate of development—is this child a fast-maturing child or
a slow one? The faster-maturing child may
need opportunities to go ahead of his age
group. The slower one may need to be
watched for fear he will be pushed too hard
or overstimulated in an effort to keep him
with the majority of his age group. We are
usually aware of the need for the mentally
retarded child to be allowed to take things
at a different pace from his age group. We
are not always so keenly aware of such
special needs among children in the normal
group who merely mature slowly.

Nor do children always grow evenly in
all aspects of their development. Some
children seem to grow more smoothly than
others, so that at any given age they are
mentally, emotionally, and physically at an
equal level. There are indications that these
children may have less difficulty in growing up and show fewer behavior problems
than those who grow rapidly in one area
and more slowly in another. A child may
develop rapidly mentally so that he seems
ahead of his actual age group, but at the
same time may be immature in his social
growth. It would not be fair to judge such
a child by one area in which he is advanced,
and scold him for not living up to the
same level in all his activity. We must know
all sides of a child's development if we are
to understand him and meet his needs.

Growth does not always go smoothly
ahead. It is always continuous, but it is
not always steady. Sometimes there will be
weeks or even months during which the
child seems to stand still in his development. At other times the child may even

seem to go backwards; he may not seem
as independent today as he did last month.
Sometimes these slowing-up periods come
before a new spurt in growth. There is a
pause in growth, for instance, before the
growth spurt which marks the beginning of
the adolescent period. In order to get a
true picture of the growth of the child we
should not look at the immediate present,
comparing this week with last week, or
today with yesterday, but take the long
view—look back six months or a year or
two years and observe the growth which
has steadily taken place. The nine-year-old
may baffle adults with his bad language and
his untidy appearance, but he knows more
about truthfulness and honesty than he did
at six or even seven; he is more cooperative
in his work and play, and he is more
self-reliant.

Numerous clinics and research centers
have contributed to our understanding of the normal stages of child development. One of the best known is at Yale,

sectional" studies involve comparing and studying large groups of children and isolating those characteristics which seem to appear almost always at certain age levels. The "longitudinal" studies are those which follow individual children over a period of years, so that their patterns of growth are charted, and certain patterns of growth are observed. Both types of study have made valuable contributions to our understanding and knowledge.

Another approach to the understanding of children's development and problems is that of the psychiatrists, clinical psychologists, and social workers. They are concerned not so much with what behavior to expect as with why these reactions occur, and why growth is sometimes slowed up in a child, not from any factors in his own make-up, but from environmental causes. Thus they add to our understanding of both normal emotional growth patterns and unhealthy ones. They work both with children who have problems and with parents who need help in guiding their children.

From the many specialized workers in this field has come valuable information on how children feel, on their relationships with their parents, with brothers and sisters, with teachers, and with children of their own age. From case studies of individual children there has come to us a body of material more subjective and less easily measured than that which has come from the laboratories of child development, but of great importance in understanding the point of view and the reactions of our boys and girls. This material has been gathered through interviews between the worker and the child in which the child has been helped to talk of his feelings, his memories, and his reactions to the experiences of his life. From such revelations we have been given greater understanding of

under the leadership of Dr. Arnold Gesell. The insight and understanding which he has brought to us concerning developmental growth is both helpful and significant. His books *The Infant and Child in the Culture of Today* and *The Child from Five to Ten* are recommended to all thoughtful parents and teachers who would further their insight and understanding.

Among the other centers adding to our knowledge of children, their needs and their development, are the Institute of Child Welfare at the University of California; the Experimental School at the University of Michigan; the Child Welfare Research Station at the University of Iowa; the Institute of Child Welfare at the University of Minnesota; the Merrill Palmer School, Detroit; the Brush Foundation at Western Reserve University; and the Fels Foundation at Antioch College. Most of the studies which have been undertaken by these and other research centers follow two types of patterns: "cross-sectional" studies and "longitudinal" studies. "Cross-the basic needs of children and of the manner in which tensions and anxieties can temporarily block growth or distort it.

Among the outstanding child-guidance clinics of the country are the Judge Baker Foundation of Boston, which was established under the direction of William Healy; the Philadelphia Child Guidance Clinic, under Dr. Frederick Allen; and the Institute for Juvenile Research in Chicago, the first and oldest clinic of this type in the country. Dr. David Levy of New York and Anna Freud and Susan Isaacs of England have made significant individual contributions, as have Dr. C. A. Aldrich and Dr. Benjamin Spock of Mayo Clinics, and Dr. Fritz Redl of Wayne University.

We need both types of understanding— the one to give to us the general pattern of development and the individual variations within that pattern, and the other to help us understand the emotional life of the child and the interplay between this life and the growth process.

IF A CHILD'S growth seems to differ greatly from that of most children of his age, it is wise to pause and look for the reasons. Children cannot be made to grow, but growth can be encouraged by good physical and emotional care. Growth itself comes from an inner force and is inevitable. The child will grow in some measure and in some fashion whatever care is provided for him, but he may not fulfill his growth possibilities unless he receives adequate care. He will grow best if his home and school provide an environment of affection, in which he can feel that he belongs, that he is loved and needed. A child needs to feel that the adults about him like him and are interested in him. If this feeling is lacking and if the child feels unwanted or unloved, growth may be retarded.

The child needs good physical care, for we know that a fatigued child, a poorly nourished child, or a physically ill child cannot develop as fully as he might otherwise. Good food, fresh air, protection from disease, the correction of physical defects, plenty of exercise and outdoor play, balanced by relaxation and rest—all these are essential for the best development of a child's personality.

The child also needs opportunities to reach ahead, to take the next step, the right amount and kind of stimulation at the right time. He cannot learn either reading or independence until he has reached a stage in his growth at which he is ready to learn these things. If he is pushed ahead too soon, if too much is expected of him before he is ready, the discouragement may react against growth instead of helping it. On the other hand the child may be slowed up in his growth if his parents or teachers do not recognize when he has reached a point of readiness for the next step. If the child is

kept dependent when he has shown a desire to be independent, he may either rebel and take the independent step himself, or hold back and lose interest. The little child who reaches for his spoon shows a readiness to take a first step toward independence from Mother in feeding himself. If Mother will not give him the spoon because he is "messy" in using it, the child may later refuse to feed himself when Mother decides he is ready to do so. If a child is ready for the next step in arithmetic, and is kept back until the slowest member of the class is ready, he may lose interest in trying to take the next step, and fool away his time.

Growth is influenced by many environmental factors. Sometimes the child may be experiencing too much competition with older brothers or sisters, so that he is discouraged at the comparisons and ceases to try to compete. Sometimes there is a new baby in the family, and the child is feeling the burden of being the oldest or is feeling a bit less loved. Sometimes, by even well-meaning parents or teachers, he has been criticized and scolded for his mistakes and

failures, without enough balancing praise for his successes. If a child is tense, anxious, unhappy, out of harmony with his parents or his environment, his growth will not proceed as fully or as well as if he were emotionally secure and happy.

In the following sections we have tried to give to parents and teachers pictures of normal children as they grow from year to year and go from kindergarten through the elementary school. This is a guide to help you know what to expect of your children from year to year, what their needs will be, so that you may be ready to meet them. Through case studies we have attempted to suggest the variations within the pattern, the problems of the individual child, or the interactions between the child and others around him. We have tried to bring an awareness of the individual differences between children, differences in environment, background, endowment, and emotional needs. Alert teachers and parents will always keep the individual child foremost in their minds, seeing him against the background of the normal developmental picture. Sometimes if the child seems very far from this picture, both teachers and parents will feel the need to use the resources of their community or state to help the child adjust and work through his problems. We need to be aware that some problems are due to a particular phase of development and that others have a serious emotional basis. The nine-year-old boy who is noisy and untidy may just be trying to show his independence, to be like the other fellows; but the boy who is aggressive to the point of being unable to get along with other children, or the boy who withdraws into himself and cannot make friends, is in need of special help.

As a child enters kindergarten, then, we need to be aware that he is still growing, developing, and maturing and that as he changes from year to year, his needs and potentialities will change too. He is *not* merely an adult in miniature.

Much of the behavior that is typical of normal children is exasperating and irritating to adults. We object to the six-year-old's being quite so noisy and boisterous, and we wish he wouldn't fidget so. And when our preadolescent loses all the good habits of orderliness and cooperation that we have worked so hard to build up, we find it very discouraging. But if we can learn what may legitimately be expected, we will save ourselves and our children much unnecessary heartache and bewilderment. We will not make the mistake of regarding as wrong or abnormal, behavior that is perfectly normal for the child's age and level of development. If, in addition, we study the special needs and growth patterns of the individual child, we can help guide his development against the background of our knowledge of the whole sequence of growth. We cannot make children grow, but we can understand their growth needs and cooperate with growth.

17

CHAPTER TWO

Five

is a comfortable age

Pᴿᴼᴮᴬᴮᴸʏ at no period of life does a child accomplish as much as during the preschool years. When we look back over the years from two to five, we realize how far a child has come, how much he has learned and absorbed. As a toddler of two, he was barely beginning to talk; he had words but only a rare sentence. He could walk, but still fell down if he ran or tried to turn quickly. His parents had to take almost complete responsibility for his physical care. His concepts of good and bad did not yet exist. He did not relate himself to the past or future but lived in the immediate present. He had not even learned how to play with other children. He could not yet really cooperate or even share. He knew nothing about the world outside of his immediate environment; without Mother or some other responsible person he would have been utterly lost.

How different the five-year-old when he starts off for kindergarten. In three years he has developed a definite personality of his own. The kind of person he will be is beginning to show definitely, not only in his appearance but in his way of meeting situations, his approach to life. His speed of learning, his potentialities of intelligence, some of his special skills and talents are beginning to be noticeable. Those individual characteristics which make him different from everyone else are already evident.

He usually goes to kindergarten eagerly looking forward to the new experience. He may hold his Mother's hand tightly as he approaches the building the first day, but rarely does he try to turn back. Not only does he want to know what kindergarten is like, but he enjoys other children and wants to be with them. He is relating what he sees to his past experience and is anticipating the future. The five-year-old is no longer a baby, but a child who is ready to be away from home for two or three hours a day as an independent person.

✗The five-year-old youngster has entered a period of slow growth, very different from the rapid growth of the first eighteen months. If he is a boy, he will be between 37 and 45 inches in height and will usually weigh from 33 to 45 pounds. A girl will be from 36 to 44 inches in height and will

weigh from 31 to 42 pounds. The five-year-old may be expected to grow two or three inches during the year and to gain from three to six pounds in weight. Children vary greatly in the amount they gain, depending partly on the total body size.

✗Although boys are often slightly taller and heavier than girls during the years from five to ten, the girls are usually about a year ahead of the boys in their physiological development. The skeletal development of the five-year-old girl approximates that of the six-year-old boy. When puberty is reached, girls are about two years ahead of the boys physiologically and often socially too.

The five-year-old is beginning to have good control of his body; he can use it quite purposefully and skillfully. He can run and skip and dance; he can climb and jump. His body growth is not even. His legs are lengthening more rapidly than other parts of his body, but they are straight and firm. His posture may need watching. His

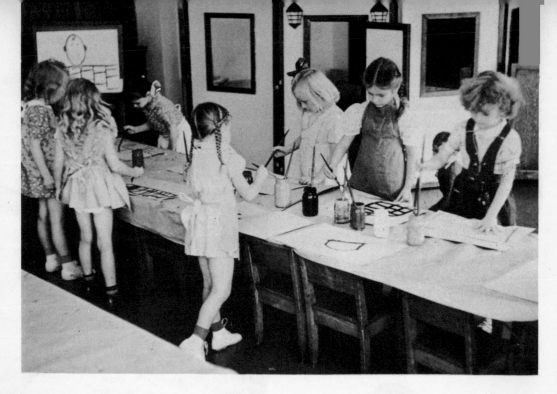

lungs are still relatively small, and his heart is growing rapidly. His large muscles are much better developed than those that control the fingers and the hands, so that he should still be encouraged in those activities which strengthen the large muscles of arms, legs, and trunk. He is not yet ready for such activities as writing. Painting with a large brush on a large surface is desirable; holding and manipulating a pencil and trying to make small letters might produce an undesirable strain.

Handedness is usually determined by the time the child is five and should not be changed. Ninety per cent of youngsters are right-handed. The left-handed child may need special help in learning to write.

The hand and eye do not yet work with complete coordination. The child may still have difficulty when he tries to reach for things beyond arm's length and may sometimes spill or knock them over. The eyeball is still growing in size. It will not be fully developed for several years. The kindergarten child is far-sighted and should not

be expected to spend much time looking closely at small things. If he reads, he should not be expected or encouraged to read print which is less than 24 point (24 point is roughly ⅜ inch in height). When he looks at picture books, care should be taken to develop in him the habit of sitting in a good light and of holding the book properly.

The five-year-old is an active child, but without the restlessness which he may have had at four. He responds to his growth needs by being noisy and vigorous, but his activity has definite direction. He is usually not just tearing around, but playing something or doing something. He runs and climbs, he shouts and jumps, and he enjoys games in which there is plenty of movement.

He needs equipment which gives him an opportunity for purposeful and planned activity—a tricycle which he will handle with skill and take much delight in, a wagon to pull or push or haul his playmates around, plenty of large planks and boxes so that he may make bridges for climbing, boats for sailing, or just something to jump from. He needs ladders or a jungle gym to climb unless nature has provided a tree of just the right height with large, spreading branches. He is learning to throw and catch a ball and may greatly enjoy a low basketball basket in which he can try to toss it. The more adventurous five-year-olds will be experimenting with roller skates and perhaps stilts. The little girls enjoy trying to jump rope, though their efforts are not often successful. By recognizing this developmental need for activity and cooperating with it, both home and kindergarten can help the strengthening of the large muscles and the development of body control, as well as give the child constructive channels for expression.

PERIODS OF strenuous activity need to be balanced with periods of quiet activity, even periods of rest, for the five-year-old gets tired rather easily in spite of his vigor and eagerness to use his body—or perhaps because of it. A five-year-old will often withdraw from play of his own accord and either just watch or seek a quieter activity; occasionally he will even lie down. His fatigue is often shown by crossness or

irritability. Few children of this age take regular afternoon naps, but many of them will take a nap one or two days a week, as fatigue seems to pile up. Most five-year-olds sleep about eleven hours at night. In a kindergarten program a rest period is advisable. If the child is at home during the afternoon, he should have a "quiet-play" rest time even if he is not able to sleep. If he attends afternoon kindergarten, it is usually wise to bring him in from play at about eleven in the morning, clean him up, and let him have a quiet period or a rest before lunch and afternoon school.

During these periods of quiet activity, the child needs an opportunity to feel free to move from one activity to another. He cannot yet be expected to sit still for a long period of time, but his attention span is increasing rapidly so that he may remain interested and absorbed in the same project up to twenty or even forty minutes. Blocks, paints, clay, "work-with" tools, puzzles are all satisfying to the growing interests of the five-year-old. He no longer runs from one activity to another, experimenting with this and that, but knows more fully what he wants to do today and will even carry over a project until tomorrow. He may work for

a period of time at the easel or settle down at the puzzle table; he may try to make a bowl of clay or spend time with the blocks working out a plan which he has in mind.

The five-year-old usually has an idea before he goes to work. In his painting he may start out by announcing what he is going to paint. He will often be very critical of his work, and may even express dissatisfaction with it or ask for directions. Many five-year-olds have passed the stage of just smearing and dabbing paint: they try to create and have a definite feeling of accomplishment when the picture is finished. They like to show the finished product to the teacher and receive her praise, or save it and take it home to Mother and Daddy.

THE CHILD of five likes stories related to the here and now and will respond eagerly to "Let's have a story" whether at his home or at school. He enjoys stories that answer his questions about the things he sees around him—steam shovels and engines, grocery stores and boats. He also likes stories of the activities of children and of family life. Some imaginative stories delight him, especially those about animals, but he rarely enjoys the more fantastic and unreal fairy tales; he is too much absorbed in orienting himself to the realistic world about him to be able to relate himself to a too-distant world of fantasy. That will come later. He will listen to poems with much pleasure; the rhythmic swing adds to the child's joy in listening. The youngster becomes quite absorbed in the story or poem and does not like interruptions. He wants to see the pictures in the book and is disappointed if there are none. Some of the children will begin to try to read; others will pretend that they can read and will tell a story as they turn the pages of a picture book.

Rhythms and songs are greatly enjoyed

by the five-year-old group. They like to "make up" dances to music and will enter enthusiastically into singing and rhythmic games. Many of the children are beginning to follow a tune and will even correct a child who does not know it. Often a five-year-old will chant a little rhythmic song of his own as he goes about his play. He likes to take part in a rhythm band.

The five-year-old loves dramatic play. He is ready to act out the story which he has heard—very simply and with plenty of action and spontaneity. His love of dramatic play is the keynote to many of his activities. Such play will often be very practical; five is very much interested in his home and acts out this interest by playing house, being mother and father, playing doctor, or going to the store. Both boys and girls enter into this type of home-centered dramatic play.

THE KINDERGARTEN child is greatly interested in group activities and group play. He likes to play with other children, but he is still very much of an individual and does not often really cooperate with others. He stays in the group as long as he enjoys it, but his interests are still self-centered. If he tires of the group activity, he will become restless or will seek something else which pleases him more, even if it means leaving the group without a father in the home or a delivery truck for the grocery store. The kindergarten child is capable of taking part in the activities of the large group if it is well supervised, but he gets along better in small groups of five or six children who are playing together, or with just one other child. At this age three is often a crowd; a child can adjust to one playmate or the other but often not to both. Thus on a rainy day it is wise for Mother to invite one friend over rather than two. The five-year-old is getting along well in taking

turns, respecting other people's belongings, and asking for the use of things rather than snatching or hitting. His sense of property is developing. There is still quarreling and fighting, but he is learning better ways of getting along and is increasing in his ability to handle situations himself. Mother and teacher can usually remain in the background while the children of this age work through their own problems.

A five-year-old is beginning to use language well. He talks freely, carrying on conversations and expressing ideas. He loves to tell a story, and he will tell the teacher about something that happened at

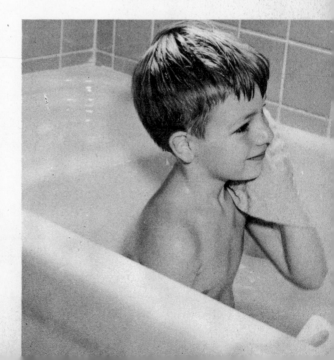

23

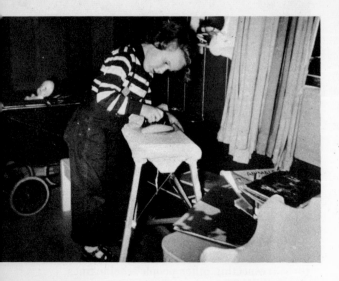

home or will enjoy telling Mother about the happenings of the day at school. He has learned to put his needs into words. Speech is beginning to be used in an adult manner. Pronunciation is usually clear and easily understood. Parents can help by listening to their youngsters when they try to tell about things, by encouraging conversation in the family, and by avoiding an overemphasis on correct speech. That will come later and largely from example. Speech at this age should be spontaneous.

A CHILD OF this age is beginning to be quite independent and to enjoy doing things for himself—if he has not had too many demands made upon him during the past three years, if he has not been pushed too hard or had too much expected of him. He can usually wash himself, although Mother will have to help in the hard-to-reach spots and behind the ears. He is able to take care of his own toilet needs, although sometimes he needs a reminder, as he finds it hard to leave his play. He feeds himself well, although he has definite likes and dislikes. Most five-year-olds prefer foods that are not mixed together. They do not enjoy creamed vegetables as much as raw

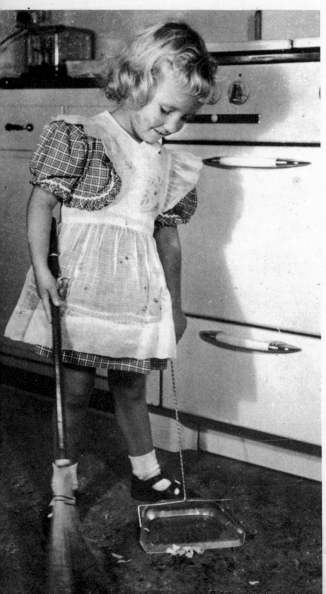

vegetables, or puddings as much as fruit or jello for dessert. They still like to eat many things with their fingers, although they are becoming increasingly skillful with fork and spoon; some fives even try to use a knife.

Youngsters of this age can dress themselves, although they still get things twisted sometimes. They cannot tie their shoelaces or manage difficult buttons or small fastenings. There will still be many times when they need help getting into a difficult snowsuit, especially when they are tired or out of sorts. Parents can help by trying to provide clothing with self-help features, good-sized armholes, large buttons or snaps in places which can be reached, and either two-piece underwear or drop seats which the child can really manage, rubbers which are loose enough to put on easily, and open-front rather than pull-over sweaters. If this is done, dressing can be a source of great fun and pride to a child.

When one takes care of a child from babyhood on, it is sometimes hard to keep pace with his growing ability. Many a mother does not even know until she visits kindergarten that her youngster can put on his own snowsuit. It requires great self-control on the part of mothers to refrain from

garten. They enjoy their friends, they enjoy teacher and kindergarten, but Mother is the important person. Her support and approval are constantly sought.

FIVE IS AN age of conforming, a comfortable age. Dr. Gesell points out that it is a stage which parents enjoy because children seem to "behave as they should." It seems to be almost a resting point between the experimenting of the four-year-old and the extremes of the six-year-old. The five-year-old wants to do what is expected of him. He will often ask whether he is doing something in the right way, or he will turn to Mother or teacher with "May I go?" "May I do this?" He wants to fit into his environment and is usually in surprisingly little rebellion against it. This is the age when he is beginning to be able to take some responsibility for his own actions and to know the difference between right and wrong. It is often said to be the age at which his "conscience" is developing. Until now he has been dependent upon Mother or Father or some other adult to tell him what is acceptable behavior; now he seems to be beginning to understand for himself, although he often turns to the adult for guidance and reassurance. He still thinks of good and bad in terms of specific situations—it was bad to do this or good to do that. Because the child is interested in conforming at this age, it is a year during which he may be taught to adjust to the needs of the group and to accept a need for respecting authority in necessary situations. The child who goes to kindergarten during this year of good equilibrium has a better chance of learning to adjust to the schoolroom situation with a minimum of strain than does the six-year-old, who goes to school for the first time during a year generally marked not by good adjustment but by conflict.

quickly doing for a child something he is doing slowly and ineptly. Yet such help robs him of one of his greatest sources of satisfaction in successful accomplishment, a kind of satisfaction we all need for building self-reliance and courage to meet difficult situations. Five wants to feel and rely on his own powers and should be encouraged, though never pressured, in this desire.

The five-year-old also shows his independence by liking to be trusted with errands or by performing simple tasks in kindergarten and at home. He may go with great pride to a nearby store and bring home a loaf of bread for supper, change and all. He will usually carry out directions faithfully and be proud of his success.

The five-year-old is home-centered in spite of the fact that he is quite an independent little person. When he was four he sometimes ventured out of bounds to explore the neighborhood, but at five he likes to stay near home base. Mother is very much the center of his life—he likes to be at home and near her. Some five-year-olds show anxiety if they think that Mother will not be at home when they get back from kinder-

A good day in kindergarten

THESE children are having opportunities to grow as five-year-olds should. The climate of the room is friendly and cordial, yet businesslike. There is a nice balance between individual and group activities, between active play, quieter fun, and rest. There is time for observation, time for sharing ideas and working together, time for building, painting, and handicraft, time for dramatic and rhythmic play, time for books and stories, and time for songs and records. The day starts easily and happily with free activity, each child following his own bent.

"Let's give the little fellow a swim now."

Trucking on a big scale.

Books are good friends already.

Mary Eleanor, drink your milk!

Records are rarely broken.

There is always time to talk things over and make plans. Through such informal discussion and through observation the teacher can make a careful study of each child's mental capacities, work habits, emotional stability, social adjustment, and physical well-being, and plan needed help.

These boys have been trained to use tools with safety to themselves and each other.

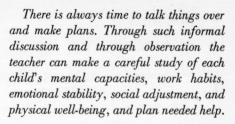

Clay has limitless possibilities.

Peg boards and puzzles are perennial favorites.

Crayons are shared as well as ideas.

David likes planes.

"... along came a spider."

Time to start putting things away.

*Part of learning to be a good worker is learning
to clean things up afterwards and put tools away carefully.*

Rest is short but complete.

Everyone welcomes milk-time.

"We always wash hands before we eat."

". . . and then Little Black Sambo met another tiger."

Holidays are gala occasions and fun to plan for.

Time to go home. Kindergartners can manage snowsuits alone.

This is a good life for the fives. Their basic human needs are being met. They are learning to work and play together and are building confidence through successful efforts. They are learning techniques of personal problem solving and satisfactory human relations through opportunities to learn and to practice intelligent self-direction.

Mama's baby

TODAY'S five-year-olds have had unusually varied backgrounds because of the upsets of the war and the period following it. Many parents have been disturbed and worried. As a result there has been inconsistency in many homes, and in some a marked instability or little love. Sometimes the adults in charge have been too severe. Sometimes they have been too busy, or too worried. Sometimes they have been too protective. During the war years many mothers, separated from soldier husbands, clung to their babies for their own comfort, keeping them close to gratify their own parched emotional lives.

This situation was the start of difficulties for Larry Drake. His father was drafted when he was only a few months old, and his mother gained such comfort from her baby that he was rarely out of her sight. She devoted herself to him. She slept with him, petted him and babied him.

As he grew older, play with other children was rarely permitted: he might get hurt, he might "pick up a germ," he might learn something naughty. He cried for whatever he wanted—and got it. He made unreasonable demands—and was never refused. His mother taught him to need her, to be helpless alone. He depended upon her for everything. For more than four years she encouraged this. Then her husband's tour of duty was over and he came home.

When Larry entered kindergarten at five, his speech and general behavior were like those of a two- or three-year-old. His mother did not realize this. She told the teacher proudly that the boy could recite many nursery rhymes, could count correctly to fifty, recognized most letters.

But Mrs. Drake did not realize that she had failed to help Larry learn a most essential thing—how to get along without his mother. She brought him to school the first day, a tense, frightened, shy little boy with curly hair that looked like a little girl's, and a suit much too dainty for swing or slide. She announced that she planned to stay with him until he was accustomed to the new surroundings, saying in the child's hearing, "He's not used to rough children. And he'll miss me so, he might cry."

Until mid-morning Larry clung close to his mother. He seemed mildly interested, yet kept tight hold of his mother's hand or skirt. Mother had impressed him with the fact that he would miss her if she left him.

WHEN IT came time for orange juice, Miss M suggested that Larry join the other children at the little tables and led the reluctant child to a chair next to hers. While he was drinking his orange juice he momentarily forgot his mother, who took advantage of the opportunity to slip out of the room, unnoticed by anyone.

Suddenly Larry pushed back his chair, stamped both his feet, stiffened his whole body, and cried loudly, "I want my mama! I want my mama!"

Miss M took his hand to lead him away from the others, knowing that he needed patient reassurance that his mother would return. But as she did so the door opened and Mrs. Drake rushed in. Larry stretched his hands to her. "Mama!" he shrieked. "I want to go home, I want to go home!"

"Mother's precious!" Mrs. Drake cried. "You don't have to stay in this horrid school if you don't want to! We'll have fun at home." And to Miss M: "He's too little for school. I told his father so, but he insisted." And she swept from the room with the boy in her arms.

As Miss M was preparing to leave that afternoon, a man came to the kindergarten and introduced himself as Mr. Drake. He had heard about Larry's unfortunate introduction to school and was anxious to see what could be done. He spoke very frankly.

He told Miss M how appalled he had been on his return from military service to find his wife making such a baby of Larry. The boy had never learned to do anything for himself. He cried a great deal and was entirely undisciplined. His mother hovered over him constantly and he clung babyishly to her. And she did not really want things any other way.

"They both need help," said Miss M. "I think when Mrs. Drake sees how differently other boys Larry's age do things she'll agree it's time she allowed her boy to grow up. I doubt if she has any realization of how much five-year-olds can do."

They talked at length about the best way to help Larry make the adjustment to being away from his mother. "There is no hard and fast rule about these things," said Miss M, "because no two children are alike. In most cases we find that a child adjusts most easily if Mother leaves right away. Then there's no constant looking to her for cues as to whether she is expecting him to be fearful or rebellious. Even if a child is uneasy and perhaps cries a little

at first we find he usually gets over it very soon because there are so many things to interest him. And he sees other children having a good time. Such a youngster needs a lot of extra attention at first, but usually only for a rather short time.

"But in Larry's case, his terror is deeply seated. He's five and of course should be willing to stay without his mother, but emotionally he's as dependent as a three-year-old, so we can't expect his social behavior to be any different right now.

"Let's try having Mrs. Drake come and stay here with him until Larry feels more sure of himself in his new surroundings. And it might be wise not to plan on staying through the morning at first; especially after what happened today Larry may feel reluctant about coming back at all. So let him know ahead of time that he's coming 'just for a little visit' and may leave whenever he wishes."

When they arrived the next morning, Mrs. Drake was half embarrassed, half hostile toward Miss M. She had resented her husband's interference and had finally consented to return to the kindergarten only after much bitter and tearful debate.

Miss M, suspecting this general attitude, said very little to Mrs. Drake that day beyond welcoming her and saying again that they might stay just as long or as short a time as they wished. She established them comfortably and then left them.

Larry sat on his mother's lap, nor did he once let go of her hand or venture forth to join the fun. In a short time he became restless and they left.

The next day, Miss M sat down beside them briefly, chatting impersonally about kindergarten routines. When they were preparing to leave, Miss M asked Larry if he would like to take a little car home to play with and bring it back the next day.

Larry looked down and said nothing, and Miss M added, "Perhaps one of these days you'll bring one of *your* cars from home to show us."

Slowly, very slowly, changes could be noticed. One day Larry was at school before nine, and played with some toys while the other children were coming into the room. But he retired to the safety of his mother's side when they had all arrived and group activity commenced. Another day soon afterwards Larry played most of the morning, close to Mother, it was true, and claiming her constant attention and continuous comment on whatever he was doing, but nevertheless following by himself the activities engaged in by the other children who played in small groups. Finally he entered into things with the other kindergartners—singing, listening to stories, joining a game now and then.

It was not easy for Larry to learn the give-and-take, the sharing, the waiting turns, that most of the children had been learning for many months before they started kindergarten. He had no concept of the rights of others, and would cry and pout when he wanted to use the easel and another child was there first. It was a novel experience for him when such behavior did not produce immediate solicitude and aid, but only his teacher's matter-of-fact statement, "Maybe you'd like to work on this puzzle while you're waiting."

He found it disconcerting that Miss M did not tell him what to draw, and he did not like to have to stop coloring when it was orange-juice time. But he soon found that if he kept on coloring he missed his juice. He resisted putting away things he had used, until he found that if they weren't picked up, he wasn't ready to take part in the next activity. Larry was learning.

Had all this happened earlier, Mrs. Drake would have often flown to his aid and showered him with sympathy. But she, too, was learning. She could now accept the suggestion that her rôle at kindergarten should be as passive a one as possible, if Larry were to become part of the group and learn to conform to its standards, and she agreed now that such belonging and such conformity were desirable.

Larry began to experience real enjoyment in his new capabilities. It was no longer upsetting to him to have his mother leave after she had visited for a time in the room, nor did he fret when she did not return until almost dismissal time. Finally he could happily say good-by at the school door and go in with the others.

Miss M had several conferences with Mrs. Drake alone, and the school psychologist also talked with her. She was helped to see how she had tried to meet her own emotional needs by clinging to her child. Through these talks and with her husband's encouragement she was helped to a new viewpoint and helped too to enlarge her interests and activities. Larry continued to be an important part of her life. But he was not *all* her life.

It is of course not only in wartime that mothers are overprotective. The problem is only accentuated then. The same tendency can be seen at any time—mothers driven to oversolicitude by their own need, yet believing they are benefiting their children. The outcome is that children are deprived of opportunities to learn to be independent, self-reliant individuals.

Often adults' problems prevent their children from leading healthy emotional lives. Causes reaching far back in the development of both need understanding if their lives together are to be smooth and peaceful and happy.

Carla and the twins

A SITUATION puzzling alike to parents and to teachers is that of the kindergarten child who has acquired certain habits and skills which suggest that he is well on the way in the growing-up process, but who "suddenly" loses all those good traits and capabilities and returns to ways of response apparently outgrown.

The disturbed parent may be unaware of anything which might account for the situation. The puzzled teacher may think over all details of classroom activities and find no element which might be the causative factor. But if home and school come together and talk over the total situation, there will often be revealed the basis for the change in the child. Frequently one is too close to a problem for the perspective necessary to understand it.

This was true in the case of Carla Hughes. Carla was not quite five when she started kindergarten. She was a sturdy little girl, and quite independent. She adjusted easily to the group and played well with the other children. She responded readily to the teacher's directions and learned new facts and skills quickly. She soon took upon herself the task of preparing for the mid-morning orange juice and graham cracker period. She set the tables with the help of another child whom she managed pleasantly. She saw to it that everything was neatly cleared away when the group had finished.

Miss R, the kindergarten teacher, thought that here was a child who must have a happy home life, and she recalled the conference she had had with Mrs. Hughes the previous June, when arrangements had been made to enroll the little girl in school for the fall term.

"Carla's a good little girl," the mother had said, "and so helpful! She keeps her belongings neat and tidy, and she's always willing to help as much as she is able—she empties the waste baskets and dries the spoons and that sort of thing. She loves to be with other children, although there haven't been many occasions when that has been possible. I hope she'll get along nicely in kindergarten."

FROM THE earliest September days Carla had adjusted so well that Miss R had given no thought to not having seen the mother since that spring visit. Since Carla was one of the bus children, her traveling to and from school did not require Mrs. Hughes' presence. There had been no difficulty or disturbance of any sort, and Miss R had had no reason to ask Mrs. Hughes to come to school. Although usually she liked to have parent conferences at rather frequent intervals, sometimes with large classes not every mother was seen regularly, because of lack of time. And when a child seems as happy and capable as did Carla, it is understandable if a busy teacher does not add extra hours to a full schedule.

But late in the fall Miss R began to note a change in Carla. One morning she found her shoving a smaller child off the swing. Another day she had to separate her from another kindergartener when both children were struggling furiously for the same book.

Other changes became apparent. Carla asked for frequent help with her wraps, although she had previously managed even rubbers alone. And she seemed to weary of the responsibility of the tables and serving, although she had earlier begged to be permitted to continue it. Lately, too, there had been a great deal of spilling when she filled the paper containers used by the children. And there appeared to be frequent arguments between Carla and her "helper" for the day. Carla would whine if she couldn't have her own way. At the beginning of the term she had been remarkably reasonable about necessary postponing of what she wanted to do. Hard falls she had formerly met without a murmur. Now she whimpered when she was bumped.

Miss R decided to write a note to Mrs. Hughes and suggest a conference. Perhaps the child wasn't getting enough sleep and so was less relaxed than she would be with sufficient rest. Perhaps there had been some change at home which might account for the change in the little girl.

At the appointed conference hour, Miss R was startled to have an elderly lady appear, introducing herself as Carla's great-aunt.

"Mrs. Hughes is so busy, she asked me to come in her place," she explained. "Twins two months old don't allow much time for anything else. I'm not surprised you're complaining about Carla. She's a handful at home, certainly! Ever since I've been there, she's made things difficult for everybody. Wets her bed at night and makes more laundry at a time when there's plenty anyway, keeping the babies sweet and fresh. Won't do as she's told during the day and wears us all out wanting help with things she's well able to do herself. And naughty! She'll purposely run against a chair and

knock it over, just when the babies have gone off to sleep. She'll raise a fuss whenever her mother goes out without her. I'd soon take care of her, if she were mine!"

"Why, I didn't know about the twins. Carla never said a word," said Miss R. "But I thought she was a good little girl at home. When her mother came last June, I understood that there was no trouble at all. And when Carla came to school in September, she was good as gold, and so helpful! Why, she was able to do things many other children couldn't do. I've thought of Carla as a sweet and capable child."

"Then why did you send for her mother?" demanded the visitor severely. "We've got plenty to do at home these days without being called to school for that Carla!"

Miss R was puzzled and did not prolong the interview. As graciously as possible she discussed general kindergarten procedures, stressing some of the little girl's good points and making no mention of her changed behavior.

Later she telephoned Mrs. Hughes to set a time when she might visit the home, and the following Saturday morning she and Mrs. Hughes had a long talk while Carla was out with her father and her aunt was giving the twins an airing in the nearby park.

Mrs. Hughes, too, was concerned about Carla. "She used to be so self-reliant," she said at one point. "Now she doesn't help herself washing or dressing, and she's more care than she was two years ago. And she cries so much and fusses about every little thing! She isn't eating properly any more either, and lately she refuses her milk unless she can have it in a bottle. I'm so ashamed! At five, my little girl taking milk from a bottle!" And young Mrs. Hughes laughed in embarrassment.

Further sympathetic questioning brought out several facts which Miss R felt might have a great deal to do with the difficulties Carla was having both at home and at school. She had been accustomed to being the sole interest of her mother, and the twins made a radical change in her life. She had to share her mother now, and she had to share her room, too—her great-aunt had occupied a bed there since she had come to help with the new babies. And Carla had not been prepared for either of these big changes in her life.

TALKING it over, it became apparent both to mother and teacher that a great deal had been expected of Carla. The happy hours she had formerly spent with her mother were now changed to perplexing hours spent with Great-aunt Gertrude. Breakfasts were hurried affairs, and she was sent out of the kitchen to be quiet in her own room as soon as she had finished. She used to stay and "help." Kindergarten might well have seemed to the little girl a means of getting her out of the way so her mother could spend more time with the twins. Mrs. Hughes confessed that lately she had had little time with Carla—the frequent excursions to the park, the zoo, the beach, had stopped entirely; even the former cozy moments on Mother's lap were now few and far between.

"I'm afraid I don't manage very well," said Mrs. Hughes ruefully. "I can't get along without Miss Curry here. I know she's more strict with Carla than seems necessary, but Carla isn't the nice, sweet little girl she used to be. I just don't know what to do."

Miss R suggested that if Mrs. Hughes could arrange to come to school someday, an appointment could be made to talk over the entire situation with the school psychologist. Perhaps they could plan a way to help Carla regain the happy, independent ways

so characteristic of her before the birth of her twin sisters.

This plan was carried out, and when the picture was made clear to them all it was not hard to see what Carla needed and how she could be helped.

The coming of a baby had not been explained to Carla. She had had no share in the preparations, and no forewarning of her mother's going to the hospital or of Great-aunt Gertrude's coming to live with them or of the changes a new baby was bound to make for everyone.

The first weeks of the twins' life had been anxious ones for all the grown-ups, for the infants were tiny and Mrs. Hughes was not very strong after their birth. But Carla was given no explanation for the concern and flurry of the adults. It confused her to be shunted aside, to have her questions ignored, to be left to her own devices for long periods at a time. She felt no one loved her any more. Accustomed for so long to having Mother for herself, Carla was upset that now Mother was always too busy or too tired or too distracted to play with her.

In her confusion and distress she tried to find a way back to the former happy times she remembered wistfully. A great deal of Mother's time was spent feeding the twins. What more natural than that Carla, capable though she was in feeding herself, should resort to a baby's way of getting food—having her milk in a bottle, being given it by Mother? The twins got attention that way. Losing the dry habit was also an unconscious effort to get more of Mother's time and care. Carla's demands for help in washing and dressing routines could be accounted for in the same way.

IN HER resentment at the intruding twins, it was not strange that Carla was noisy at moments when she well knew that quiet was desired for the sleeping babies. She wasn't concerned with their comfort. They interfered with everything she wanted to do, and Mother didn't care about her since they came. Disturbing them was one way she could give vent to her feelings.

And because she resented the twins, she came to feel hostile toward other children, too. Her play was no longer peaceable and friendly. She snatched things from other children. She was rough and aggressive with them. This was another way she could relieve her feelings. She behaved with them as she wished she could behave toward the twins but didn't dare.

Few children go through the event of the coming of a new baby without a very real emotional involvement. They cannot put into words the feeling of rejection which grows and grows, for they do not understand it. They do not specifically ask if the parents love the baby more than they do their big girl. But they often feel that it must be so. Jealousy and hostility develop. These are natural, normal reactions. If they are anticipated and understood by the parents, they can be in large degree forestalled. And what cannot be prevented must be given sympathetic understanding, if the older child is to be happy.

THE OLDER child should be told of the new baby's coming. Every effort should be made to make the youngster feel he can share in the preparations before and the attention afterwards that revolve normally about a new baby. But he needs a great deal of reassurance that all the excitement and the many changed routines do not mean that there is any less love and devotion for himself.

It is essential that a specific plan be worked out to permit a daily period when Mother spends time exclusively with the older child. This is when he must sense that he is as important as ever to her. This is when he must derive the feeling of security so important for contentment during childhood and in later years, too. And this is when he should be permitted to verbalize the wholly normal antagonism aroused by the newcomer.

When the first-born says of the new baby, "Let's send him back," take it as calmly as possible. What he means is, "Pay some attention to me, too." When the older child is asked if he loves his baby sister, and answers honestly, "NO! I wish we didn't have her," don't be shocked. He is telling you the baby has made such a change in his own life that he finds it intolerable.

WHEN YOU reprove him or punish him for expressing his resentment, you do not end it. You only encourage its continuance below the surface. It is then that hostility is really hazardous. It should be recognized and acknowledged and accepted. The child should be helped to understand that he is not wicked for feeling as he does, but that the feeling is not warranted, because he is indeed still loved and still wanted by his parents. And the parents' actions must prove this. Then the older child can tolerate his own feelings and can learn to tolerate the baby. Otherwise he can do neither.

Carla's regression to baby ways needed this understanding. She had been punished for "being a baby" and scolded for jealousy of the twins. Instead, Mother now planned time with her alone each day, and there was fun no babies shared. Now Carla felt wanted and loved. She regained her old sense of security. And because she was happy again, she was good again.

There are always problems to be solved in living with children. Sometimes a new baby creates a new one.

CHAPTER THREE

When they are six

BEING SIX years old has a special significance for almost every child. He has looked forward with eagerness and pride to the time when he could say, "Now I am six and I can go to school."

This is one of the great turning points, because here he steps beyond the family circle into the larger world of the school and the community. Until now his relationships have usually been limited to his own family, the few children on his block, and perhaps to playmates in a carefully supervised nursery school or kindergarten. In each of these situations his mother has been closely involved. But now that he is six, the child must find his own place and make his own friends under new conditions. Whereas in the home the child is loved and accepted because he is a member of the family group, he now finds that he must win acceptance among others of his own age. Just being Billy Smith is no longer enough; he must succeed because of his own worth as an individual and because of the contribution he can make to the group.

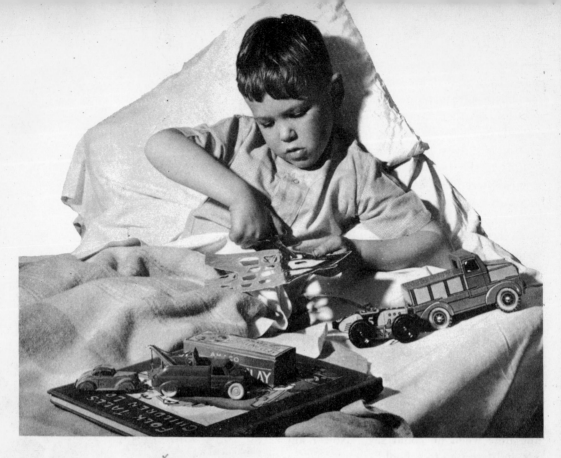

The sixth year is one of transition between the home and the school, between the life of a little child protected by the home and that of a first-grader, who must meet the often rigorous demands and competition of school life. Many factors combine to determine the nature of the child's adjustment to this new environment, but the two of probably greatest importance are his patterns of individual growth and the kind of home experience he has had.

Progress in physical development is uneven, but by six the child has usually lost most of his baby contours. His legs lengthen and there are gains in both height and weight. Although this growth is less rapid than that of earlier periods, mothers are still sighing over quickly outgrown clothing. The broad, closely knit boy or girl can be expected to weigh more in proportion to height than does the slim, rangy young-

ster, and yet neither is under- or overweight. While the child's body is gradually changing in shape, so, too, is his face. The jaw lengthens as permanent teeth replace baby teeth and as new molars come in.

The organs and framework of the six-year-old's body are growing and changing, even though this development is not easily observed. The heart is still in a period of rapid growth, but the brain has almost achieved its full weight. During the sixth year, eyes are not yet mature in either size or shape, and their relatively shallow depth probably accounts for a tendency toward far-sightedness. This defect is corrected naturally when, sometime between eight and ten, the child's eyes attain adult size and shape. Although eye and hand preferences are well established, a six-year-old still finds the coordination of eye and hand movements difficult. Muscular development is also uneven, and, in general, large muscles are more advanced than are small ones. Precise movements are therefore a matter of considerable effort and strain for him.

Partly because of this uneven physical growth, a six-year-old is particularly susceptible to the various contagious diseases he encounters. With his tremendous energy, he makes a difficult patient, especially during convalescence, when it requires great resourcefulness and a quick shifting from coloring books to toy trucks (or dolls) to clay modeling or cutouts, in order to keep him as quiet as he should be.

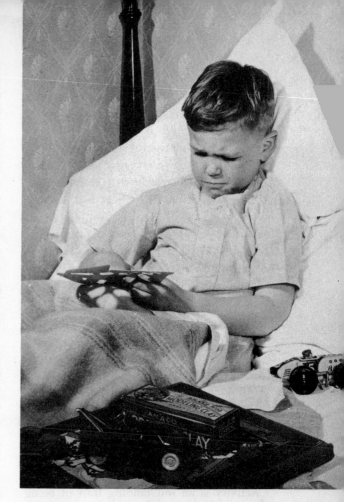

PATTERNS of growth have many variations, fast and slow, steady and irregular. These differences in rate are true not only of physical growth but also of mental, emotional, and social development as well. A child of good mentality whose overall pattern of development is slow may be mentally ready for school at six but, in emotional and social ways, he may be more like a four-year-old, with school life too hard for him. The big, physically well-developed boy may be immature socially and mentally. Too often such a boy is judged by his size alone, and pigeonholed accordingly: we are likely to say, "A big boy like Jack shouldn't act like such a baby."

Such variations in growth patterns as these make it necessary to know not only what children of his age are like in general, but what each child is like in particular. Many behavior problems, both at home and at school, develop because the adult in control, either mother or teacher, does not recognize the level of maturity reached by a certain child. In a classroom for six-year-olds some children will still be babies, immature emotionally and unable to adjust socially, while others are secure, self-reliant little people who are able to hold their own

in their group. Many youngsters are regarded as special problems or as difficult children incapable of adapting to first grade when, in reality, they either are passing through a phase of growth natural in their development or have not as yet reached the point of maturity attained by the majority of the class.

THE TYPE of home experience a first-grader has had is the second crucial factor in school adjustment. If a child has grown up in a warm, friendly home, if his parents have shown him affection and acceptance so that he comes to new experiences with the security of his home to help him, then he will usually be able to cope with the new and larger environment of school. If, on the other hand, his early years have been a period of strain—if his family has moved often or has had to live in cramped quarters or with relatives, if his parents have been separated because of the war or for other reasons—this child is likely to come to school tense and fearful. The boy or girl who has been severely disciplined, over-rigidly trained, or made to feel unwanted, will also find it hard to adjust to the class-room. So, too, will there be troubles ahead for the child who has been overprotected and babied by a mother who has failed to recognize his early needs for independence.

Obviously six-year-olds cannot all be treated alike. *Each child is different, bringing to school a special native endowment, a special rate and pattern of development, and a special home background.*

ALTHOUGH it is true that there is no typi-cal child, still there are certain charac-teristics which do seem to be predominant in the six-year-old group and which do give us an indication of what we can expect from many of these youngsters.

Activity is an outstanding trait of being six years old. Children at this age rush about in their play, jump up from the table at mealtimes, wriggle in their seats at school, gesture freely as they talk. Their whole bodies seem to be involved in everything they do. When they read, their lips move, their feet shuffle, and they twist their fingers in their hair. When they write, they may screw up their faces, bite their lips, and pull themselves back and forth in their chairs. They may try hard to sit still, but they are not able to do so for long, because it is difficult for them to control their motions voluntarily. It is clearly unwise to put a strain on these youngsters by expect-ing them to sit still for more than a short period of time. Restlessness at home and at school is often a sign that not enough opportunity for activity is being provided.

Even in their thinking, six-year-olds seem to carry over this pattern of activity. They learn much better through being active than through sitting and listening. First-graders count more easily if they have objects to move. They absorb ideas better when dis-cussions and explanations are accompanied by, or grow out of, many chances to handle all sorts of materials, to experiment with all kinds of tools and art equipment, to look after details of housekeeping, and to care for such living things as a pet duckling or even a class garden.

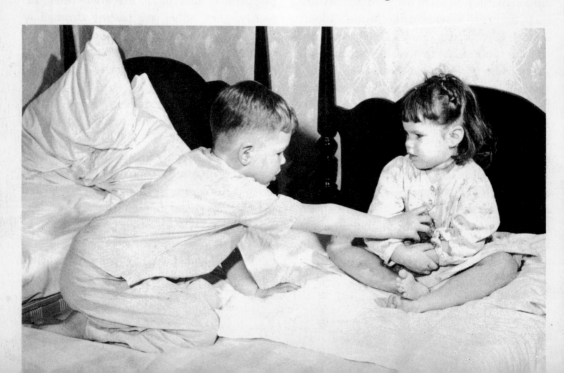

Six-year-olds enjoy using their hands. Although they like to try to make things, they are still clumsy and cannot be expected to produce perfect products. And even if their skill were greater, their relatively short periods of interest would make it hard to carry an activity through to a conclusion completely satisfactory by adult standards. Their work, then, will be crude, but creative efforts should not be discouraged by placing all the emphasis on perfection. Since the small muscles of the arms and hands are not completely developed, it is still hard for many children to write or cut well or to do handwork that involves much skill or control. Children vary considerably in this sort of physical maturity,

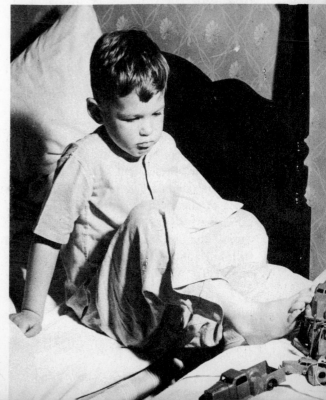

and standards should not be so high that the girls and boys having slow muscular development are discouraged or pushed to the point of tension. It is well to remember that muscular development cannot be forced; we can only cooperate with the degree of maturity found at any level. Most children of six, however, can learn to paste and cut, to use paint and crayon, and to handle tools with a fair degree of skill.

Activities which require use of the large muscles should be stressed throughout the sixth year. There should be plenty of opportunity for climbing and hauling, for running and jumping, and for free, active play. Six-year-olds like to pull and push, to use wagons and scooters, and to build with large blocks and boxes and boards. Their physical skills are not too well coordinated, and they are just learning to bat a ball or to jump rope. Mastery is far from complete. If you watch a six-year-old throw a ball, you will see that he uses his whole body. His actions are quite different from those of the twelve-year-old, who handles the ball in a sure and direct manner. But even if the movements of six-year-olds are still rough and jerky, they do enjoy learning new skills. We should encourage and give

opportunities for this learning, but we should not try to force or push girls and boys of this age to accomplishments beyond their ability. A well-developed child may perform easily on the trapeze while other youngsters, not yet ready for such stunts, stand by, watching with envious interest. Someday they, too, will try.

The playground has been called the training school of childhood, and it shows not only the kind of activity children of six need and enjoy but also the behavior patterns which they are developing. They climb, jump, and run; they also shout and fight for their rights. Taking turns, a social technique which may have seemed mastered in the nursery school or kindergarten, appears to have been forgotten. Now every child wants to be first, and there is a scramble for the apparatus, with pushing, fighting, and quarreling. Each girl or boy wants to be the leader; each one wants to win and finds it hard to lose. Children of this age need to be taught again how to take turns and how to get along together. Some of this rough-and-tumble play and aggressiveness, however, is necessary, for it is part of learning to hold one's own as a new independence is being experimented with.

Competition is often keen, and it is not surprising that many children boast and compare possessions, heights, and even families in trying to assert themselves and achieve status in the group.

The play of six-year-olds calls for wise adult supervision with a minimum of interference. The shy child or the slowly developing one who might be overwhelmed by the usual playground activities may need special help for a year or two until he is able to hold his own in the active group.

CHILDREN of six are trying to leave babyhood behind and to free themselves of the behavior of little children. They do not want to be treated as they were during the preschool years. We would be concerned if this growth drive did not appear, because children must drop baby ways and change their dependence upon their mothers for the increasing independence and vigor of childhood. Adult help is needed to show them that self-assertion does not have to be rough and rude to meet the challenge offered by playmates of their age.

Group activities gain popularity in the first grade. Many children enjoy projects and games undertaken together, although there is little group loyalty or responsibility. These will come later. At six a child often enters a game with enthusiasm only to leave if he does not get the part he wants or if he loses, or perhaps because something else attracts his attention. His behavior shows that this is still a transition period between the individualistic play of the pre-school child and the team play of the middle-grade boy or girl. Some immature children will remain at the level of individualistic play throughout this year; for them group participation will be hard. A child should be encouraged to take part but not compelled to do so.

In spontaneous play, girls and boys tend to show different interests. Girls play house and dress up, while boys play cowboys-and-Indians and cops-and-robbers. When girls and boys do mix in such free play as housekeeping or store play, there is an awareness of sex differences. The boys will be the storekeepers, the fathers, or the delivery man. A boy will rarely take the part of the mother or nurse. Occasionally girls join in the chasing and fighting games of the boys. Best friends, however, are almost always of the same sex, and play in small groups is preferred. Although friendships are still shifting, they tend to persist among especially mature children.

Dramatics have a prominent part in the spontaneous play of six-year-olds, as in that of five-year-olds. This delight in simple, informal acting develops out of the interest and activity of the moment. Dramatic play goes on in the classroom, where it is a source of learning as well as of fun and pleasure. Rehearsed or elaborately planned affairs are likely to destroy this rich,

creative means of teaching and learning, and a child of six quickly becomes self-conscious in a directed situation.

The love of dramatization carries over from play to conversation. A six-year-old tells a story with gestures, often moving his whole body expressively as he talks. He likes to add his own touches, and it is a mistake to scold him for telling what is not completely true. Actually he is giving expression to his imagination as he weaves his story. The differences between reality and fancy are only gradually being realized. The adult can bring the child back to the here-and-now with an understanding wink and "Was it really that way, Jimmy?"

Eagerness to learn is one of the most endearing traits of six-year-olds. Theirs is the age of *why*. First-graders come to school wanting to learn and eager to know—we wish they could keep this eagerness all through school. How the questions of these children are answered, how their curiosity is stimulated and encouraged determine their subsequent attitudes toward learning. Asking *why* is not enough for these youngsters; they also try to find the clues and answers to their questions. In this way they are trying to orient themselves to a world which is much bigger than the family or the block. Their efforts to express themselves need encouragement and serious response by the adults around them.

What is within the children's own environment challenges them first. The faraway remains vague and only slightly understood. These children learn by concrete situations and direct participation. Time, like distance, is not a clear concept; their interest is in the present, in what is happening *now*. Six-year-olds cannot plan much for the future, nor should they be expected to accept responsibilities which

involve a perception of time. "We will do this after recess," is more meaningful to a roomful of first-graders than "in half an hour." Perhaps because time still has so little meaning, many of these children are likely to dawdle, and, if made to hurry, become irritated or upset.

Six-year-olds like responsibility. Because they want to identify themselves with adults and do what they think is grown-up, these children like to help set the table, wash the dishes, or make a simple dessert. At school they want to feed the goldfish, erase the blackboard, and pass the papers. Even cleaning up is a coveted task if a word of praise makes the workers feel they have really accomplished something. There is direct imitation of the mannerisms of Mother, Father, or a beloved teacher. Although a child's behavior at home may disturb his parents, he may appear quite grown up when he is out. This ability deserves praise but should not be taken to mean "He can act that way all the time if he wants to." The effort of being grown up all the time is too much for active, restless six-year-olds and should not be expected.

Decisions and choices are hard for these children to make. It is wise not to expect too many decisions from youngsters who are still so little beyond babyhood. Routines may eliminate the need for making some decisions and give six-year-olds a feeling of security. It is reassuring to know that meals come at certain times and that one activity follows another in regular order in the schoolroom. This does not mean that programs for this grade should be rigid. On the contrary, much freedom and adaptability within the program is needed even while broad limits and sequences are clearly marked.

PRIMARILY, the sixth year is one of transition. The child is not a more integrated, better-adjusted five-year-old. He is a different child, actually less well balanced, less robust, less decisive, and often less cooperative. He is changing physically, mentally, emotionally, and socially. He is trying to identify himself with older children and even with adults. He wants to be grown up, but at the same time he feels very small and dependent upon the affection of adults about him. He needs this love and warmth for maximum growth and development. Rigid discipline or a severe atmosphere at home or school holds him back. He wilts under criticism and disapproval and becomes discouraged easily. When he is nine he will be able to take criticism in his stride, but now he needs encouragement. His explosiveness and violent changeability are normal and must be expected.

Affection, warmth, friendliness, and a sense of humor can all help us live happily with girls and boys who are six. They love to laugh and they enjoy a joke. Because their coordination is not fully perfected, they still need help—help which may seem out of proportion to their size. Mothers, for instance, should be on hand at dressing times, and teachers may need to offer a bit of help when coat sleeves and snowpants are hard to get on. These children need praise, encouragement, and understanding.

Emphasis on academic achievement can destroy a first-grader's confidence. Grades or marks should not be mentioned, but each child should be helped to read and write and do numbers when he is ready—and not all first-graders will be ready at the same time. Any effort to force a child to learn and to show independence before he is ready only defeats itself, rendering learning more difficult than it should be. If we wait for the point of readiness, the child will pass more smoothly and efficiently from the years of early childhood into the more complex and more demanding school-age period.

This is a time for learning, not one of final achievement. Adults are often impatient, expecting too much of six-year-olds. Success should be judged by direction of progress rather than by a particular achievement at a particular time. Steady growth is a sign of success—has the child made progress over a period of months? If we expect more of a six-year-old than he is ready to give, tensions may be set up which will slow the process of learning and affect the child's whole relationship to the school situation. A flexible program to meet the needs of all the children in the first grade cannot be overemphasized if each child is to have a good start in school.

Jimmy is always up in time for a good breakfast.

Jimmy is six

Sᴉɴᴄᴇ his birth, Jimmy's parents have given him the love, affection, and understanding all children need. At home he has always been a respected member of the family group. He has had a chance to grow within the pattern of his individual characteristics and rate of development without pressure, and to grow in his own style. Standards have never been demanding but there have been standards. There has been freedom

Off to school on his new two-wheeler. Not all six-year-olds can handle a bike, but Jimmy's parents felt he was ready. He can ride it to school because he takes a path where there are no cars.

51

but he knows where he stands and the limits of his freedom.

Both at home, and now at school, Jimmy has known success, status, and the feeling of belonging. Giving and sharing have been a part of his life. He is a normal, happy, healthy child of six-going-on-seven.

His first Progress Report indicates Jimmy's fine physical, mental, and social well-being —the goal we all seek for children.

Jimmy likes to fix an after-school snack.

CHILDREN'S SCHOOL
NATIONAL COLLEGE OF EDUCATION
Report of Teacher

Name of Child ___Jimmy Martin___

Physical Status

Jimmy is a handsome, red haired lad with bright blue eyes and winning smile. He has excellent coloring and a healthy look. School attendance is excellent which again suggests physical strength. Jimmy is well coordinated and well developed. He uses both large and small muscles with skill. He has excellent posture. He does, however, tire easily and is not always as vigorous in his play as the other boys.

Emotional Status

Jimmy certainly has his feet on the ground. He is very stable, very secure, and has the poise of an adult. He has every situation in hand and if caught or in a jam is able to climb out without the other children realizing his predicament. He is serious about everything he does. He is a sensitive little boy with a normal reserve.

Social Adjustment

Jimmy enjoys working and playing with other children. He has a particular group of boys he enjoys working with. He shows ability in leadership with these boys. He is, however, a good follower when someone else takes over. He has a fine gift of speech and carries on an intelligent conversation with the adults about the room. He is well liked and accepted by all because he has such a pleasing disposition and a happy out-going personality.

Capacities, Attitudes and Interests

Jimmy is a very capable little boy. He has an abundance of informational material based on actual experiences. Consequently he is right there with the answer when the group meets a problem or a teacher asks a question. He learns the information and values in the new experiences he is given. Jimmy takes advantage of all room equipment. He particularly enjoys the dramatic play connected with the group activity. He is well ready for reading, writing, and number experiences. He is reading at school with ease and interest in the Primer material. He absorbs all number experiences.

Jimmy loves the music periods. He sings happily the many songs. He learns the words quickly. His voice range has increased and his pitch is more accurate. He particularly enjoys the cowboy songs. Rhythmic response is good. He is, however, sometimes self-conscious.

Jimmy makes many voluntary oral contributions to our discussion and planning periods. He often brings things from home to share at this time. He has poise when speaking before a group. His sentence structure and vocabulary is advanced. He makes many voluntary contributions in the visual training periods. His vision is good.

Recommendations

Jimmy has matured greatly this semester. He has gained a confidence and poise. His academic progress is steady. He is a fine, cooperative boy to work with.

Reprinted by permission of The National College of Education

In the back yard both Jimmy
and little brother Bobby
enjoy the bars.

Jimmy surprised his mother
by getting out the vacuum and
cleaning up all by himself.

He likes to play
with his little
cars and trucks.

And now teeth need
a good brushing
before he goes to bed.

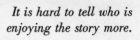

It is hard to tell who is
enjoying the story more.

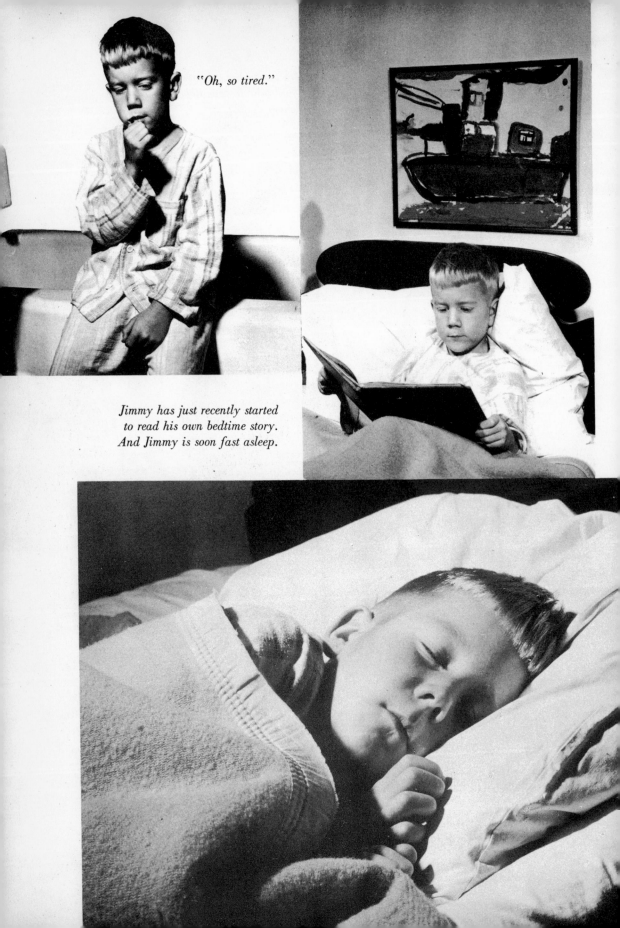

"*Oh, so tired.*"

*Jimmy has just recently started
to read his own bedtime story.
And Jimmy is soon fast asleep.*

The case of Patty Morris

SOME ASPECTS of a child's behavior depend upon his individual responses—for example, whether he meets situations shyly or eagerly, passively or aggressively. Other aspects of behavior can be understood as reflecting the standards of the family and neighborhood from which he comes.

Patty Morris entered first grade shortly after her sixth birthday. She was a stocky, square-built child. She was reasonably clean, but her straight, unbrushed brown hair was dull and lifeless. Four of her brothers and sisters had attended the school, but nothing in their behavior had prepared Miss H for Patty's aggressive, uninhibited, rough, stubborn, defiant ways. The other children had been awed, appealing, submissive, and anxious to please in the classroom. But from the moment Patty reached the first grade, she was a troublemaker.

When Miss H asked a few children to come to the reading circle, Patty shoved her way to the center seat. She then insisted that Jean, a doll-like child with carefully combed curls and starched pink pinafore, sit beside her. She pushed and shouldered Paul aside to make room for Jean. Before the week was over she had grabbed an apple away from Carl, used unbelievable language in "telling off" an older child on the playground, shoved two children out of their seats, and kicked another on the shins.

During the first few days she seemed to want to be near Jean and appeared pleased to be placed at the same table. But within a few days this was all changed. Jean did not accept Patty's overtures and Patty began to take delight in calling Jean names, threatening to beat her up and yanking her long curls until she cried for help.

BY THE END of the first week Miss H was at her wits' end. She began to review all she knew about "normal" six-year-old behavior. On the surface, Patty's behavior seemed far different from other six-year-olds Miss H had known. But Patty was certainly fundamentally much like them: they generally liked to run and shout, to push and shove, wanted to be first, to brag and show off. Like them, she wanted approval; and like them, she did not yet know how to cooperate in a group. When Miss H finished her checking, it looked as though Patty might not be so "different" after all. What was disturbing was that Patty exhibited the usual traits in such excess and with such disruptive effects.

Perhaps something in her background was responsible. Miss H thought over what she knew about Patty's home. But she found that although she had taught four Morrises before Patty, she really knew very little about their family life, except that they lived in an old ramshackle tenement district.

The other children in the family had caused no trouble. Paulie had been a docile child. Jim was cute, a bit slow, but she had rather liked him. She could not remember much about the two older girls. That was really all she knew about Patty's family. Because they had presented no problem, she had never been impelled to search further. But now the situation had changed.

THE FOLLOWING Saturday Miss H visited Patty's home. She had never been in the district before and felt a little uneasy as she picked her way through swarms of children of all ages. As Miss H neared Patty's house, she spotted the child with her fists doubled up and her shoulders hunched. Egged on by June and Robert, Patty was cursing a boy who had shoved her.

The Morris family lived in three rooms facing the railroad tracks. Miss H learned that in addition to Patty and the four brothers and sisters in school, there were three children younger than Patty and another was expected soon. The father and mother seemed to be hardworking, poor, and ignorant. But they loved their children and gave them some security through their affection. Few restrictions had been placed on them from earliest infancy.

Ever since she could walk Patty had taken care of herself in the neighborhood and on the street. She had grown up with little attention to toilet training, food habits, or personal hygiene. Indeed, there was little now. The children slept together, three and four in a bed. When four shared a bed, they slept crosswise instead of lengthwise. There were no regular hours for going to bed—the family might settle down at nine or twelve or even later. Meals were an irregular, haphazard affair, and often there was not enough food to go around. Sometimes a sweet roll, a hot dog, or a hamburger constituted the entire meal. Frequently Patty supplemented this by fruit snatched from a nearby store, a procedure which was commonplace in the neighborhood.

The entire family considered Patty a "good kid." She had spunk, she could take care of herself, she was "honest," she could sing and dance and fight with the best of them. She wasn't selfish or sneaky or sly. In fact, there was no suggestion in anything

related by Mrs. Morris that she saw any reason for concern about Patty.

Clearly, what was acceptable behavior at home was unacceptable in the classroom. Miss H could see that Patty faced a problem too big to solve alone: the necessity of tempering her aggressiveness, frankness, and lack of feeling of "mine and thine," to adapt to a new kind of experience, a new kind of discipline, and a set of standards without precedent in her life. She needed whatever help Miss H could give.

ON MONDAY morning pandemonium broke loose in the cloakroom. Patty was hitting out at two girls, shouting at the top of her lungs, "She did too! She did too!" Miss H assured the two girls that she had really visited Patty on Saturday.

The morning went fairly well, but the moment the children left the room at recess, Miss H heard Patty's strident voice, "Yeah, yeah, she likes me better than anybody." She reached the door in time to see Patty give Jean a mighty shove as she said, "Miss H don't like you—she likes me." With that, she ran off with the apple which Jean had planned to eat.

Miss H wondered what Patty's family meant when they said she was honest. It was obvious that the honesty admired by her family ignored property rights. Patty came at once when Miss H called her. When asked why she had taken the apple, her answer was direct—"Because I was hungry." Her reply to the question "Do you always take something to eat when you are hungry?" was equally direct and honest —"Yeah, why not? Don't you?"

Why not, when the reward for stealing was the satisfaction of hunger? Miss H didn't have the heart to tell Patty to throw away the other half of the apple. In perplexity she put an arm around the child, wondering how best to handle the situation. At that, Patty threw her arms around Miss H and said, "I love you." She was blissfully unaware of any reason for reprimand or censure for her actions or attitudes.

Miss H felt that perhaps she had a clue to handling matters. That night she drew up a detailed analysis of Patty and her problem, culminating in a definite plan of action. Patty's health and physical condition were good despite inadequate diet and care. She had good average intelligence. In her family she had affection and approval, definite status, and a firm sense of belonging and being like the others. In school this was not the case. She showed normal six-year-old traits, and at home was used to giving and sharing, independence and success. She was frank and open, direct, and used to responsibility. The conventions and standards of the classroom were completely alien to her, but Miss H could see that in Patty she had a great deal to work with. Patty's characteristic ways of meeting her problems must be channeled into constructive adjustments. She must be helped toward a greater feeling of accomplishment in activities acceptable in the schoolroom, and must at every opportunity be given recognition for constructive effort.

The next day Miss H asked Patty to distribute the reading-readiness books to the group and took occasion to thank her with a word as to how carefully she had handled the books. During the music period she asked Patty to sing a phrase of a song alone, and urged the other children to try to do as well.

Each day Miss H found something in which Patty could excel or participate acceptably. Patty's good muscular coordination made it possible for her to shine in rhythmic activities. She was good in active running games. The other children began to seek her out when choosing sides. The day Jean asked to be Patty's partner was a high spot for Miss H as well as for Patty.

IT WAS HARD work, requiring much patience and ingenuity, but as the year progressed, Miss H gradually helped Patty to learn—on a six-year-old level—a new set of behavior standards. Because Miss H understood that Patty had to learn these in addition to her school work, she gave Patty much attention and extra work in this area, just as she gave extra help to Jean, who found learning to read difficult.

She gave Patty responsibility and helped her toward the satisfaction which that offered. She guided her aggressiveness into leadership in games. She helped her to control her outbursts toward other children by helping her to recognize their rights and privileges, as well as her own. At every opportunity, she helped Patty acquire status and group acceptance.

As the year progressed, the group came to admire Patty's honesty, frankness, and generosity, her independence and skill in games, singing, and other activities. During the personal development discussion periods the group helped Patty to understand herself. She, in turn, learned new ways of giving and sharing. As she acquired new possessions of her own, she acquired some sense of property rights and learned new standards in regard to "taking" things.

Patty was not changed in a week or a month. She was not a consistently cooperative child at the end of the year. But she became a happier, more productive one who could live in a group without being the perpetual nuisance that she had been at the beginning of the year. Miss H was well pleased with Patty's progress, and there were hopes of an increasingly better adjustment in the next grade.

57

Robert Blake—a six-year-old veteran

IT IS GENERALLY recognized that within every child lie certain limitations as well as certain potentialities for growth and development. Whether these are *innate factors* —poor vision or low intelligence or an imbalance of the glandular system, for example —or whether they are *environmental factors*—such as extreme poverty or a broken home or lack of opportunity for social relationships—they must be considered in any attempt to help a child with problems.

Sometimes one condition will offset the unfortunate influence of another. A frail body, for instance, need not be an insurmountable obstacle in the path of good adjustment. But, of course, there are not always factors capable of counterbalancing the unfortunate ones. High mental ability, let us say, cannot be expected inevitably to overcome handicaps of a physical or a social nature. There are times when, despite excellent potentialities a child is nevertheless overwhelmed by the circumstances of his life and his behavior gives no hint of his latent capacities.

Robert is a case in point. Entering first grade at six and a half, this frail, sallow, unattractive boy cried frequently and whined even more often. He chewed his nails incessantly. He was destructive. He shuffled when he walked, and his speech was confined to low monosyllables. His whole demeanor suggested a reluctance to meet the unfamiliar and a fearfulness in social situations. He did not join in the playground games. He seemed unable to follow the procedures in the classroom. He showed little interest in the teacher's instructions, rarely held his attention on any activity for more than a few moments, and fidgeted restlessly wherever he was.

WHEN THE passing of weeks brought no change in the youngster, Miss M became almost certain that she had a mentally retarded child in her group. However, the results of psychological examination proved her wrong in this conclusion: Robert, in spite of the forlorn, helpless, inept picture he presented, was actually a child of superior intelligence.

Miss M, challenged by the incongruity of the situation as well as by the unhappiness of the youngster, determined to find out why the boy was not living up to his potentialities. This bright boy must be helped, she felt, to have a brighter life.

A call at the Blake home one afternoon rather surprised Miss M. Despite Robert's usual untidy, ill-kempt appearance, the home was extremely neat and clean and was nicely furnished. The baby in his playpen looked clean and healthy. Mrs. Blake was a pretty woman, attractively dressed, and Mr. Blake, who came home from work while Miss M was chatting with his wife, was a pleasant enough man.

How did a child as unhappy, unhealthy, and unstable as Robert develop in this kind of home? Robert's mother looked cross and resentful when she was asked about the boy: she declared petulantly that she did not see why she deserved such a burden. The boy's father said bluntly that Robert was the most exasperating kid he had ever known and that no matter what they did, they seemed unable to make him change.

"We do what we can for him," he said, defensively, "and it's a lot, too. Why, I just bought him a new bicycle, and he's afraid to ride it. I took him to a baseball game with me a couple of weeks ago, and would you believe it, he didn't seem to have any fun at all."

"Tell me about the way he grew up," suggested Miss M. "Was he hard to manage when he was a baby?"

The mother launched into an account of Robert's early life. "He was a terrible child to take care of, nothing like our baby now," she began, her voice full of resentment. And then a long and bitter recital followed, the story of thousands of other little boys whose fathers were drafted into military service and whose mothers took them traveling about the country, leading—however necessarily—hurried, emotional, irregular lives. Not all little boys react in just the same fashion to the same experiences. Robert had not been able to meet the demands which were made upon him during his preschool years. It was now apparent that the unhappy results were influencing sadly his beginning school years.

How can a sense of security come from a life spent in day coaches, in rooming houses, in tourist cabins, one following the other in bewildering succession? How can an affectional attachment grow when a child is left in charge of one stranger after another, and when always his mother is worried, impatient, indignant at the turn of events which she is powerless to control? How can social relationships be easily established when there have never been any playmates, and grown-ups have always frankly found a child a bother and a nuisance? How can respect for property come when he has never had a toy of his own which could certainly be taken along traveling to his next "home," when there has never been a bed of his own, a familiar place which by its very familiarity offered reassurance that troubles would end?

Miss M, listening, could understand that Robert whined in protest. He cried with frustration. He had not understood his mother, and he had feared his father, whom he saw only occasionally and who treated his son as he treated the men for whom, as a sergeant, he was responsible.

When Robert was five, the uncertain existence was changed. His father was about to be released from the army. His mother and he went to the pleasant little home where they were now living. She fixed up a room for him alone, and told him their train trips were over.

But Miss M could see that Robert's troubles had continued. He found that the big man whom he had seen now and then during the past few years was coming to live with them, too. The boy had always been fearful of his father, and their daily contacts did not change his attitude. His father had a quick temper and a quicker hand. Punishment was frequent when his demand for instant obedience was not met and when Robert found it impossible to meet the adult standards which his father sternly set. There were threats, too, of being deprived of the nice new possessions if Robert did not mend his ways. "We do what we can for him," his father had told Miss M defensively. But unfortunately they had not done the right things.

Soon other demands were made on Robert. He had to share his mother with a new baby brother. He had to keep quiet because the baby was sleeping. He had to give up a promised trip to the park because Mother was tired after the baby had kept her up most of the night. Home did not live up to his expectations. It had its problems, even as the tourist cabins and rooming houses and day coaches had had theirs. Mrs. Blake's story made that clear.

But not even the imperfect home was really to last, from Robert's viewpoint. He was told one day that tomorrow he was going to school. Little explanation was given him; he was simply warned to do as his teacher told him and left at the schoolroom door to meet the new experience alone.

Now Miss M could begin to understand what life had done to Robert. She saw that both home and school had to work together to rehabilitate a war veteran of six.

Fortunately, Robert's parents were eager for help. Their distress about the boy was genuine, and although their methods thus far had been poorly conceived, they had no thought that their ways were the only ways of treating a child. They agreed that spankings had not helped; they would stop them. They granted that they had thoughtlessly set their standards too high. They could see that their love for the boy had not been proved to him. And they could appreciate that the new baby had been so appealing that the older child had often been ignored or given little consideration and had inevitably felt rejected, unloved, and uncertain of his place in the family group. They were most receptive to Miss M's explanation and suggestions, and chagrined at their part in Robert's difficulties. And they were relieved that the boy was definitely not dull.

Miss M assured them that she recognized that some changes were called for in the way Robert was being handled at school, too. Until knowledge about a child is reasonably complete, anyone is likely to misunderstand and misinterpret behavior, she told them. And they felt better about their own mistakes when they heard the teacher admit her early misconceptions.

Miss M was well aware that school could help Robert enormously. She planned first of all to show Robert that she was his friend. She selected one of the children in the class who was an easy-going, protective sort of boy, and saw to it that Robert was seated near him and was his partner in some of the group games. She made it a point to help Robert go over again the beginnings of the reading approach, so that his lack of accomplishment during the early part of the school year did not penalize his progress for the remainder of the year. She took occasion to praise him for the effort he made to pay attention, and she made sure that the class knew of his achievement when he made his first recognizable drawing and when he stayed at a puzzle long enough to make the picture fit together just right.

When she noticed Robert squirming and wriggling in his seat, she sent him to pile up the blocks. Whenever he very evidently had come to the end of his limited capacity for concentration, she suggested that he go to another activity of a completely different kind in which he had shown interest.

As the weeks passed, Robert gradually took more of a part in the group and became more relaxed. A group discussion one day revealed the fact that he had never had a birthday party. That gave Miss M an idea. She could bring home and school together in still another way, for Robert's seventh birthday was not far off. Suggesting to Mrs. Blake that a party at school might be planned for the occasion, she was delighted at the response: Mrs. Blake promised ice cream and cake and favors.

The children entered wholeheartedly into the plans for surprising Robert, and on the day of his birthday, while he was out of the room on an errand, they quickly helped his mother set the tables with the paper plates and napkins and spoons which Mrs. Blake had brought. The birthday cake, decorated with candles, was put at Robert's place and as he came back to the room the children all sang "Happy Birthday" fervently. Robert's eyes shone.

When Robert left school that day he thanked Miss M shyly. "I had fun," he told her. "And I liked it best that my mother was here, too. They all said 'Happy Birthday' to me. And she did, too. And she made a cake for me. She never paid any attention to my birthday ever before."

Robert's alert intelligence stood him in good stead when his emotional problems were eased. Once he could use the good ability which was his, he made progress in his school work. Once he could feel accepted by others, he participated well in group activities. He learned the rules of games quickly. He generally had a good suggestion when the children could think of nothing to do. He learned to plan and carry through an activity, and he had pleasure in doing so.

Robert did not come through the war unscathed. But once his difficulties were understood and given attention, persistent joint effort on the part of his parents and his teacher showed results. He took strides toward becoming a well-adjusted veteran; he began to learn to take his rightful place as a more capable and a happier child. By the time he entered second grade, he was losing the helplessness, the fearfulness, and the unhappiness which had characterized him when he first entered school.

CHAPTER FOUR

Slowly and steadily ahead

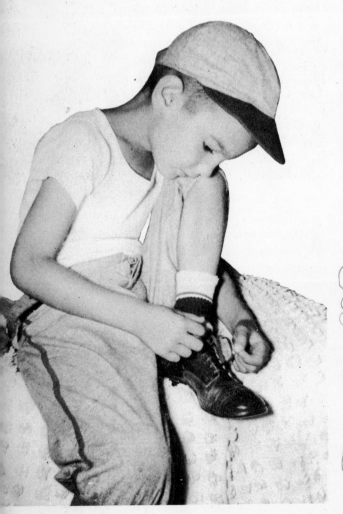

THE SEVEN-YEAR-OLD in his physical growth is much like the six-year-old, but in his feelings and his attitude toward life he is a more mature little person. He has entered another phase of his development, so that his experience in the second year in school will be on a different level from that of his first year. Both teacher and parents should be aware of his new growth needs so that they can be prepared to anticipate and understand them.

Physical growth continues steadily and slowly; there is nothing spectacular about it. The annual expected growth in height is still two or three inches, with a weight gain of three to six pounds. The legs continue to lengthen rapidly. The large muscles are still ahead of the small muscles in their development, but the child is gradually developing greater skill in the use of the small muscles. He can hold a pencil, although he grasps it tightly and shows a good deal of tension when he writes or prints. Eye-hand coordination is also improving. The eyes are not yet fully ready to accommodate themselves to near work, and a considerable amount of eye-rubbing is noticed among seven-year-olds. This may indicate that the eyes are under some strain, and it certainly suggests the need for not overemphasizing schoolwork which requires too constant eye work.

This is the period when the child is losing his baby teeth. He will have an increasing number of gaps as the months go by. Most of the children will have acquired their six-year molars and the central incisors will be appearing. Most children do not experience great difficulty in cutting these teeth, although a few may feel some soreness or show some irritability.

The seven-year-old tires easily and often shows fatigue during the afternoon session of school. He no longer takes an afternoon rest even on Saturday or Sunday. Most children of this age sleep approximately eleven hours at night, usually starting for bed between seven and eight o'clock. Care needs to be taken to provide rest through a change of activity, especially during the afternoon session at school, and to balance active play with quieter activities.

A HEALTHY seven-year-old is full of vitality and energy. Although he is not as continually active as the six-year-old and is more likely to balance his activity with periods of relatively quiet play, he still feels the drive to rush around, to climb, to do stunts on a trapeze, or to jump from heights. On the whole, though, he is more cautious and less likely to take chances than he was when he was six. The tricycle is usually put aside by this time in favor of roller skates, a jump rope, a scooter, or a coaster wagon. Most seven-year-olds look longingly toward owning a bicycle; a few can ride a two-wheeler, but most of the group are not quite ready for it yet. Seven likes to do tricks,

turning somersaults or hanging by his knees from the trapeze, climbing to the top of the jungle gym or the higher branches of a tree, or even a garage roof if one is available.

A child of this age often appears restless, as his general need for activity seems to carry over into all his behavior. The seven-year-old is often fidgety at the table; he may jump up during the meal or find it hard to sit still and not wriggle. He often uses gestures when he talks. When he is reading he may move his lips, shuffle his feet, hitch his chair back and forth, or play with his hair. When he writes he may screw up his face, bite his lips, or squirm in his place. Many youngsters try to sit still, but are not able to do so. Both parents and teachers need to make an allowance for the need for movement at this age and not plan a program that calls for too much sitting still.

The seven-year-old also learns better if he is encouraged to be active while he learns. He counts more easily and effectively if he has objects to move. He understands better if he can make things in a sandbox or take some part in other projects. Abstract thinking is barely beginning. He wants to use his hands, explore things with them, make things with them, learn things through them. He enjoys painting, clay modeling, and carpentry and is learning to handle tools well.

LANGUAGE has developed rapidly during the past year. The second-grader carries on vivid conversations. He likes to talk, although his conversation usually centers

64

about himself and the things he has done, or about his family and their possessions. His story will often be quite dressed up and will be related with eagerness and gestures. He still enjoys dramatic play both in school and in spontaneous play with other children.

Language is now a tool which he can use effectively in expressing disapproval. Instead of always fighting, the seven-year-old will sometimes hurl words and walk off the scene. He expresses his feelings toward his mother and her requests in no uncertain terms if he feels that something is not fair or if he doesn't want to do it.

He still enjoys songs, rhythms, and stories. He knows a tune now, and comments if other children do not sing correctly. His interest in stories has widened; he can now listen for a longer period of time and can carry over the thread of a story from day to day. Now that he can read some books himself, he may find much pleasure in reading alone, although he still enjoys being read to by teacher or Mother. This is the age

when fairy tales and myths are enjoyed. Poems are still favorites, and the child will call for the ones he likes; he may even know a good many by heart. His interest in stories about things that really happen is increasing and broadening: he wants to know how things work, what electricity is, all about

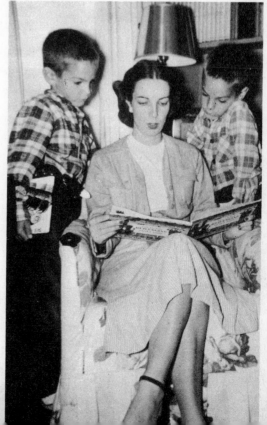

trains, airplanes, and cars. He still likes animal stories, but now he enjoys nature stories about real animals. He likes stories about other children and perhaps is beginning to be absorbed in the various series of books about boys and girls. The comics are coming on the scene; they are read, exchanged, and borrowed back again. Each child has his favorite which he may read and reread. This is the time to encourage his going to the library and choosing the book he wants alone.

The child's interest in stories carries over to radio listening. Many seven-year-olds come dashing in from play toward the end of the afternoon eager to hear the next installment of a favorite program. Many can listen to the radio without being concerned; others are upset by the overexcitement of some of the programs. Some children have disturbing dreams following an overstimulating hour of listening. It is sometimes necessary for Mother, or for teacher through discussion at school, to help choose the more desirable programs. If a child is very high-strung, Mother may have to say "You may listen to any of these programs" instead of leaving the choice entirely up to the child.

Movies are beginning to become part of the life of the seven-year-old, but they also are too stimulating for many youngsters of this age. If the seven-year-old attends them, the movies should be carefully selected and the child should arrive after the previews of other pictures. Movies, more than either comics or radio, seem to cause tension in many children of this age.

THE SEVEN-YEAR-OLD is learning to stand up for his own rights on the playground and will sometimes stand up for the rights of another child, especially where property is concerned. Most seven-year-old boys will fight for their rights if necessary, or else will walk off in indignation and refuse to play. Each wants his turn and demands it if he doesn't get it. A certain amount of aggressiveness and ability to hold one's own is necessary at this age, for the child must

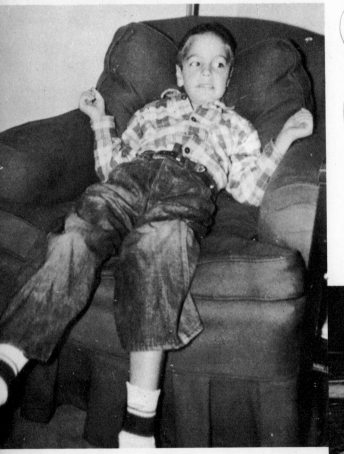

make an adjustment to the rougher ways of the playground. In another year gangs will be forming, and the youngster, especially the boy, will find it even more necessary to hold his own with the crowd. The problem of the adult is to help children do this without becoming too ill-mannered, crude, or rough. It is not an easy task and it causes much distress to some children. Some of the shyer, more withdrawn youngsters may need considerable help during this year and, in some instances, protection from situations that are still too difficult for them.

There is a good deal of competition among children of this age. They like to be first— to get the best grade or paint the best picture. They like to win the race or have first turn on the swing.

Seven is sensitive to what other children think about him and to whether or not he is liked. Many children become quite anxious for fear they will not be liked by their classmates. Boys and girls still play together, especially in group games, but their interests are diverging and best friends are almost always of the same sex.

At the same time that he is trying to learn to hold his own with other boys and girls the seven-year-old is also reaching for the approval of adults and is becoming increasingly sensitive to their approval or dis-

approval. These two desires often conflict, as the pattern of the adults and of the child's own group is not always the same.

Because the child is trying to reach out toward adult patterns and to think of himself as related to the adult world, it is more important than ever that his relationship with the adults about him be a warm, friendly, encouraging one. The teacher of the second grade has an especially important role to play in the development of the child under her guidance, for he will seek a close relationship with her and will want to please her. If she is rigid or repressive, the child will be less likely to develop into an independent personality, less able to think for himself. The seven-year-old often finds it hard to take criticism from an adult and will sometimes cry or blame the adult if he is scolded. On the other hand, he will accept and follow leadership and guidance quite devotedly. If the teacher is kindly, understanding, and responsive so that the child is encouraged and allowed some freedom and independence, he will be helped to develop well during this year.

It is important to recognize the seven-

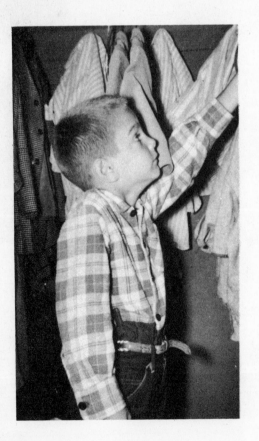

year-old's drive toward independence—a drive that is often overlooked because of his outward dependence upon his teacher for directions and reassurance. He may even be very impatient and irritable if she doesn't help. He wants to be independent, but doesn't quite trust himself. Yet if there is too much adult control he will be rebellious and hit out against it. He wants to grow up and become part of the adult world, to leave behind the manners and dress and behavior of the little child; yet at the same time he seems anxious for fear he will not do things correctly, and therefore he turns to the adult to be sure that he is right. If he is not reassured he may temporarily give up trying, until a little redirection or encouragement gets him started again. His teacher and parents need to be supportive in their attitude and yet at the same time encourage him to be independent and spontaneous.

THIS IS a good year for schoolwork because the child is anxious to do well and to learn how things are done. Gesell calls it the "eraser" age. The seven-year-old erases as much as he writes, trying constantly to make his work more nearly perfect.

It is a good year at home, too, for the seven-year-old has learned to do many things for himself, although he often dawdles and dreams while he is doing them. He still needs a patient reminder from Mother that time is slipping away and that he will be late for school, or that dinner is almost ready and hands should be washed. But he is beginning to see the need for washing hands and even for helping around the house. He likes to have a "job" at home, just as he likes to help teacher at school. Again, he may not always carry it out efficiently, but with a little help and encouragement he is learning to do his share. He can take care of most of his physical needs. He can bathe himself, brush his teeth, dress himself, and tie his shoelaces.

Although the seven-year-old is beginning to develop a concept of time, he still lives pretty much in the immediate present and cannot plan well for future goals. He understands what time is and is learning to tell time. He may worry about being late for school, but he cannot yet take full responsibility for getting there on time. He still dawdles and moves slowly as if time meant nothing. Sometimes he will hurry up if he is told that he must leave for school—the dash into his clothes may be a sudden contrast to his dreamy dawdling.

The second-grader is ready for a small allowance. He understands what money is for. He knows that food and clothes and other things that one wants must be paid for. He usually knows the names of the more frequently used coins, and their relationship to one another—that a nickel and

five pennies are the same and that a dime is worth two nickels. With a weekly allowance seven-year-olds begin to learn about spending and saving.

THE SEVEN-YEAR-OLD is much more sensitive to feelings and attitudes of others. One of the most striking contrasts we see between six and seven is the fact that whereas six lives in a world of activity in the here and now, seven is reaching out for new experiences, trying to relate himself to his enlarged world. But he seems to be taking things into himself rather than going out

toward them. He is often dreamy and absorbed as if he is thinking things over and trying to adjust himself to a new world of ideas and feelings. He likes other people and wants to be with them, and he is gradually becoming more sensitive in his feelings toward them and more aware of their feelings toward him.

His ethical sense is beginning to develop. He is able to take some responsibility for his own actions. He is concerned about right and wrong. He often criticizes his playmates if they do things which he does not think are right, and he may tattle to teacher or Mother. Sometimes this tattling is an attempt to win the approval of the adult, but frequently it seems to be an outlet for his anxiety and concern about these things, and an attempt to reassure himself that whereas the other children are wrong, his behavior is still desirable. He may also ask, "Is it all right to do this?" "May we go there?" He is still seeking for patterns of behavior and wants to be sure that he is getting the right ones. He still does not have a complete understanding of truthfulness or honesty. He may pick up little things that he likes, a pencil, a piece of chalk, an eraser, and slip them into his pocket. He is more truthful than he was at six, but he is still learning.

SEVEN is a good age, and a responsive one, but it is very easy to impose upon the child's eagerness to do what the adult wants. He often becomes overanxious because he fears he will not be able to achieve the standards set for him by his parents or teacher. He is becoming more critical of himself and is sensitive to failure or being made fun of. There is no place for sarcasm or ridicule on the part of an adult toward a seven-year-old; even too much teasing is unwise. Because he turns to an adult for guidance, it is easy for him to become too dependent upon adults, too inclined to give in to adult authority at the expense of his own feelings and drives. It is up to the adults to steer a middle course which gives him the support and encouragement he needs so much at seven, yet induces independence and self-reliance on his part.

Seeing double

JACK and Jerry are twins who have known only pleasure in their twinship. They are happy, active boys, well liked by their friends and cooperative at home. Their life has been fun, predictable and consistent in its rules and regulations, always challenging and always within their powers to cope with. Small wonder that they look on life confidently, with zest and eagerness.

Pull those laces good and tight.

The floor is a wonderful place to dress.

Whistling is a brand-new achievement.

No need to argue about it.

It's a great game.

*If you fold an airplane just right
it will sail every time.*

A left-hander is usually left-footed too.

*Digging was hot work.
We really earned this.*

*How can so much new dirt get
in those ears every day?*

72

Compliant Johnny

JOHNNY GIFFORD was seven, in second grade. He had had an uneventful school career thus far, seeming to keep up with the class without trouble. But now, gradually, he was showing increasing difficulty with his work. He took a long time to get started with a lesson, erasing time and time again the word or number he had written, never seeming satisfied with the results of his efforts. When a period was over Johnny had rarely completed his work, although the others in the class would often finish long before the bell rang.

Miss E was a very young teacher; this was her first assignment. She thought of Johnny chiefly as one among her thirty-eight children who never made her day difficult, and whom she considered "good as gold" and so never worried about. She was aware that lately the child's schoolwork had fallen below his earlier accomplishment, but she hoped it was a passing phase and that he would manage to advance with the class at the end of the term.

But when Johnny's report card indicated his slow and unfinished work, Mrs. Gifford accepted no such casual interpretation. She appeared at the school early the next morning and announced firmly to Miss E, "He's never given any trouble before, and we're not going to have anything start now. He can learn as well as the others. If it's necessary, you punish him. He must get a better report card next month. Perhaps he should have special tutoring."

Mrs. Gifford spoke quickly and decisively. Her chief reaction to the school report was

indignation that her son was not bringing credit to his family. He had disturbed the routine of doing exactly as she expected, and she found this intolerable.

Mrs. Gifford had always considered Johnny's docile obedience as reflecting the "good job" she was doing in bringing him up. Quiet, self-effacing Johnny had followed all the regulations imposed by his mother at home. She was determined that he would meet her standards of good schoolwork. A plan of tutoring was arranged, although she was greatly upset that such special attention should be necessary.

Johnny accepted the new arrangement submissively, although it meant giving up a good deal of his playtime. He wanted to do better in school. He had been worried because he tried hard and never seemed to do what his teacher expected.

After a few sessions, however, the tutor felt that Johnny's knowledge of basic skills was really adequate. He read well, and his number work was good. It was the amount of time he required that interfered with his being successful in the classroom. And his slow progress with a lesson was generally due to the fact that he was not satisfied with his own work and would copy again material which had already been carefully reworked, or erase what another child would have considered acceptable.

YOUNG MISS E felt challenged by the situation, partly because she thought she might have been somewhat at fault, partly because she sensed that the mother's attitude was unwise. She discussed the matter with the school principal, Mr. Jamison, and an appointment was arranged for Mrs. Gifford to talk to him. At about this time Johnny developed a heavy cold, and because he stayed home during an entire week, Miss E went to the home to take some schoolbooks to him. Her report of the visit suggested to Mr. Jamison the possible basis for Johnny's troubles and for his tense, anxious manner.

"Johnny was lying on the living-room sofa," Miss E related, "and his mother said that as long as I was there with him she would go out to do some errands which Johnny usually did. She said it as if he had caught cold just to inconvenience her.

"When she had left, Johnny told me worriedly that his illness was making his mother do a great many extra things. It seems he cares for his own room every morning, making the bed and dusting and using a carpet sweeper before he leaves for school. And he always sets the table, helps with the dishes, polishes ash-trays and plant holders and that sort of thing, and keeps the bookshelves in perfect order. And in the past month another chore has been added to the list; he helps with the ironing, doing the handkerchiefs and pillow slips as his share. Every minute is planned for him!

"Of course Mrs. Gifford is a wonderful housekeeper," Miss E continued. "I telephoned only a few minutes before I went over to their house, so nothing special could possibly have been done. The place was spotless, everything exactly in order and looking as if it had just been polished or pressed or scoured."

WHILE Miss E was chatting with Johnny, who had been delighted to see her, she picked up a book, glanced through it and replaced it. A little later she fingered a lovely pottery bird, examining the exquisite workmanship. Johnny became disturbed and restless, and when Miss E questioned him, he blurted unhappily, "The book should be on the next shelf, not where you put it. And the bird you were looking at— it should face the window, and you made it face the wall. My mother won't like it if things aren't right. She says there's a place for everything and everything should be in its place. She scolds if I don't fix things right after I dust."

Johnny was apologetic for his implied criticism of Miss E, but he apparently could not risk displeasing his mother. Miss E cheerfully replaced the articles as he directed, and Johnny relaxed. She asked him then if his father, too, was particular about everything, if he was strict. The reply was unexpected.

"Daddy tries hard," answered the child, seriously. "But he's different. Mother says it's the way he was brought up. She says she's going to bring me up right. I heard her tell Daddy so one night," he added confidentially. "That was when he wasn't being neat, and Mother told him I was just like him, and he was a bad example. No, Daddy's not strict," said Johnny, coming back to the original question which had started his comments, "Daddy's nice."

BEFORE Mrs. Gifford returned from her errands, Johnny's father came home. He entered cheerfully, tossing his coat on the end of the sofa, placing his hat on the table, letting his newspaper slide to the floor. But an anxious look soon appeared on his face. He talked nervously, asking innumerable questions. Had Johnny taken his medicine? Had he eaten his lunch? Had he given Mother any trouble? It was nice of Miss E to bring books for him; he was so far behind in his work, and Mother didn't like that. She wanted him to be promoted!

Johnny sat up excitedly. "I have to be promoted!" he said shrilly. "I have to be! Mother said nobody in her family had ever *not* been promoted!"

Miss E soothed him. "We'll help you, Johnny. You'll be back at school soon. And I'll leave these lessons for you to do while you're home."

Mr. Gifford went to the door a few moments later, as Miss E said good-by. Johnny was out of hearing and Miss E observed that she wondered if standards had been set too high for the boy. She told the father about the earlier conversation.

"My wife's a wonderful woman," he said, a little uncomfortably. "I know she's set in her ways, but really, she means everything for the best. She wants John to be different from his untidy father," he said with a self-conscious smile. "And she's right about this schoolwork, too. Of course she's right."

Mr. Jamison felt that this visit of the teacher's was very enlightening. It suggested a home situation which was difficult for the boy, and which was perhaps tied in with his school failure.

He made an appointment with Mrs. Gifford to come to the school, and when she came he talked the situation through with her. Talking with her, he was sure his surmise was correct. He tried to show her how Johnny was caught between the opposing standards of his parents. In trying to please both of them, the boy was having a hard time of it. Punishment was not the answer, as his mother seemed to think.

"Maybe you're right," said Mrs. Gifford finally, though grudgingly. "But Johnny will have to do as I say. I can't change at my age. I've learned to put up with his father's careless ways, but I won't have my child spoiled."

It was not easy to persuade Mrs. G. that her overexacting ways not only were creating a too demanding situation for Johnny, but had confused him because of the friction they brought about with her husband. A balance between the standards of the parents was urged as being more wholesome for Johnny. At least outward accord between mother and father was essential to establish a feeling of self-confidence and security in the child. Without these, his schoolwork was not the only aspect of his life which might be affected. His total adjustment was likely to suffer.

PARENTS are not always as rigidly demanding as Mrs. Gifford, yet whatever their standards, they affect their children. For children want to please their parents because that is how they win the good will and approval so important to them. Thus when parents have opposing viewpoints and one home has two standards, the child in that home becomes confused. His confusion can be shown in many ways.

In Johnny's case, the mother was a stronger willed, more dominating personality than the father. Johnny was zealous to meet her demands, and tried hard to live up to her expectations by being meticulously clean and orderly. The other parent was gentler and more affectionate, a casual individual. His ways were vastly different. In seeking to meet his mother's requirements, Johnny often felt as if he were implicitly criticizing his father. That made him feel guilty. And when he occasionally left a toy on the floor or neglected to hang up his coat immediately upon entering the house, he felt disloyal to his mother. That made him unhappy. It was a problem he could neither understand nor resolve.

It was a dilemma which gave the youngster considerable worry. And he did not leave the worry at home, where it originated. Often in school something would remind him of one or the other parent. He would begin to wonder a little resentfully whether he had done everything he was supposed to before leaving the house that morning. And he would speculate—was Daddy really a bad example, as he had heard Mother assert? Then he would feel wicked to have such critical thoughts about his parents.

His docile behavior at home had been the outgrowth of both his guilt over these reflections and his fear of arousing his mother's wrath. He had learned that if he did what he was told and said little, things moved more smoothly. But he could not control his thoughts as he did his actions. Often he felt angry or rebellious even as he was carrying out instructions. Frequently he disliked his mother intensely while he was doing exactly as she directed. He wondered about his father, who clearly did not live up to his mother's expectations. But he admired him greatly and wished he could accept his ways for his own.

It was a very disturbing state of affairs for Johnny. At school he had been "good as gold," as Miss E said, because he was fearful that he would hear criticism from his teacher as well as from his mother. His own demands upon himself for perfect papers created a large part of his difficulty with class work. And the demands were a reflection of his mother's standards, which were beyond the child's achievement and so troubled him constantly.

None of the grown-ups with whom Johnny had daily contacts had really understood the boy. They had the faulty concept, often held, of considering a child's behavior indicative of a problem only if it is behavior which disturbs or annoys or interferes with others. It is entirely true that obvious reactions, such as temper outbursts and disobedience and quarrelsomeness, are evidences of poor adjustment and suggest the need of help. But it is equally true—although not always remembered—that behavior which is always yielding, submissive, and compliant is also evidence of poor adjustment and also needs help.

Johnny's docility was a symptom. It needed recognition and understanding. For the healthy and happy small child is eager and responsive and active. Tractable and submissive moments can be observed in all children, of course. But when they are not punctuated by more enterprising, alert, investigative moments, when the child never chafes or protests or murmurs, the situation is suspect.

It is easier to handle the compliant child than the rebellious one. It is easier for the time being, at least. But his very passivity, his resigned acceptance of what is demanded of him, is unhealthy. The withdrawn, meek, acquiescent behavior may cover angry and resentful thoughts, or puzzled and anxious ones. A wholesome environment at home helps to eliminate such reactions. Parental accord at least in the presence of the child is important. Arguments and recriminations between parents confuse children, and injure their healthful emotional growth. When a child is not good, but too good, there is trouble somewhere.

No place like home?

THERE IS an old couplet which tells us that "East, west, Home's best." And certainly it is true that in general home *is* much the best place for a child to grow up. Most parents love their children and want to provide adequately for happy, healthful development. Few situations suggest taking a child away from his home. If it is possible for him to live with at least one parent, he is usually better off there if arrangements can be made for his care and supervision when the parent must be at work.

But it is wise to consider every situation individually. Sometimes unusual circumstances make foster-home placement far more wholesome than a child's own home. Sometimes it is better for him to leave his family, despite the traditional counsel that "Home's best."

Huntley Williams lived in a large, comfortable apartment. There was a playground nearby, and school was conveniently located. His family was in good circumstances and able to provide him with more than ordinary necessities. But by the time he was seven, Huntley had a long history of troublesome behavior—a type of behavior not infrequently found when a child lives under conditions of deprivation with no recreational facilities. He was defiant and impudent at home. He had twice run away. He was flagrantly disobedient, told lies, appropriated whatever he fancied, and never showed any remorse when he was scolded or punished.

It was the aunt who finally approached the school. She said that since he was three,

Huntley had been a problem. He would throw his food on the floor. Without apparent reason, he would throw things out of the window—fruit from a dining-table bowl, the telephone pad, a number of guest towels. He was destructive with his toys, careless of his clothes, and would not take responsibility, forgetting errands, neglecting piano practice, ignoring meal hours.

The aunt considered that the climax of his misdemeanors was his taking a ten-dollar bill from her purse. Huntley denied knowledge of the money until confronted with clear evidence that he had changed it for smaller bills and spent them for cokes and dime-store toys for the neighborhood youngsters. When it was useless to deny it any longer, the boy shrugged and refused to talk about it further.

ALL THIS was utterly baffling to his family. It was only too apparent that their method of constant scolding and frequent whipping, of depriving the child of allowance and movies, had been wholly ineffectual. They felt puzzled when the school said Huntley was not considered a problem: he was up in his work, and while he argued and quarreled considerably with the children and was inclined to be noisy and talkative, he had not been thought very different from most boys his age.

It was decided to consult a child-guidance center. Not infrequently a child who is considered "bad" in one situation will show such acceptable behavior in another. This apparent paradox can be understood only when all the circumstances are known. We need to study thoroughly both the child himself and all the conditions of his daily living—not only current conditions, but happenings throughout his life. For the behavior of a child at any time may be the result of what has occurred many months or years before.

THE GUIDANCE-CENTER staff found Huntley's physical condition to be excellent. His mental ability was superior. But when social relationships were investigated, it was very apparent that Huntley was not liked by his schoolmates.

Huntley had apparently taken the ten dollars to buy things for other children which would, in effect, buy their friendship. It was therefore necessary to understand why such a step seemed necessary to him, why he had not been able to make friends without resorting to bribing. That brought into the picture the boy's family situation and the emotional interrelationships there.

The surface circumstances included a comfortable home, zealous medical provision, and piano lessons, with a very fine teacher. But they did not include even one acceptant, understanding, sympathetic adult through whom Huntley might have achieved emotional security. Beneath the surface of his everyday living smoldered bitterness and resentment and unhappiness.

Huntley's parents were divorced after his mother had deserted her family to live with another man. The boy was then two. His father had never wanted a child and had always resented the added burden. When his wife chafed under the restrictions imposed by an infant, he was even more bitter. Yet when his wife left them, he saw no recourse but to make some plan to care for Huntley. He arranged to live with his mother, an aged, eccentric widow, and his older sister, also widowed, who was a high-school teacher.

HUNTLEY was undoubtedly confused by the many changes which occurred during those days. He clung to his nurse, the most familiar and the most attentive of all the people around him. When she left—unable to get along with the demanding grandmother—the little boy cried for days and could not be consoled.

Elderly Mrs. Williams had never been anything but coolly interested in Huntley. She had disliked her daughter-in-law and rarely saw her; she was indignant that her only grandchild should have his mother's maiden name. She had finally agreed to sharing a home with her son only after considerable inner struggle, because, she said, she "knew her duty." Small wonder that the baby cried for his nurse and feared his grandmother. She rarely smiled at him, rarely expressed either affection or approval. Her "duty" did not include loving the boy.

She was a rigid disciplinarian and was in complete charge. Huntley's father was increasingly absent from home, and when there, never questioned the grandmother's demands or decisions. If she complained about the child, he was spanked. When this had no effect, he was deprived of privileges or locked in his room.

THE AUNT remonstrated with her brother once or twice when she noted marks on the boy's body after he had been struck by his father with a doubled clothesline or a thick leather thong. But she had little to do with the child and was often away weekends and evenings as well as during the day.

When she spoke to the social worker at the child-guidance center, she mentioned that on several occasions, after he had been punished, Huntley had failed to come home until very late at night. "His father punished him severely," she said, "but it did no good. The next day he'd come home even later!" It evidently did not occur to her that there was little at home to attract the boy.

When the psychologist at the center met Huntley, it was hard to convince the boy that he was there not to be punished but to be helped. However, his sullen manner finally changed to responsive friendliness. He wanted to be liked.

He spoke about wanting the children on the playground and down the block as his friends, and he told how his grandmother was making things difficult. She ignored his protests that errands and tasks were always required when he wanted to go out to play. Nor was he ever permitted to bring a child to the house to play. His grandmother said he "showed his poor blood" by seeking the company of the neighborhood boys.

He had real need of them, need of being accepted by them. But they called him "sissy" and "stuck up" when he did not join them at play. At home he was rejected, and to be rejected by the children too was more than he could bear. To treat them, and so entice them to be friendly, had suggested a way out of his misery.

IT WAS IMPOSSIBLE to convince the family that Huntley was not a confirmed delinquent, an incorrigible thief and liar. They would not grant that the vastly different behavior shown by the boy at school and at home involved them seriously.

The grandmother refused to concede that she had played any part in the unhappy developments. The father said frankly that he stayed away from home so much because "The devil himself couldn't live peaceably with the old lady," and he did not blame the boy entirely for his transgressions. Nevertheless he was too distraught by his own emotional problems to be really concerned about his son. The aunt said bluntly, "I don't suppose we could expect him to grow up normally in our abnormal household," and thus summed up the situation.

Fortunately it was possible to arrange for the boy to go away to a summer camp and to plan on his living in more favorable surroundings in the fall. In another city a family was located who could use the money Huntley's board and supervision would bring them, and in return would give him a new chance at more normal development. They had two children of their own, were understanding and sympathetic.

FOR HUNTLEY, home was clearly not best. One can only speculate as to what might have been accomplished if the father had accepted his own need for psychiatric help, or if the grandmother had been less rigid and resistant, or the aunt a warmer and better-adjusted personality.

Huntley at seven had been asocial, yet sought sociability. He had sensed rejection, and sought acceptance. Because he was young, it was not too difficult to help him. By the time he was ten many of the scars had healed.

He continued to do well in school. He did better outside of school than he ever had before. There was no longer any need to rebel against unfair authority. There was nothing to lie about, nor did he have to appropriate what did not belong to him in order to buy friendship. He lived as an accepted member of a well-adjusted family. He felt loved and wanted. He had time to play. He had an allowance.

He had been given an opportunity to develop in wholesome surroundings. Away from his own family, all went well. It was the home situation that had been the problem, not the child.

CHAPTER FIVE

Eight

is an eager

year

THE THIRD year in the primary school is the dividing line between early childhood and the more mature middle years. The eight-year-old is "halfway up the stairs." He is not a little child, nor is he yet quite so settled down and responsible as he will be when he is nine. He does not like to be treated as a little child and greatly resents being talked down to by his parents or his teacher, but he is still very dependent upon praise and encouragement and needs to be reminded of his responsibilities if he is to carry through. Because he looks and seems so much more grown up than he was at seven, adults often grow impatient when his actions are less mature than his appearance.

The eight-year-old is very much aware of the adult world and is trying to find his place in it. He wants to behave in a more grown-up way. At home his manners may be lacking, but when he goes out he may surprise his parents with his courtesy and good behavior. He is not so dependent upon his teacher for emotional support as he was at seven, but seems even more dependent upon his mother. During this year he often seems demanding upon her. He continually wants her to play games with him, to do things with him and for him, to listen to his talk, and always to be at hand when he wants her. Perhaps this is part of being neither a little child nor quite ready to be grown up. While he resents being dom-

80

inated or overdirected, eight still needs his mother's support and wants to feel close to her.

Eight is an eager year. It is a year when the child seems ready to tackle anything, and he often shows more enthusiasm than wisdom in what he tries. For this reason it seems to be a year of hazards, during which accidents seem to take place in greater proportion than in other years. The eight-year-old wants new experiences; he wants to try things out, to see how they work, to know how they are made. Often he may attempt more than he can do, and so the results disappoint him or he is not able to complete his project. If this eagerness is wisely directed, it can be a profitable year in the development of the child. Wise adult guidance which knows how to cooperate with the enthusiasm of the child, how to channel his curiosity and vital interests, can be invaluable during this year. On the other hand, the adult who dominates, over-directs, and is overcritical can cause much tension and anxiety in children of this age. Parents and teachers who are working with eight-year-olds need to be aware of the sensitivity of these children, their desire for guidance and help in achieving their goals, together with their inability to accept too much criticism. Tears are near the surface if correction is too harsh, and resentment wells up at being "bossed."

Physically the eight-year-old is still developing steadily but slowly. His arms are lengthening, and his hands are growing larger. His eyes are beginning to accommodate more readily to both near and far distances, so that he is better able to handle reading and other forms of schoolwork that require the near focusing of the eye. Eye-hand coordination is definitely improved. Near-sightedness often develops during this

year; the eyes should be checked and glasses prescribed when necessary.

The permanent teeth are continuing to appear, usually the incisors first and then the lower bicuspids. Care of the teeth should be stressed during this year, as the novelty of brushing teeth has worn off and many children grow careless and neglectful. The

81

craft work with tools which require some skill in manipulation. The girls will enjoy simple sewing and weaving and will usually spend many hours with paper dolls and other cutouts, cutting carefully and efficiently.

Some children, particularly the tall, thin youngsters, develop poor posture during this period. However, they can be interested in learning to sit and stand well, provided this is done not by nagging and scolding but rather by capturing their interest in the development of the body and the reasons why good posture is desirable. Sometimes poor posture is a sign of too much fatigue, of emotional tension, or of poor nutrition. In all cases of poor posture it is wise to study the child and try to remedy the cause.

Baseball, soccer, and other organized games delight the eight-year-old. He tries to learn the rules and may become quite bossy in trying to see that they are kept. Sometimes his group will invent variations of the rules or make new rules. On rainy days or in the evenings he is becoming an enthusiast for table games—monopoly,

necessity for regular dental check-ups should also be emphasized.

Since the large muscles are still developing, the children still need much opportunity for movement and active, outdoor play. They continue to run and shout and climb, and there is much wrestling and punching of one another. At the same time the small muscles are much better developed and the children are able to use them more effectively and with better coordination. Writing is much more even. They can do

parcheesi, rummy, hearts, and all the old and new favorites that children have played through the years. Erector sets and chemistry outfits, models of airplanes, trains, and boats keep the boys busy. The girls have countless involved games with their paper dolls.

The eight-year-old wants a "best friend." There may be many quarrels and much arguing between best friends at this age. Boys often fight with each other, and girls call names and have battles of words, but a sense of loyalty to each other is beginning to develop. The children can usually work out such situations between themselves without adult interference. Many of the friendships will shift during the year, but some of the youngsters will remain best friends and carry the friendship over into another year.

Just as they desire a best friend, so children of this age also seem to enjoy having an "enemy." Sometimes two children will single out other children as enemies, sometimes a group of children will single out one child or another group. If the feeling toward the "enemy" gets out of bounds, some

adult intervention and adroit redirection may be necessary.

UNTIL THIS year although boys and girls have chosen their best friends from members of their own sex they have also played together some of the time. Now we see a marked difference. Boys and girls are pulling definitely apart in their interests and their activities. Sometimes they will even gang up against each other and

gangs and clubs but will utilize their potentialities for helping the child learn how to relate himself to others and work cooperatively with them.

The adult-supervised group cannot take the place of the children's own group, but it can be of great additional value during this year. The eight-year-old responds well to group activities of many kinds. His teacher finds that in the classroom he is a willing member of the group, with the result that she can plan and think more frequently in terms of the group as a whole. Projects in the classroom, club activities after school, organized games, and recreational projects fit the children's needs and interests. Competitive games such as spelling bees or arithmetic games or simple desk games are entered into with zest. Through games the eight-year-old can enjoy wholesome competition and can learn to be both a good winner and a good loser. A well-planned program of games, both indoors and out, provides not only fun but valuable learning for the third-grader.

A full program of after-school activities is particularly valuable during this transition year. Eight-year-olds are not always mature enough to carry through such planned activities by themselves. Although

call names or tease. They are entering the period when their interests will focus upon friends of their own sex. It is the beginning of the period of gangs and clubs. At this age the gang or club may not be well formed, and its purpose and membership may change frequently. But the desire to be a member of the gang is emerging and will grow in intensity during the next few years. At this point it is beginning to be very important to be like the rest, to belong to the group. Both parents and teachers sometimes find this difficult, for it becomes increasingly evident that the child may follow the pattern of his group rather than the directions of parent or teacher, in cases where the two do not coincide.

However, there are great strengths to be gained from this belonging to the group. The child needs the sense of security it gives, the opportunity to identify with others of his own age and sex, the opportunity to make plans and rules not established by adults and to carry them through, and the valuable lessons in cooperation which he learns better in his own group than in any other way. The eight-year-old cannot take much criticism from adults, but he is capable of considerable self-evaluation at his own level and he is able to take and give criticism within his own group. The wise parent and teacher will not put pressure against the establishment of

they may start an organized game of base-ball or soccer on the corner lot, they get mixed up and confused and usually end with much squabbling and disputing. Much of this they can work through in some measure by themselves, but they usually respond well to friendly adult guidance and direction which gets them out of the muddle. When they are older there will be increasing value from self-direction in such activities.

PLAY IS frequently dramatic. The child's earlier interest in "acting" becomes very strong during this year. The boys may copy the radio programs and movies in which they are becoming absorbed, the girls still dress up, play house, or act out scenes with paper dolls. In addition to the dramatization in their informal play, eight-year-olds are also ready to take part in simple dramatics in the classroom and thoroughly enjoy putting on a "play." These dramatizations, of course, should be kept simple and within the abilities of the children, participation being more important than a finished performance.

Movies, comics, and radio have become a definite part of the life of the eight-year-old. Many eight-year-olds go to the movies once a week. They are addicts of western and Indian pictures, stories of war and of adventure. The girls like musicals, and both boys and girls enjoy animal stories. Neither boys nor girls like love stories; they wish "all that stuff" was left out. At this age they do not want to be too frightened and often will not look or will cover their ears. Most youngsters of this age listen to radio programs in the late afternoon or early evening. They follow with enthusiasm their favorite serials and also enjoy some of the comedy and quiz programs. Some eight-year-olds have bad dreams and disturbed sleep follow-

ing movies or radio programs that are over-stimulating or too frightening. Individual reactions should be considered in permitting or denying this activity.

Comics are exchanged back and forth and are read and reread. The child who does not read well may prefer comics to books, but most eight-year-olds read and enjoy many other books if their interest and delight in them has been encouraged. At this age it is particularly important for parents and teachers to be aware of the competition of the comics and to select for boys and girls books that are full of adventure and humor, so that a wider reading interest will develop. Fairy tales, stories of long ago, tales of animals and children, of Indians and western adventures, appeal to the third-grade child. Reading aloud is still enjoyed by many; others prefer to read to themselves.

COLLECTIONS of all kinds also intrigue the child who is eight. His pockets will be full of odds and ends, but his interest is also

beginning to focus upon real "collections." These may vary from bottle tops or playing cards to interesting stones, bugs, or stamps. His interest is not always prolonged, and his collections may change frequently, but it is an activity to be encouraged. At home Mother can help by providing a place for the collections and by not throwing away things because they seem useless to her. Teacher can help by encouraging the youngsters to bring their collections to school and tell the class about them.

Money is beginning to play a significant part in the life of the eight-year-old. He understands now about money and its use in our culture. He has some conception of saving for something which this week's allowance will not buy. If his allowance is not big enough for his needs, he will seek opportunities to earn small sums of money. He plans ahead, counting the weeks it will take him to save enough to buy a bicycle or a pair of roller skates. Often he is quite unrealistic and starts off saving for unobtainable items. Often, too, he will spend unwisely the money that he has. But he is beginning to learn the value and purpose of money and how it may be used. He needs to experience owning money and spending it in his own way. A small allowance is a "must" for the eight-year-old. Discussions at home and at school about how money can be used and saved can be of great interest and help to him. The ideas the adults present must be in the realm of reality for the eight-year-old mind: saving for college is beyond his interest or understanding; saving for a dollar baseball bat is within both his reach and his comprehension.

The eight-year-old is developing a better understanding about time. He can tell time and can relate it to the events of the day. He knows at what time meals are served, when school begins, and when he must

be in bed. Yet he still does not seem ready to take complete responsibility for going to bed, getting up, or arriving at school on time. There still have to be reminders from his parents if his routines are to function at all smoothly. He has the habit of putting things off. "In a minute" and "soon" are much used words.

He understands also about days and months and years, and he is trying to relate himself to a past and a future. He is showing an interest in things that happened "long ago," although he is often very confused as to just when past events occurred. He may think that his grandmother lived in the time of the Pilgrims, that she used a spinning wheel and was afraid of Indians. But at least he realizes that there *was* a past in which people lived and did things; his horizons are extending. His world now extends definitely beyond the present; he

the differences but laying stress on the many similarities.

Not only is the eight-year-old beginning to understand other people better and to develop sympathy and acceptance of others and of their needs and rights; at the same time he is beginning to understand himself better. He sees himself in relation to other people. He realizes now that some children do things better than he does, that others are not so capable, and that different ones excel in different activities. He is usually fairly accepting of himself and is not too concerned about his weak points unless the adults about him have put too much pressure on him, made too many comparisons, or disturbed him because of their concern over his achievement or ability. He shows a capacity for self-evaluation and will even sometimes laugh at himself for something he has done. He alibis a good deal and makes excuses for himself, but often makes plans for doing better. He frequently sets rather high standards for himself and tries to live up to them, as well as to the standards which are being set by the adults around him.

The eight-year-old is full of energy. He may not be so easy to guide as the seven-year-old. He may be more argumentative and have more spirit, but he is also alert to the world around him, interested in people generally, full of curiosity and the desire to know. He may not practice his skills as carefully as he did at seven, but he is eager to find out about things and is stimulating to be with. He may be careless about his clothes, unwilling to help at home, noisy and bossy; but he is also lovable and friendly. The third year in school can be a good one for parents, teachers, and children, for the child will respond well to wise and kindly adult leadership and guidance.

realizes that people live and die, that there have been people before him and will be people after him. This is an adult concept and shows that he is growing up.

At this age the child's thinking is reaching out beyond his immediate environment. He knows now that there are children living in other parts of our country, some living much as he does, some very differently. Stories about children in other parts of the United States interest him, and he may pore over maps of the states and pictures of other places. He is beginning to notice the differences among his own classmates; sometimes, through the influence of the adults in his environment, he may have begun to develop feelings and prejudices concerning these differences. Because he is noticing people, this is an excellent year in which to develop a friendly interest in boys and girls of other lands and other races, pointing out

Marlene

MARLENE is as happy and active an eight-year-old as one could wish to see. She is doing well in third grade and has reached the point where she would rather read to herself than be read to. At home she is a busy, participating member of the family group. Marlene had polio when she was two and will always wear a brace on her leg, but no one seems to pay much attention to her handicap, least of all Marlene—she is too busy doing the many things that all girls her age like to do.

Pictures still help make a book interesting but reading has come to be a lot of fun.

Dolls were an early love and still claim much time and devotion.

Marlene's mother has just bought new hoops and is teaching Marlene to embroider.

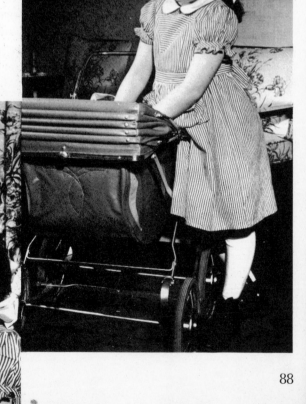

88

Everyone helps in this family.

She has taken piano lessons for two years
and enjoys it, all but the practicing.
Drawing is a favorite occupation.

Marlene is a good match for brother John
in the many games they play.

Isabel had no friends

THERE IS increasing acceptance of the concept that every behavior reaction has some cause. But sometimes it is not understood—or at least not remembered—that no single cause can explain so complex a result as a child's behavior. There is always an intermingling of circumstances.

Mrs. Warren first became worried about eight-year-old Isabel because the child had no friends. When other girls had birthday parties or asked each other to come home after school to play, Isabel was never invited. And in the morning when groups of children trooped toward school, Isabel always walked alone. Finally Mrs. Warren talked the situation over with a close friend.

"She's so much younger than the others in her class," said the latter. "Children like to feel grown up, and they probably resent having a younger child around."

Mrs. Warren was impatient with herself for not thinking of this before. It was perfectly true. Isabel was eight and in fifth grade. Most of her classmates were at least two years older. Accordingly, after some deliberation, Mrs. Warren enrolled Isabel in a beginners' music class, with other children seven, eight, and nine years old.

But Isabel's early interest in the music group did not last. She learned quickly and soon became bored with the repeated instructions and demonstrations. And the children did not seem to care for her.

MRS. WARREN now sought help from the school. Isabel's teacher had been aware that the little girl was not particularly popular, but she did not know that any real social adjustment problem existed.

"I always try to give her a chance to shine here in the classroom," she told Mrs. Warren, "because I've seen that she doesn't get along on the playground. Perhaps the play club would be a better plan than music lessons. Isabel isn't very good at games, and I've noticed the children don't choose her for sides. She might be better liked if she had more skill running and playing ball and that sort of thing."

So Mrs. Warren enrolled Isabel in the play club with a group of girls about her own age. But this plan did not work either. One cannot play ball or run races without other children. Isabel was irritated by the proficiency of the others and found it disconcerting to have the others laugh at her clumsiness and shout at her to hurry.

AND AGAIN nothing changed in the social picture. Isabel continued to walk alone to and from school, to be alone with a book most of the time, and to be restless and irritable weekends. Mrs. Warren talked again with the child's teacher, and they decided to consult a child psychologist.

Isabel was the older of two children. The mother had few memories of the child's first years. Mrs. Warren went out a great deal socially, accepted many responsibilities in club work, and made a point of never missing a lecture series. So, obviously, she had left the care of the child largely to nurses. She had not been anxious for children—her life was full enough without them.

Isabel's nursery-school experience was uneventful, and at four she was placed in kindergarten. She was admittedly young, but she was big for her age and well along in the skills learned in nursery school, and it seemed appropriate to put her with the older group. Isabel did well and entered first grade the next year, at five.

About .this time, the mother recalled, things became increasingly difficult at home. In the family group Isabel was always demanding the center of the stage: she talked incessantly at the table; she ordered around her little brother Richard, then aged three; she had to be first to greet her father when he came home evenings, first to get in the family car when they went for a drive, first to kiss Grandmother when she came to visit.

ISABEL did outstanding work at school. Her progress was so rapid and her knowledge so extensive that she was given a double promotion at the end of second grade. Then, in a class with nine-year-olds, but only seven herself, Isabel began to make a point of seeking acclaim in any way she could. She was the first to put up her hand when a visitor was in the room, the first to call out answers to the teacher's questions. Her air of tolerant superciliousness was amusing to the grown-ups. But it was decidedly annoying to the other children, who were thus made to feel inadequate and less capable than Isabel.

It was not surprising that as such behavior continued, their resentment toward her grew. Miss T had contributed to the problem, she saw now to her chagrin, when she had tried to make Isabel feel better for her unsuccessful playground experiences by making her academic skills overly conspicuous in the classroom.

Little wonder that Isabel preferred to stay in during recess periods. She would read widely and arrogantly parade her knowledge before the others.

A vicious circle had become well established. The children, by their behavior on the playground, were not so much seeking for Isabel's discomfiture as unconsciously seeking to prove themselves adequate. Isabel was not so concerned with making the others feel "small" in class as she was unconsciously helping herself to forget her failures at play by displaying her superiority at studies. And neither school nor home had until now stopped to consider the causes of the home unpleasantness or of Isabel's poor social relationships, or to wonder whether they might be remedied.

THE PSYCHOLOGIST was concerned also about an aspect of the case which had not been given more than passing notice by the others: The child was decidedly overweight. She was clumsy, her breath was short, and she tired quickly, all from the same cause. It was not surprising that she had not been good at active running games.

An increase in Isabel's weight had been particularly marked during the past eighteen months, although she had always been chubby. Food was her comfort. If no one liked her, she didn't need company to stop at the drug store on the way home and buy a double chocolate sundae.

After several interviews with the child, it was clear to the psychologist that the overweight factor was exerting an influence not only on her physical health, but also on her emotional and social adjustment. Because the children avoided Isabel or at most accepted her only as a last choice in group games, she felt unwanted and disliked. They jeered at her clumsiness, they called her "Fatso" and "Baby Tank." So she had become inwardly convinced that no one liked her—at home her family preferred

Richard, she felt certain. At school her classmates preferred anyone to her, it was all too apparent.

I T WAS possible to explain not only to Mrs. Warren and Miss T but also to Isabel, in terms she could comprehend, that the tremendous food intake and frequent desire for excessive sweets were not evidences of a hearty appetite, but of unsatisfied emotional cravings. It became clear that especially on occasions when Isabel felt humiliatingly unsuccessful with her schoolmates, or unfairly ignored at home, she ate ravenously. The more she ate, the more excess poundage was accumulated, the less skillful she was on the playground, and the less attractive she was even in new frocks carefully chosen for color and line. She needed help to work through the reasons for her emotional distress and discontent so that she would no longer have to meet her emotional needs by turning to sweets. Understanding and sympathetic encouragement and recognition of the total situation were all essential.

Mrs. Warren had had her pride pampered by hearing "So young to be in fifth grade!" and "How bright your little girl must be!" She had found it difficult to accept the fact that while Isabel was certainly a very bright child, she was definitely not a very happy child. But she was sincere in wanting to improve the situation, and agreed that there were many ways in which the home could provide more wholesomely for Isabel.

Both parents took care not to suggest any favoritism for the younger child. Mrs. Warren frankly admitted that Richard was so friendly and responsive that they might perhaps have made it appear that they preferred him to his sister.

They cooperated in the exercise recommended. Both Mr. and Mrs. Warren arranged to skate and bicycle and hike with her, choosing places where her acquaintances were not likely to be.

They observed strictly the diet prescribed by the doctor. Meals were planned to make Isabel feel as little different as possible from the rest of the family. Her pleas for sweets were deflected by offerings of fresh or dried fruits. Both parents somewhat shamefacedly admitted that often in the past they had stopped for a coveted soda or sundae because they "felt so sorry" for Isabel.

Mrs. Warren altered her schedule of many activities to give more time to Isabel. Not only did they ride and walk and skate together, but there were cozy times when they talked over daily happenings and made plans.

T HEY MADE a conscious effort to show the deep affection and love they had for the child. They drew her into the group at home instead of tolerantly (perhaps sometimes proudly) watching her go to her room to read while they and visiting relatives or friends chatted sociably together. They knew now that it was not because "Isabel's so studious," as they had thought, but because Isabel had been so ill at ease and dejected, that she had left company.

Not immediately, but after a period of time, all these changes, along with Isabel's continued interviews with the psychologist, began to show results. Loss of pounds and loss of discontent went together. Increase of real self-assurance replaced former cockiness, and when Isabel was invited to go to a Saturday movie with two other little girls, all concerned counted it real progress.

No single factor should ever be considered the cause for poor adjustment until a child's entire life situation has been reviewed. The many causes which will be disclosed need understanding in all their interrelationships, if a child is to be helped to achieve better adjustment.

Margaret—a case of a visual handicap

THE REASONS for a child's behavior may be clearly discernible when all the factors involved are known. On the other hand, failure to take into account some one factor may leave concealed the one significant condition that could explain continued undesirable behavior. Sometimes even so obvious a factor as sensory impairment remains unnoted for a long time.

Individual health records, based on periodic health examinations that include attention to vision and hearing and metabolic rate, are not always available. And without the information afforded by such records even the most conscientious teacher may find it difficult to establish the real basis for a problem situation. Physical factors should never be ignored if understanding of a child is to be reached.

Margaret was eight years old and about to repeat the work of the second grade before the cause of her school failure was recognized. Miss W had made an intensive study of her during her first year in second grade, providing a detailed picture of the child—a dainty, graceful little girl with blond curls, fine features, and a delicately built body. Yet the condition causing her to present a problem was not revealed until further investigation was undertaken. Miss W's data did not include the kind of information obtainable only through technical investigation.

Margaret was the smallest child in her group. Although she seemed somewhat frail in physique, she had excellent muscular coordination and surpassed the performance of other children in all rhythmical activities. For several years she had had dancing lessons and showed definite skill in both ballet and tap dancing. She enjoyed this activity very much and responded readily to the instruction provided. In dramatic play, too, Margaret showed real ability. The freedom and naturalness of her behavior in such situations gave the impression of self-assurance and poise.

HOWEVER, in other situations Margaret was not at ease. There was frequently a troubled look in her eyes, and she was inclined to withdraw in social situations. She was obviously anxious and insecure in group activities other than rhythms and music and showed no aggression or initiative in games. Rarely taking an active part, she appeared very retiring, seemed vague and helpless. With younger children, however, she was somewhat more at ease and a little more sociable. Playing with them, she showed less reluctance to take part in games than she did in her own group.

During class hours Margaret was very restless. She rarely contributed in reading or discussion periods. She would pick at a loose thread in her sweater or pull at her hair ribbon. She continually shifted from one position to another, twisting her legs around each other, crossing her knees, or drawing her feet up on the chair rung. She squinted and frowned and chewed her fingers.

Margaret was a poor reader and did not seem to try to improve her reading. At times she showed resentment and flipped the pages of her book crossly. When called upon to read aloud, she hesitated with almost every word and asked for a great deal of help. She lost her place, frequently reread a line, or skipped to the line above or below where she should have read. Often she coughed or cleared her throat nervously. She developed a slight stutter when asked to read aloud, although at other times her speech showed no impairment of any kind.

W EEK AFTER week the other children gained facility in reading, while Margaret continued to stumble along miserably. Miss W was at a loss in trying to understand Margaret's behavior. The child showed genuine pleasure when dancing or taking part in dramatic play, and she was quick to learn in such situations. But she did not respond readily to other learning requirements, nor did she seem to enjoy any other activity.

The home situation did not appear to be the source of the difficulty. The child seemed healthy and well cared for. Her parents were not exacting and did not become irritated or impatient with her school problem. Whenever the school had approached them, they had been most cooperative and willing to accept any suggestion offered.

When it became apparent that Margaret would not be able to do the reading required in third grade, Miss W talked the matter over with her parents. All felt that it would be better for Margaret to repeat the work of the second grade. Her mother and father were aware of her lack of concentration. They had tried to help her with her reading at home and knew how resistant she was. They were puzzled and concerned, and wondered if some other type of investigation could not help reveal the cause of the problem, since the school had found nothing to explain it.

Not until after school opened in the fall was it possible for arrangements to be made to take Margaret to the Reading Clinic at a nearby university. There experts administered a battery of tests to ascertain why the child learned some things easily, yet could not seem to learn reading at all. They attempted to uncover the reasons for her poor social adjustment and for her general anxiety and lack of self-confidence.

P SYCHOLOGICAL examination showed that Margaret had superior intelligence. Results on both the Stanford-Binet Scale and the Pintner-Paterson Performance Scale agreed on this finding. Mentally Margaret seemed ready for work of fourth-grade difficulty. Yet she could read only at first-grade level, and then but slowly, frequently asking the examiner to tell her a word.

The impressions of the psychologist coincided with Miss W's observations. He found Margaret uncertain and unresponsive verbally, fearful of each new, unfamiliar requirement. This was especially noticeable when reading was involved. With the easier performance-test materials she managed fairly creditably, but as soon as they became even a little more demanding, she became tense and worried.

The speech specialist found no problem, despite Margaret's occasional stuttering when trying to read. This tendency he explained on the basis of the tension caused by her marked reading disability. Hearing was perfect. Enunciation was clear.

Margaret's basal metabolic rate was +10. While this was within the normal range, although in the upper range of normalcy, the endocrinologist thought it might contribute in some measure to the nervous reactions apparent. But the pediatrician found her general health to be excellent: weight was normal for her age and body build; there were no food allergies; all physiological functioning was normal; teeth were in perfect condition. Thus far, even this extensive investigation had revealed nothing to account for the puzzling and disturbing situation at school.

However, the problem finally was disclosed when a visual examination was made. A condition of alternating internal strabismus was found. (This is an eye disorder in which the eyes cannot readily be focused on the same object because of incoordination of the eyeball muscles.) In addition, it was discovered that glasses were needed to correct hyperopia (far-sightedness) and astigmatism (a structural defect in which rays of light are not focused to a single point, but over a diffuse retinal area).

These visual defects were the basis of Margaret's difficulties. When attempting to read, she would look first with one eye, then with the other. They did not coordinate. During this process she would lose her place, skip lines, reread a line. The ophthalmologist felt that the visual problems alone were sufficient to have caused the serious reading deficiency. The resulting personality and behavior problems, of course, exaggerated the difficulty.

In evaluating all factors disclosed by the examination, the clinic group was agreed that Margaret's essential difficulties lay in the visual area. They recommended that glasses be secured immediately.

They further advised that the child be permitted to continue with her own class at school, going on to third grade. It was the opinion of the group that with her vision corrected, Margaret's superior intelligence would permit her in a relatively short time to reach the reading skills now shown by other third-graders. With a changed attitude toward reading—to be anticipated once the child experienced some success in it— remedial reading would probably be effective as it could not be while visual impairment was making the process so uncomfortable and well-nigh impossible.

With this counsel, Margaret's parents and teacher felt greatly relieved. The child was fitted with glasses, and arrangements were made for remedial instruction. After thirty hours of remedial work, given in thirty-minute periods twice weekly, rapid progress was evidenced. In a four-month period of time, Margaret's reading advanced as much as would generally be expected in a two-year period. She was soon on a par with her classmates in reading and was progressing in her other schoolwork, too.

Significant changes were now apparent in her attitude toward the other children, both at play and in class. Margaret began to show self-assurance not only in the special fields where she felt competent, but in all activities. Her fearfulness disappeared. Her earlier helplessness was no longer apparent. She no longer seemed tense or anxious.

Specialists can frequently aid the teacher in helping a child realize his full potentialities. Had Margaret's visual handicap been discovered and corrected earlier, it is likely that she would have been spared many unhappy moments of tension and anxiety, and that her behavior would have been acceptable, her attitudes healthier, and her scholastic progress wholly adequate.

All areas of response must be investigated if a child is really to be understood. Omitting even one possible contributing factor can create grave difficulties for the child and cause much concern for those charged with his training. Complete knowledge of a child makes it possible to plan wisely for his progress in all activities—at school, at home, and at play.

CHAPTER SIX *The mature child*

NINE IS the year for which many parents have been waiting. As Gesell says, "Nine is finally becoming what his parents have been striving for."[1] He is no longer a young child, but a boy or girl who is able to be fairly responsible and dependable. He understands explanations, he is interested in trying to do things well, and he is beginning to have a strong sense of right and wrong. His abilities are clearly apparent; his real interests are beginning to develop. Individual differences are distinct and clear. The nine-year-old is an individual with a very real personality of his own.

[1]Arnold Gesell and Frances Ilg, *The Child from Five to Ten*, Harper and Brothers (1946), p. 200.

At nine the wide variations of development which will become increasingly noticeable at ten and eleven and twelve may be beginning. In his interests, the nine-year-old is closer to the ten- or eleven-year-old than to the seven- and eight-year-olds, whom he considers young and sometimes refers to as "the children." This is especially true among girls, a few of whom may be nearing the beginning of puberty.

Physically most nine-year-olds are very much like eight-year-olds, but a little more long-legged, a little better developed, and a little closer to body maturity. Those who are more mature will be nearing puberty and during this year may reach the plateau in

96

their growth which precedes the growth spurt of preadolescence. A very few girls may menstruate during this year. Girls are gaining in growth maturity over boys and may be one to two years ahead of boys the same age. The lungs and the digestive and circulatory systems are still growing and are almost mature in function. The heart is not yet fully developed, and some children may strain it during this year if allowed to compete physically to any great extent with older children. The eyes are much better developed. Although they will not reach adult size until ten, they are able to accommodate to near work with less strain. The first and second bicuspids are appearing. Teeth often need straightening; if this seems indicated the dentist should be consulted, as treatment is sometimes started during this year. The whole body is continuing to grow steadily and is much nearer its adult functioning.

The hands are becoming increasingly skillful. Eye-hand coordination is greatly improved, so that the child is often able to use his hands with real skill. Some children are beginning to show much greater skill than others in the use of their hands. Both boys and girls enjoy crafts and shop work and will carry out quite careful and well-planned craft work of many kinds.

THE ATTENTION span of the nine-year-old has greatly increased. He may spend a morning or an afternoon with his erector set, his chemistry outfit, or his tools. The girls may sew, or work with weaving, or even attempt the more intricate bead-loom work. The fact that attention can be sustained does not mean that adults should plan activities of too long duration, for interest and self-motivation are important determiners of attention span. Although the child may be capable of prolonged interest, forced or required attention for too long a period of time can be very wearing to him and usually results in tension and restlessness.

The nine-year-old has ideas and interests of his own and is capable of carrying them out. He often makes his plans and goes ahead without any adult direction or encouragement. He will carry on a project over quite a period of time with sustained interest, thinking through and planning each step with almost an adult carefulness. At the same time, as soon as a project no longer interests him he may drop it without finishing it or giving it a further thought.

Nine-year-olds still need and enjoy much active, rough-and-tumble play. But sex differences are showing up increasingly. The boys shout and tear around. They like to wrestle and punch each other—in fact, punching is often a mark of extreme affection reserved for best friends. The girls, on

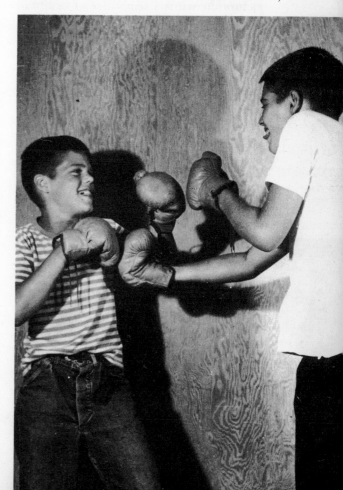

the other hand, enjoy active group games but are usually less noisy and less full of spontaneous energy than the boys. They turn to quieter activities or to roller skating, ice skating, jump rope, and jacks. Both groups are talking more. They may rush onto the playground with shouts, but will soon congregate in groups and begin to talk. Sometimes they will just sit around talking at random; at other times they will make plans or discuss the activities of the secret club or gang. Their plans are often elaborate and not carried out, but the talk is good and the youngsters enjoy it and grow with it.

AT NINE the child is a bit of a perfectionist. He wants to do things in the right way. He may work hard to perfect a skill or will recopy, on his own initiative, a piece of work that looks "messy" or "sloppy" to him. He is no longer satisfied just to paint a picture: he wants a semblance of reality in what he paints. He will ask for help now and will be interested in techniques and skills. This interest applies not only to his schoolwork, but also to his play skills. He wants to be a good ball player, to know how to pitch and catch well. He wants to learn how to swim; he is no longer content just to splash around. He is anxious to know how to ice skate or ski. Children need to develop skills that other children appreciate and admire, and so this is a good year for Father and Mother to take time with both boys and

girls, encouraging them to learn how to do things and helping them do them well.

Parents and teachers can overdo the teaching of techniques and skills at this age, however. For although the child wants to know how to do things, his ability and his capacity for sustained interest may not equal his enthusiasm and desire. The adult must be aware of the child's ability and capacity in order not to set standards or offer techniques that discourage the child instead of encouraging him in his desire to learn. It is extremely important that any teaching of skills be done in a spirit of enjoyment, for the cultivation of a skill through overinsistence, through driving too hard, or through demanding perfection of performance can destroy the initial desire to acquire the skill and the pleasure in using it, whether it be playing the piano or pitching a ball. The child's own interest and enthusiasm will make him responsive to learning. Let the child lead the way and the adult supply the knowledge as the child expresses an eagerness and readiness for it.

MANY nine-year-olds are great readers; others are hardly interested in books at all. The wide developmental variations that are beginning to be apparent at this age are very evident in both reading interest and reading ability. There may be a reading span of four to five years in the fourth grade. Some children will be able to read as well as adults and will be enjoying their first experience with the classics; others may still be at first- or second-grade level. The choice of reading materials for children of this age is difficult because of this wide range in their needs.

This is the year at which marked reading disabilities sometimes become evident and may begin to affect the total personality of the child. Parents and teachers need to be on the alert for signs of reading disability so that the child may receive help if he needs it. Holding the child back will not meet the problem, nor will forcing or scolding him, as various developmental and emotional factors are usually involved in a reading difficulty. The help of a special reading or guidance teacher may be necessary if the child is not to be handicapped in all his schoolwork and subsequent personality development. Certainly everything must be done at home and at school to keep him from feeling discouraged and ashamed of his failure to learn to read.

The nine-year-old is beginning to put aside fairy tales and much of the fantasy and imaginative play of his earlier years, and is relating himself not only to his immediate environment, but to his community, his country, and even other countries. His interest goes beyond that of the third-grader. The alert fourth-grader is eager to know about other countries. He likes to study maps and play travel games. He enjoys writing letters to children of other countries either as a member of a group or as an individual. He may ask keen and discerning questions about world conditions and about other peoples.

H E IS beginning to understand about his own country and to develop a feeling of loyalty and pride in it. He wants to know about the different parts of his country. He is interested in business and industry, in farming and shipping. He enjoys trips to a dock, a factory, or a farm and will ask innumerable and intelligent questions about the things he sees. He is beginning to be interested in biography, in heroes and great men. He wants to know about Washington and Lincoln, and often shows as much interest in them as he does in Buffalo Bill.

It is a stimulating year for parents and teacher, even though the growing independence and individuality of the child may sometimes make it a difficult one. He is beginning to think for himself, to develop his own ideas and point of view, and to realize that sometimes there is more than one opinion, and that perhaps Mother, Father, or even teacher may not have all the answers or be always right. The nine-year-old may be quite outspoken and critical of the adults he knows despite genuine fondness for them.

The nine-year-old responds best to the adult who treats him as an individual and approaches him in an adult way. He enters eagerly into making plans, whether for a project or party in the schoolroom or a trip with the family. He is more cooperative and responsive when he is included in making the plans than when he is told "This is what we are going to do." His ideas and suggestions are often worth considering. In the same way he is willing and able to take some responsibility. He likes to be trusted with the handling of the family baggage on a trip, going to market, repairing something for Mother, or getting the props together for a play at school. He likes recognition for what he has done and responds well to deserved praise. He is apt to be bashful about public recognition; he likes praise to be more of a

private affair. On the other hand he is often very fair and will refuse to accept credit for something he has not done. He will even give the credit publicly to his friend or to the person who he feels deserves it.

HE IS also beginning to understand more about truth and honesty, about property rights and the personal rights of individuals. He is developing sympathy and loyalty for others. Fairness plays a large part in the thinking of the nine-year-old. He will take criticism or punishment if he thinks it is fair, but will be most indignant and outspoken if he feels that his teacher or his parents or another child is being unfair. There are many arguments between the children themselves over fairness in games, with the youngsters taking sides and upholding one another. This is a good sign, for it shows that these children are really beginning to understand right and wrong and are trying to develop standards. Nine is a good year in which to help youngsters develop those standards which build character. This is best done through specific situations and experiences rather than through "sermonizing." (In Chapter Ten there is a fuller discussion of the methods most helpful in developing these concepts, as well as detailed suggestions of what concepts a child can be expected to grasp at each age level.) Nine is a critical year for this type of teaching, for it is at this point that some youngsters, particularly those who are unhappy, unsuccessful, and insecure, may turn in the direction of delinquency. Teaching character is of course not all these children need, but it may strengthen and guide them.

The nine-year-old is able to make up his own mind and come to decisions. He should be allowed to have as many experiences as possible in which he can have a measure of

independence and make decisions for himself. He will not always be right, but he is ready to learn from the occasional failure of his judgment, as long as the learning takes place in situations where failure will not have too serious consequences. He is able to be on his own quite a bit now. An overnight visit to a friend's house, a trip by himself on the bus downtown to carry out an errand, the purchase of his school supplies, or even a well-planned train trip to Grandmother's is not beyond many nine-year-olds. They will respond well to increased independence and opportunities to make choices and decisions.

THE NINE-YEAR-OLD is not only responsible: he is also beginning to be reasonable. One can talk things over with him and present a point of view. If he is not involved too emotionally in a situation, he will frequently be capable of modifying his plan or changing his mind if another course is suggested to him. He will listen to the reasons presented by an adult, but he will also want the courtesy of being allowed in turn to present his reasoning. He is able to accept the need to put something off, to plan to go to the country for the picnic next week if the weather is poor today. He can understand a reasonable explanation in regard to the family budget. He may be disappointed that he cannot have a new bike now, but he can understand that this fall the family cannot afford it and he can accept a promise that it will be given on his birthday in the spring. He is even able to see the necessity for contributing some of his birthday money toward the bike, or earning his share. He is best guided by a reason, simple and clear cut, for a decision which must be made. He is reasonable in accepting punishment if it is fair and may even see the need for a reminder that his conduct was not

desirable. If punishment must be given, the most effective is that which has a reasonable tie-up with the situation for which he is being punished.

Because the nine-year-old seems so mature and capable in many ways, the adults about him are sometimes apt to overestimate his maturity and to expect too much of him, with a resulting impatience when he seems "childish" in some of his reactions. He is beginning to show maturity in many ways, but he is still not far from being a young child. He may have a greater understanding of truthfulness, but under pressure may not remain truthful. He may be independent in many of his decisions but turn to Mother or teacher for help in some little thing which she feels he should be able to do for himself. Because the nine-year-old is still half mature and half a child it is best to let him lead in the direction of independence, to encourage

him when he shows that he wants to go ahead, but be willing to help without ridicule or criticism when he occasionally turns back toward his more dependent, childish ways.

CLUBS AND GANGS are stronger than when these children were eight, although they are still of rather short duration and the membership and purpose may change frequently. Some firm and loyal friendships may develop during this year. The influence of the group on the child is becoming greater. He wants to be like the others, to talk like them, to look like them. If his friends wear their shirttails out and use slang a bit freely, Mother may temporarily lose the battle for neatness and gentle talk. She may have to be satisfied with a compromise to "look nice" on Sundays and use no rough words at home. The girls, on the other hand, are usually becoming more interested in clothes. The basis is the same—wanting to be like the others, but in girls this may take the form of a greater interest in well-brushed hair and a more attractive appearance. Some girls even talk with great superiority about "those awful boys, aren't they messy?" Not all girls are neat at this age—some will be regular tomboys, just as careless and indifferent to their appearance as the boys.

Just as children copy each other in clothes and interests and mannerisms, so they may also absorb and follow loyally the whole pattern of the gang. Usually this pattern is not undesirable and can give the child many valuable experiences. There is danger in some neighborhoods that the pattern will not be a satisfactory one, and in this case a delinquent or semidelinquent gang may develop. In most neighborhoods this is not a problem, but teachers and parents should be aware of the possibility so that the youngsters in such a group may be redirected in their activities and helped in their personal adjustments. Success is usually possible only if the entire group is redirected; work with an individual child or his removal from the group is not usually satisfactory, as the pull of the group is strong, and if a child is forbidden to be with his pals, he is likely to feel defiant or rebellious and find ways of joining them. The difficult gang is a community and neighborhood problem which must be worked out by parents and teachers together by constructive planning.

FRIENDS and membership in a group mean a great deal to nine-year-olds. They are generally conformists, afraid of that which is different. Often they will leave out the child who is in any way different from themselves, whether the child is unusually bright or a bit slow, whether he speaks with an accent or dresses differently, whether he has a special talent or is handicapped in some way. In the earlier grades the children were not so keenly aware of differences as they are now when belonging to a group has be-

come so crucially important. For this reason parents and teacher need to be particularly alert to notice and help when possible the child who is at all different and is being left out of one of the nine-year-old groups. Sometimes the teacher will be able to help the other children to accept him. Sometimes it is possible to place the child who is different in a favorable position in relation to his classmates, so that they begin to like him and appreciate him. Perhaps by careful planning other children may be invited to the home, or the left-out child may be seated next to a friendly child or drawn skillfully into a group project toward which he can make a valuable contribution. There are times, however, when it seems impossible to obtain acceptance for a certain child; such a child will need personal help, understanding, and support in learning how to adjust to the group and to a situation which is difficult for him. Some children, even some especially attractive or talented ones, may never be fully accepted, and compensations and other outlets may have to be found for them. The child on the fringe of the group should have careful and special thought during this year.

DURING THE eighth year and more markedly at nine there is an interest in babies. Girls delight in small babies, hover over them, and want to take care of them. Even the boys often show a real interest and pride in their smaller brothers and sisters and may sometimes like to be asked to look after them. Along with their affectionate interest in babies they are also curious about their origin and are still often confused about the birth process. Children are interested in this information as part of their knowledge of the world about them. In addition, some nines are already nearing puberty and should be prepared for what to expect in their own development. If these things are not explained by the adults who are closest to them, they will ask questions and gather sketchy or erroneous ideas from other children. Much of the sex play and sex curiosity of children of this age comes from lack of information, from unsatisfied but very normal curiosity, or from wrong information and attitudes given to them by their playmates. Long before the emotional involvement of adolescence we should be laying a groundwork of healthy attitudes toward the problems it will bring. In a later chapter we shall take up this whole subject in greater detail.

Most nine-year-olds seem pretty well-adjusted youngsters, busy and absorbed in their own affairs and vigorous in carrying them out. They seem to be coordinating and profiting by what they have learned during their early childhood. At the same time they are beginning to reach ahead toward their teen years and interests. It seems to be a fairly steady, well-knit year before the turbulent preadolescent and adolescent years begin. It is a good year in which to build for the future, an important year in the development of the child.

Nine
has many interests

IT'S FUN to be nine; you can do so many things well. You can figure out and understand complex ideas and processes; both large and small muscles are ready to serve you well. And your powers for accomplishment are matched by a new resourcefulness and stability. Your interest in anything and everything is active and constructive. You will probably have not one but many hobbies, collections, and special interests.

Nine likes plenty of rough stuff.

Nine's album may contain pictures, stamps, match cases, playing cards, or autographs.

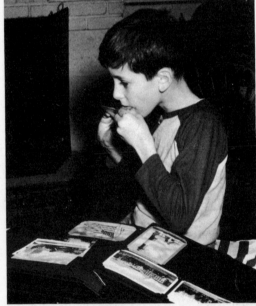

This is a hobby that's fun alone or with the gang.

How do different things act and what are they made of?

104

Many different abilities and interests are utilized in the designing and construction of puppets, stage, and scenery as well as in the writing of the lines and the actual manipulation of the puppets.

The gang likes any kind
of game or contest.

It's fun to send and receive secret messages.

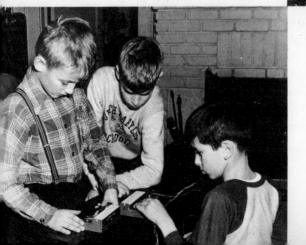

Runaway Mark

IT IS generally acknowledged that security is an important childhood need. But too often it is assumed that when a child's parents provide a home and clothes, and see to it that he is well fed and reasonably clean, they have furnished that necessary security. Physical security, however, does not necessarily bring with it emotional security. It is emotional security which children must have if they are to grow to be strong and healthful personalities.

The feeling of insecurity may influence a child's behavior in many ways not directly related to the basic problem. Sometimes he rejects social relationships, fearful of further rejection of himself. Sometimes he dreams away his time at school, and lessons suffer. The patterns which may develop are almost infinite.

In the case of Mark, insecurity was symbolized by his running away. At nine he was a year behind in school, not because he was incapable of doing adequate schoolwork, but because he had been unable to withstand the severe impacts of a home made stormy and puzzling by difficult family relationships. He had become confused by the circumstances of his life and needed help before he could face his situation rather than flee from it. And his parents needed help, too, in order to make the boy's situation less formidable, so that he could learn to handle it.

DURING his earliest years he had been pampered and indulged by his parents, and he had become accustomed to having things his own way. Discipline was rare and haphazard. There was never any sustained denial, nor any insistence on anything that he found distasteful.

The arrival of a baby sister when Mark was not quite six made a number of changes for him. Mother was busier than he had ever remembered her. Daddy was preoccupied. There was less patience and less humoring for Mark. His parents said openly that they were glad he was old enough for school; and he was entered in first grade.

Mark had never gone to kindergarten, and this was the first time he had had to meet a situation without his mother. He did not like the experiences of sitting quietly, of taking his turn, of concentrating on what his teacher directed instead of on something of his own choosing. School was an ordeal for him. His seeming inability to adjust to it led the school to advise the parents to keep him home for another semester. They indicated that he appeared very immature, and since he had not yet reached his sixth birthday Mark's parents felt there was justification for the school's counsel. So again Mark managed, in a sense, to get his own way. He stayed with Mother. He avoided distasteful activities.

But staying with Mother was no longer the same. It was not only the new baby. It was a different feeling in the home. Another woman attracted his father's interest, and there were constant arguments and recriminations between his parents. Once or twice a quarrel more violent than most frightened the boy. When one day his mother took the baby and left, Mark was completely bewildered. His confusion was increased when his father brought the other woman home to live with them.

There followed a few weeks of unpleasant scenes: scolding, neglect, impatience, denial were daily worries for the child. He decided to find his mother, and ran away. The police brought him back, and his father, frightened and remorseful, was for a time more attentive and gentle. But Mark was unhappy, and soon made another attempt to run away. This time when the police brought him home, his father whipped him, and notified his wife of what was happening. He thought she would send for the boy. Instead, she came home.

The parents now decided that perhaps the damaged emotions of all could be salvaged. The other woman left, and a reconciliation was effected.

ABOUT THIS time the new school term started, and Mark was again entered at school. His attendance was spasmodic, due to a succession of minor illnesses and also to laxness of supervision on his mother's part. Success with lessons was indifferent, and Mark was not promoted.

So the following September he started first grade all over again. This time things were more peaceful at home; he had learned to adapt somewhat better to the group at school, and he had no special difficulty. He passed to second grade.

The boy's path was still not smooth, however. He was inclined to tease smaller children and to fight with boys his own size. He did not get along very well with his teacher, who often took him to task for poor work and frequently scolded him because of his fighting. Unfortunately, she did not try to find the reasons for either his poor work or his quarrelsomeness.

Then one day, after she criticized his reading, he failed to return for the afternoon session. Another time, when he had been reprimanded for being noisy and inattentive, he became sullen, and the following day did not come to school at all. Although he missed a number of days at school that year, he was promoted. But, school became more and more distasteful.

At nine he started third grade. His absences increased, and he became adept at leading his mother to think he had been at school, and his teacher to believe his parents had kept him at home. Actually, he was wandering about, spending a great deal of time at the nearby railroad yards, learning to evade the questioning of workmen who wondered momentarily at his presence. He was joining in the escapades of older boys and getting from them both a vocabulary and attitudes which were unwholesome and undesirable.

The attendance department at the school finally brought the facts to the attention of his parents. He was whipped, and told he had to go to school. He did attend school the next day, but that night he did not come home until very late. His mother scolded him severely and Mark, contrite, promised to "be good."

But he had started a pattern which did not change for the better. He had often truanted from school. Now he often stayed away from home, too. His parents were angry and bitter at sleepless nights and time lost from work to look for the boy. They had no understanding of his behavior, and their only recourse was to "try to beat it out of him." Mark felt unloved and unwanted. He liked home less and less.

By this time he was absent from school more than he was present. He slept away from home as much as he did in his own bed. The parents could not manage him.

The repeated warnings of the school were ignored. The attendance officer who had time and again picked Mark up at the railroad yards or sleeping in a protected doorway, was concerned at this nine-year-old so defiant, so glum and sullen in voice and manner, so insistent on absenting himself from both school and home. He referred the case to a social agency, and an experienced, skilled worker was assigned to investigate the situation.

FOR THE first time since he had been a very small boy, Mark now felt that an adult was sincerely interested in him. His initial wariness gave way to friendliness. They had many conferences, and Mark responded well. He was helped to verbalize his antagonism for his little sister, his resentment of his mother's desertion of him, his fear of his father's beatings, his dislike for his teacher. And he was helped to understand that there are some situations in life which cannot be changed, from which one cannot run away, and that one must adjust to them.

His sister was there to stay, *but his mother did indeed still love him.* His parents were not always amicable, *but their quarreling between themselves did not evidence lack of interest in their boy.* His father had indeed whipped him, *but he had been worried about Mark,* and had not known how else to handle Mark's disobedience. His teacher was really interested in helping him learn, *and her criticisms had been to correct him,* not to humiliate him, as he had felt.

The social worker spoke with the boy's parents, and also with the teacher. They were given both interpretation of the boy's frustrations and insecurity, and suggestions for wiser ways of management. Arrangements were made for Mark to attend a Boys' Club several afternoons each week.

Tutoring was started, to help Mark reach the level of achievement of his class and allow him to feel successful in his scholastic work. A two-week period at camp was planned for the summer. And the parents were persuaded of the importance of spending more time with the boy, of helping him to feel an important member of the family group, of taking Sundays for excursions or trips or other recreation together, so that Mark could sense his place in their affections and accept sharing them with his sister.

CHANGE was slow but steady. Unacceptable behavior was less and less in evidence. A reassured child, Mark no longer felt the need to run away from his problems. He could now go to school without resenting his little sister's staying home with his mother, and without dreading that he would return to find his mother gone. He could now come home after school sure he was a wanted member of the family, and no longer fearful of being beaten by his father. He was able to accept the routines of school and home and to respond to the ordinary requirements of life, once he felt secure in his parents' affection.

There are times when every child experiences some degree of fearfulness and worry. Every child reacts to certain circumstances with resentment and jealousy. In homes where a good parent-child relationship provides emotional security, the sense of being loved and wanted helps the child recover from tensions which are aroused inevitably in the course of his growing up. Without such a bulwark, the child feels uncertain and unhappy.

Such feelings are often the groundwork of delinquency. Understanding of them can help channel predelinquent behavior constructively and acceptably. Delinquency need not develop.

When a child is slow and dull

WHEN Edith's family moved she was nine years old. She had gone to one school for three years. Now she had to adjust to a new school, where she knew none of the children and where she was understandably somewhat shy and hesitant. The building was strange, the routines were different, the whole situation unfamiliar. Miss T, the fourth-grade teacher, was hopeful that as Edith became accustomed to things she would be able to meet the grade requirements. For Edith was friendly in a quiet way, she seemed responsive to Miss T's efforts, and she was trying hard to do well.

The routine review at the opening of the school year was not too difficult. Miss T started from almost initial fundamentals. Edith was attentive, she did her work systematically, and the results were passable. As the difficulty of the assignments increased, however, Edith's well-sustained attention and obvious efforts were no longer effective. Although her interest did not lag, and her cooperation did not abate, her work fell far below the standard of the grade.

There was no record sent from the school Edith had previously attended. Miss T was at first uncertain whether the child was reacting to a new environment in which she felt strange and confused, or whether she could not respond other than inadequately. Over a period of time she observed Edith watchfully, alert to the patterns of behavior which she was showing both in the classroom and on the playground.

Before long her growing conviction of Edith's limited scholastic potentialities was substantiated by the results of psychological tests. Just past her ninth birthday, Edith's mental age was found to be only seven years and nine months, her intelligence quotient 85. "Dull normal intelligence," was the psychologist's diagnosis. "This little girl will be a slow learner."

EDITH did not look any different from the other children of the class. She was physically sturdy, as tall as the average nine-year-old, as attractive as any child in the room. She was pleasant and friendly, though in a passive way. But although she worked industriously, there was little to show for it. As academic work became more difficult, she failed in comprehension but was uncritical of her results. A finished lesson gave her placid pleasure whether correctly or incorrectly done. Typically, she lacked the power of self-criticism.

Her thought processes were slow and inept, her memory was uncertain. She always listened attentively, but she needed many explanations to grasp a new concept and much practice to establish it as part of her store of knowledge. Her arithmetic would invariably include mostly incorrect answers. Her spelling generally had at least as many wrong words as it did right ones. In reading, she sought help with new words, then often failed to recognize the same words when they appeared again in another context, further down the page.

Edith's muscular coordination was no more efficient than was her thinking. In rhythms she made many unrelated arm movements, and was frequently out of time with the music. She could not follow a rapid tempo or a change in the beat.

On the playground the same lack of muscular skill was apparent. She ran awkwardly, and her reactions were so slow that in relay races the others became impatient with her. She could not throw a ball with either force or accuracy, and when she tried to catch one she invariably fumbled or dropped it. She was uncertain and clumsy on playground apparatus. She made many mistakes when she tried to play a game which had specific rules.

Often Miss T observed the child on the edge of a group, watching the others impassively. Her posture seemed babyish: feet apart, abdomen thrust forward prominently, hands held up loosely, away from her body. Most of the time she was rather apathetic, wholly apart from the gay, noisy play of her classmates. If someone looked directly at her, she smiled in a vague fashion— friendly, yet somehow cautiously so.

There was markedly poor development of the small muscles of hands and fingers. Edith was inept with pencil, crayon, and paintbrush. Her coloring always went over the lines. Her painting was generally badly smeared. When she wrote, she held her pencil in tight, cramped fingers, and the result was scarcely legible. She dropped things frequently, could not use scissors skillfully, was unsuccessful with the simplest of weaving. But she always tried hard.

DESPITE the inefficiency of her thought processes and of her movements, in "Effort" Edith rated high. Even in the face of discouragingly poor results, she persisted with dogged determination. As she read, her face was a series of grimaces, her lips moved as she tried to fathom the words, her finger followed line after line methodically. In number work. she counted almost aloud, she tapped the sums with her fingers, she tried valiantly to arrive at the right answers. Sitting over book or paper, her legs twisted around the chair rung, Edith was the picture of laborious lack of productivity.

In social situations the child was friendly but passive, never protesting the loss of a turn to a more aggressive child. With adults, the child seemed a little shy, a little hesitant, but was always polite and sweet, seeming to be certain that she would be helped out of whatever dilemma might confront her. At home, her family was aware of her slowness and had been patient and understanding in the face of Edith's limitations. Their unflagging affection and attention had resulted in the attitudes the child exhibited. She felt that people liked her, and so her behavior made her likable.

When Miss T was certain of the situation, she realized that with the best will in the world Edith would always fall short in many of the skills which the other children in the room would acquire with comparative ease. Recognizing the slim foundation in reading and numbers which Edith had brought to fourth grade, Miss T decided she needed a fresh start. Not only could fundamentals be established more firmly, but Miss T felt that as this was done, Edith would find the enjoyment inherent in work done successfully.

GOING BACK to materials of second-grade difficulty, Miss T prepared a "book" with Edith which had story sequences, matching exercises, vocabulary and classification sections interesting to a nine-year-old but simple enough for a child with very limited reading skill. She encouraged Edith to tell a story, which they would then organize to put in their book. Edith looked through magazines for illustrations which she then cut out and pasted on appropriate pages. The story was utilized further as the basis for writing and spelling.

Manuscript writing was introduced, and Edith was helped materially by the similarity of the symbols she found repeated in both reading and writing activities. At first she copied stories Miss T wrote down for her. Then as she progressed, she was able to write simple stories herself. She gained facility in recognizing words and phrases and in reproducing them. She learned to spell as she learned to read and write. A typewriter with large letters was available, and slowly Edith developed the ability to find and strike the right keys. She found enormous enjoyment in thus producing straight lines and legible characters. She was stimulated by the results of her efforts as she had never been before. She grew less dependent upon Miss T for help.

With the difficulty of lessons scaled to her possible successful accomplishment, Edith was experiencing a totally new delight. She could read, and read without help. She could write, and her writing could be read. What was more, she was learning to type, a skill which most of her friends did not have. It pleased Edith to have accomplished something which the others admired. That was stimulation never before experienced.

The simplest concepts of first- and second-grade science books were incorporated in Edith's work as time went on. And together she and Miss T arranged a number book, illustrative of her own experiences. For the first time in her entire school experience, Edith was aware that she was accomplishing something, that she was learning. Miss T was generous in her praise of the little girl, and gave her much encouragement.

EDITH participated in some of the work of the class, listening to discussions, understanding more than she had formerly, enjoying the experience as never before. She even offered an occasional spontaneous comment. By the end of the school year gains were apparent in more than academic skills and knowledge. Edith became more self-reliant, was learning to resist imposition on the playground, was increasingly aware of herself as a person in relationship with other persons. She continued friendly, but gained a quiet self-assertion.

Edith will never be able to learn as effectively as other children of her actual age, or to participate in classroom activities on a par with them. But she was helped through Miss T's interest and aid to learn within the limits of her abilities, and to participate to the extent that she was capable. She retained her good qualities of well-sustained attention, interest, and effort. And she lost the helpless, forlorn dependence that had earlier been characteristic of her and grew in social skills.

Not all children are bright children. Not all are even of average intelligence. But if the limitations of a child's intellectual endowment are recognized, there is much that a teacher can do to help a child to live as a social member of a group and experience the satisfactions important to everyone— successful achievement as the outcome of effort, a respected place in the group, and acceptance by one's peers. Not only a discerning teacher is required for this. A teacher is needed who is friendly and interested in each individual child to the extent of giving more time and effort and planning to particular needs which cannot be met through class activities alone. In return for the extra time and thought, regardless of the amount of specific subject matter they foster during the course of the school year, the child's teacher will have the deep satisfaction of seeing a better adjusted and far happier child.

111

CHAPTER SEVEN

The preadolescents

TEN IS A difficult year, because it is unpredictable. Many ten-year-olds are still youngsters, a bit steadier, a bit more grown up, perhaps, than they were at nine; others have already begun their prepubertal spurt of growth and are on the threshold of adolescence. This is especially true of girls, who by this age are usually at least a year more mature than boys. All fifth-grade teachers expect to have in their class each year at least one or two girls who have started to menstruate and are beginning to experience the problems of adolescence.

For this reason, being ten can present new problems. Friends begin to notice differences in each other. Mary and Ellen may have played together for years, and now Mary notices that Ellen is suddenly shooting up taller than she is, that she is no longer interested in paper dolls or the secret club word, and is even beginning to look at boys. So gaps develop between the children; each thinks something must be wrong with the other, or with herself.

Or John, who is an early-maturing boy, begins to lose interest in his school work; he is restless over the stories in his readers and is bored with some of the projects. Instead of cooperating, he becomes difficult, perhaps even to the point of truancy.

If teachers are aware that such changes may take place in children as early as the tenth year, many heartaches and problems can be avoided. The neighbors may say Mrs. Jones is letting Ellen grow up too fast, but Mrs. Jones and Ellen's teacher will know that Ellen cannot help it. She is maturing early, and recognition must be taken of this fact. A child who has matured cannot be treated in the same way as the

112

majority of ten-year-olds, who are still children.

It takes great skill and understanding on the part of the teacher to plan a program that meets the needs of the majority of boys and girls who are not approaching maturity at ten, and yet plan also for those who are approaching puberty or who have already matured. Many behavior problems can be avoided, and many youngsters can be better understood and helped, if teachers and parents know the facts about the pre-adolescent period and are alert for the signs which show that a child needs to be treated not as a child, but as a more mature individual.

NO SINGLE PICTURE can be given of pre-adolescent children. Whereas the early-maturing child is changing so markedly both physically and emotionally, the ten-year-old who is *not* approaching puberty will be much like the nine-year-old in his physical appearance and development. His talents

rush around and be "busy." He is a loyal member of the gang; also, he has learned how to keep a secret and he feels a definite responsibility for those things which he has promised to take care of.

Girls and boys are definitely separating in their interests. Boys like rough-and-tumble games, girls usually prefer quieter ones. Although they will still mix together in school activities and planned parties, in spontaneous activities boys play with boys and girls with girls. There is often a considerable amount of antagonism between the boy groups and girl groups. This lasts longer with boys than with girls, who in a year or two will begin to show a definite interest in boys. Girls of this age, as we have noted, are more mature than boys, not only physically but in their interests. They are interested in relationships between people and will play endless games with their paper dolls, working out problems and scenes of marriage, families, and babies.

Maturity is an individual matter. During the next three or four years each classroom will contain some children who have already matured and some who are still young boys and girls, both physically and in their thoughts and interests. As we have seen, it is no longer possible to think

and skills are becoming more definite and certain. His interest in people, in his community, and in the affairs of the world is more keen than many adults realize. He is interested in an elementary way in social problems and likes to take part in discussions. He is increasingly able to take care of himself and can take longer trips away from home with greater security. He works well in school. He wants to improve his ability and master skills, but he does not take himself quite so seriously as he did at nine. He likes to do things well and efficiently. He grasps the meaning of time, is beginning to plan his time, and accepts responsibility for getting things done "on time." He is physically active and likes to

of boys and girls in terms of a certain age level: it will be necessary to think of them in terms of maturity level. This preadolescent group is difficult to handle in our present school grouping because of these different levels of maturity that are involved. These levels should be interpreted to boys and girls if they are to be spared unnecessary bewilderment, fears, and feelings of inferiority at being "different." In program planning it will be necessary to allow for the differences in interest level of those youngsters who have matured and those who have not.

Preadolescence may start anywhere between nine and thirteen. Most girls begin to show signs of maturing around eleven and will menstruate at about thirteen. The majority of boys mature at about fourteen. However, the range is great: girls may menstruate between ten and sixteen, and boys may mature between twelve and sixteen, with a few starting earlier, a few later. This variation between boys and girls points up one of the big problems of the preadolescent period. Since many girls mature earlier than boys, they become interested in boys and in dates and in dancing long before the boys who are their classmates are at all interested. Many girls begin to think they have "failed" socially because the boys are not interested in them. The girl often takes the initiative toward the boy at this age and is often met with a complete lack of response. Parents and teachers need to be aware of this problem, especially during the preadolescent years, and to interpret the situation to the mature girl, perhaps providing her an opportunity to meet boys who are slightly older and who are interested in dates. Many of the problems which we meet in young adolescent girls—overdone hair-do's, too much lipstick, too much apparent "chasing" after boys—are the result of this difference

in the development between boys and girls; they reflect the normal interest in dating of the girl who has matured before the boys she has known are ready to respond, and her resulting feeling of frustration because "the boys don't like me."

Before the onset of puberty there is usually a "resting period," or "plateau," during which the boy or girl does not seem to gain in either height or weight. This is followed by a period of rapid growth in height. The child may seem to "shoot up," and Mother is again busy trying to make clothes fit. Following the growth in height there is a period of growth in weight. In girls this may sometimes seem almost alarming, for

a girl may gain as much as twenty pounds in a year, or almost seven times as much as she has ever gained in a year before. Naturally, many girls and their parents become alarmed for fear "something is wrong" or think Sally is going to be "fat." These changes need interpretation to the youngsters, and often to their parents.

Because a girl develops sooner than a boy at this age, girls are often considerably taller and heavier than boys in their classes. This again presents problems, self-consciousness, and often heartaches for the girl who finds herself towering above the boys she is so eager to interest. On the other hand, many boys worry because they are still so small and underdeveloped—they wonder if "something is wrong" with them.

At the same time that the child is growing in height and weight the rest of the body is also rapidly developing. Arms grow long, hands grow bigger, hips in girls and shoulders in boys broaden, the breasts of the girl develop, and the pubic hair begins to grow. Since the body does not all develop at the same speed, the child may become self-conscious because of overdeveloped breasts, seemingly too-large hips, big hands, or large feet. Much of the awkwardness of this age, the dropping and tripping over things which adults often find so trying, is due to this uneven growth of the parts of the body during this period.

Very often the preadolescent may seem lazy. This is often founded in a very real fatigue. Growth is taking place so rapidly that the youngster is often tired, or just doesn't want to do anything. Ten-year-olds who are not nearing puberty are usually very alert and energetic, so that the early-maturing child who is easily fatigued because of his growth spurt may stand out in sharp contrast or may even seem a difficult or uncooperative child.

Because the preadolescent is going through so many bodily changes and is also experiencing the emotional changes of the early adolescent period, he sometimes seems difficult to live with in contrast to other children of his age who may not be so near maturity. He becomes overcritical of adults, of his parents and his teachers, although at the same time he may develop

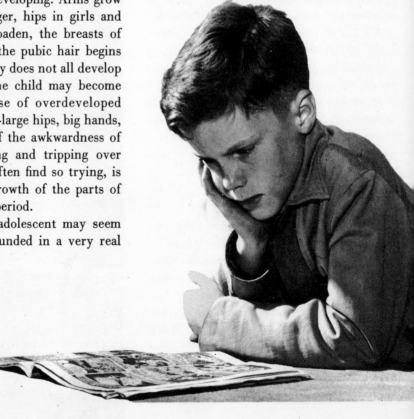

crushes on or hero-worship of an adult to whom he is particularly attracted. He wants to grow up, but he seems afraid to leave the security of childhood behind him. He may seem very responsible and capable today, but tomorrow exceedingly childish. He resents being told what to do, and yet often expects and wants help from his teachers or his parents. His moods change quickly. He may be full of eagerness this morning, and this afternoon be very blue and uninterested in what is going on. Adults need understanding and a sense of humor to meet the ups and downs of the preadolescent period. Scolding or nagging a preadolescent only makes matters worse. It is better to treat him as a young adult and to talk things over in a family or classroom council as equal to equal. It is better to give too much independence, too much trust that the youngster can and will make adequately good decisions if given the chance, than it is to treat him as a "difficult child" or show lack of confidence in him.

The gang and the group, the feeling of belonging and being like the others, is very strong at this age, whether the child is nearing puberty or not. However, for those youngsters who are nearing puberty the character of the group is changing and will change even more. The child who becomes mature loses to some degree his earlier interest in the secret code, the secret word, and all the mystery which he enjoyed in the earlier gang. Boy gangs keep this interest longer than girls. Those youngsters who have matured are beginning to be interested in the opposite sex, and although a girl will keep a girl group all through high school, it will no longer be all-absorbing. A girl will turn down a girl-group activity for a date, and the girls will accept it as a matter of course. It is much longer, however, before the boy

gang will not consider a member disloyal if he misses a club activity to take his girl out. Some trouble and misunderstanding are likely to develop during these years among the youngsters who are still children and continue their close interest in a boy or girl group, when a friend who has matured seems disloyal because his interests are changing. The more mature children will tend to group together around interests of their own. The alert teacher, parents, or community leaders will provide activities of varying types for youngsters of this age group, realizing that no one type of activity can interest children of varying maturity levels, even if their chronological age is the same.

The interest in team games is high. But skill is important. The child who does not have enough skill to hold his own will often withdraw from the game and become a spectator. Boys usually like such games as soccer, baseball, and football, rowing boats, swimming, riding bicycles, and such construction activities as making model airplanes. Girls like sewing and cooking, gardening, swimming, hiking, skating, and dancing. Both groups enjoy pets and are now able to care for them. They enjoy movies, radio, and comics, although the interest in comics is sometimes on the wane. Differences in reading ability and reading interests are very apparent. Some children greatly enjoy reading; others show little interest. The children who read seem to want facts as well as imaginative stories. They like nature stories and books on science, travel, and mechanics; many of them enjoy series of books written about boys and girls. Some of them are reading

and enjoying the classics, although most of them do not yet like "romantic" stories. Girls usually become interested in such stories sooner than do the boys.

THE PREADOLESCENT is often rebellious and difficult to guide. He will rebel at bedtime, at keeping clean, at wearing the kind of clothes Mother thinks suitable. He will often use bad language, will be untidy and uncooperative. Fritz Redl calls it a "period of disorganization." Some girls follow this pattern, too, but girls are more likely to be interested in being "cute" and "looking nice"—they will often reject the "tomboy" girl who is untidy, sloppy, or rough in her manners.

It is wise to allow these preadolescent children to let off steam a bit. Let them express their thoughts and feelings. The listening adult should avoid becoming upset and taking offense at signs of disrespect. In school, group discussions are often helpful, especially when the children can be so grouped that those who are more

mature are apart from those who are still youngsters. The interest group can often accomplish this needed separation. The teacher can listen without being shocked and can talk as "adult to adult" with the child, listening to his reasons and opinions and then presenting her point of view.

Those things which have given stability to the younger child will give stability also to the preadolescent—warm affection from parents and teacher, an understanding of his own pattern of growth and development, a recognition of his individual personality needs, a sense of belonging and of being accepted because he is himself, and an opportunity to be independent as fast as his maturity will permit. All these will help the youngster pass through the difficult years of preadolescence and adolescence without too much strain or difficulty.

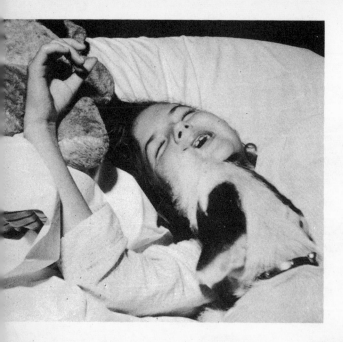

At home with Linda

LINDA is ten and in fifth grade. The new braces on her teeth are a great trial, but Linda realizes that many girls and boys go through the same thing, and she is happy that her crooked teeth are going to be straight. She understands, too, that she is changing as she grows. For example, through her health and development discussion periods at school, she learned that her too-big feet were nothing to be worried about, that it is not at all unusual for a pre-adolescent's feet to grow faster than other parts of his body. Both Linda and her mother were relieved. Even her gangling awkwardness she is taking in stride.

Time to get up! Cappy's damp kiss wakes Linda smiling each morning.

Those braces are a nuisance and so new Linda isn't yet quite used to them.

Bed made and herself almost dressed, Linda wonders if she shouldn't get a longer pair of socks.

Linda's current favorite
is Mrs. Piggle Wiggle.

"Yes, Betty,
I'll be right over."

Tuning in for "Tom Mix."

Asleep with "Dumbo," a
constant comfort "cuddly"
since Linda was a baby.

The story of Elizabeth Holmes

THAT CHILDREN change as they grow is of course recognized by everyone. But sometimes changes in behavior are so marked that the adults charged with the care of the children become disturbed. That is particularly true when the underlying cause of the undesirable change is not recognized. Once there is awareness of the reasons back of a child's reactions, plans can be made to help him reach more acceptable ways of behaving. Until those reasons are uncovered there are often many weeks of concern and discontent for all concerned.

That was the case with Elizabeth, a bright nine-year-old who stood high in her fourth-grade class. Elizabeth there was a picture of sturdy physical health. Good social relationships with her classmates and a secure home situation with understanding, college-trained parents characterized Elizabeth while she was in Miss R's fourth-grade room.

But Elizabeth in fifth grade presented a vastly different picture. She had celebrated her tenth birthday during the summer. She returned to school in September showing few of the desirable attitudes and acceptable behavior reactions so apparent during the previous school year. Both her teacher and her mother were gravely disturbed.

Elizabeth was painfully self-conscious. She kept a small compact in her desk and examined her face at frequent intervals during class periods. She applied lipstick liberally. She bemoaned her many freckles and tried to rouge them over. No longer content with the companionship of her classmates, she turned to a little clique of girls in eighth grade and sought to establish herself as one of them. They were considerably older than Elizabeth, of course. Their interests had changed from typical ten-year-old activities to whispers and giggles about handsome movie stars, good-looking boy classmates, and styles in clothes.

DURING class, one day, Miss L had occasion to correct Elizabeth's poor posture. The child burst into tears. Another time Miss L suggested that she might be more careful, after her stumbling against a table had upset a vase of flowers and damaged several books with the spilled water. Elizabeth blushed furiously and was so disturbed by the reprimand that she was unable to participate in the class discussion the following period.

Soon after this, the other girls began to tease her because of her obvious infatuation for Miss L. Elizabeth gazed soulfully at the teacher, offered to do many little unnecessary errands for her, brought one gift after another, and seemed unable to keep her hands from caressing Miss L's sleeve or shoulder whenever an opportunity presented itself.

She became more interested in romantic movies than in her school work. She collected pictures of Hollywood actors and was embarrassed when the girls laughed at her ecstatic comments and ridiculed her. She wept dramatically on an occasion when Miss L voiced rather cold disapproval of her newly acquired enthusiasms.

Her mother observed changes at home,

too. Elizabeth was demanding clothes that were inappropriate for a ten-year-old, and privileges that were unsuitable. She developed ways that had never before been hers—evasions and even deceptions, a haughtiness which was sometimes ludicrous, and a sensitiveness that made every day increasingly difficult for the entire family. Her parents were bewildered—disturbed but also annoyed, concerned and yet impatient, too.

"She's just a little girl," they said. "What are these notions she is developing? Why is she so hard to manage all of a sudden? It must be the big girls at school she has been tagging after. They have a bad influence." And they forbade Elizabeth to go around with the eighth-graders, and refused her permission to attend their parties.

But this only made matters worse. Elizabeth became increasingly rebellious, flew into a temper when she was crossed, neglected the chores which formerly she had attended to routinely. She was restless and sullen and often rude.

HER SCHOOL WORK began to reflect the entire disturbed situation. Instead of being well up in her classes, Elizabeth handed in assignments late, was so inattentive in class that she was unable to follow the group activities, and seemed unable to concentrate on new material that needed time and care for comprehension.

With Miss L at school, Elizabeth was breathlessly imploring when she was taken to task for increasingly poor achievement. "I'll try, really I will, Miss L. *Please* don't think I don't want to. I want to please you. I can't stand it if you talk to me like that!" And there was almost hysterical crying.

With her mother at home, the child alternately tried to stand on her dignity and to cajole the family into permitting her to stay up for an evening party, or to go to a movie with Carl: "Oh, Mother, he's wonderful! He's in eighth grade, and his voice is so deep and masculine! Please let me go, Mother dear!" And when Mrs. Holmes was firm in her refusal, Elizabeth withdrew. "Very well, Mother. If you insist. You simply don't understand me. You simply can't appreciate that things have changed since you were my age." And Elizabeth remained in her room with the door closed during the entire evening.

Finally Miss L and Elizabeth's parents together talked over the matter. Why these different and unfavorable reactions in fifth grade, after so successful a school experience throughout the earlier grades? Why the changed emotional responses at home, the demand for greater freedom, for social relationships which were so patently inappropriate for a ten-year-old?

Fortunately, Miss L had been sufficiently interested in Elizabeth to discuss her difficulties with the school nurse and the physical-education teacher. It was from them that the clues came which helped the family understand this little girl who seemed to want to grow up faster than her years.

OFTEN WHEN one sees a child day after day, the physical changes that take place remain unnoticed until something happens to bring them into focus—a wearable coat is much too small, or food demands change radically, or complaints of lassitude or undue restlessness are so obvious they cannot be ignored, or a peaches-and-cream complexion develops roughness and pimples. And all these things had actually been true of Elizabeth, but their gradual emergence had not been noted as specific changes.

The expensive winter coat purchased for her during the previous year was taken out on the first cold day. It was absurdly small across shoulders and chest. It was too short

123

in the sleeves. It was too short in length.

A healthy appetite grew so enormous that the child never seemed satisfied at mealtime. Candy and cookies and the richest kind of sundaes became routine after lunch, and again after school in the afternoon. Before bedtime Elizabeth was sure to be heard at the icebox or the cookie jar. In her room there were often papers from chocolate bars, and bags with only a piece or two of sticky sweets remaining.

The increase in Elizabeth's weight, her records showed, had been tremendous. She had grown more than twice as fast as nine-year-olds generally do. She had gained twenty pounds in weight during her ninth year. And during the first two months of this year, she had grown another inch and added four more pounds. No wonder that last year's coat didn't fit. No wonder that her once smooth face was marred now with patchy places and red pimples.

The changes in height and weight were accompanied by physical changes of another sort. Elizabeth's hips were wider, her breasts had developed; and together with these evidences of an early puberty she showed the muscular incoordination and clumsiness which often trouble the young preadolescent before he learns to handle smoothly the developing skeletal and muscular structures.

The occasional moodiness, the occasional spitefulness, the restlessness, the sensitiveness which had grown as characteristics of Elizabeth, were all part of the change brought about by the developing physical organism approaching maturity.

She did not understand why she should look so different from her classmates. It worried her and made her self-conscious. If she stood half stooped over, perhaps those embarrassing breasts would be less conspicuous. If she used make-up, maybe she could conceal the facial blemishes. If she

sought the companionship of older girls (girls already well along in their pubertal development and so more like Elizabeth in appearance), she need no longer feel so different, so out of sorts with herself and her world.

WHEN THE reasons back of all of these annoying reactions became clear, neither Mrs. Holmes nor Miss L felt so helpless. They recognized that Elizabeth needed aid in understanding and accepting herself in her new rôle.

It was clearly appropriate for Elizabeth to learn more of how girls grow and develop. The menstrual function was explained to her. Much of her confidence in her mother returned as the two had long talks about themselves. Her rebelliousness was replaced by a greater acceptance of reasons why some of her desires had to be refused.

As she was helped to develop new interests, her preoccupation with boys and movie stars and clothes was no longer so all-absorbing. Dancing was fascinating to her, and lessons were arranged. A dramatic group for children was fortunately available, and she was enrolled.

With her energies taken by these new and more acceptable activities, the worries of the grown-ups were lessened and Elizabeth became less depressed and confused and better able to live with her maturing self. Because she now realized that her differences from her classmates were a temporary matter, she acquired a new perspective toward herself. She no longer felt the necessity to be on the defensive against them.

Instead, with the help of her mother and Miss L, Elizabeth was enabled to substitute for her half-ashamed awareness of her increasing maturity, a kind of pride that she "had gotten ahead of the other girls."

Paul and Paul's father

WHEN IT IS possible to learn the entire story of how a child has lived and grown and developed, clues can generally be uncovered which make it possible to interpret behavior which disturbs parents and teachers. But sometimes, even after a thorough study of a child's life, the behavior remains puzzling. The clues to its origin may lie in a parent's habit of unconsciously expressing his own troubles and tensions in his relationship with his child.

Such a concept is not easy to understand, and such a situation is surely not easy to handle. When a school child is involved, he is fortunate if his teacher senses something that is beyond her province and secures the help of the expert trained in that field. Paul's story is a case in point.

Paul at twelve was repeating fifth grade. He had spent much of the previous school year lost in daydreams. He had not acquired the necessary skills for more advanced class work. Nor had he reached the quality of social adjustment which made relationships with older boys successful. He seemed immature in so many ways that it was hoped that the following year might find him more responsive and capable.

But the new teacher found Paul's behavior the same in this second fifth-grade experience. She wondered if something could not be done to bring him to the satisfaction of real experiences in place of his continuing to depend on the delights of daydreaming. She knew that until this was done he would make no further progress either academically or socially.

PAUL, according to the psychological tests in his record, was not among the very brightest children of the class. But he had adequate ability to do school work successfully. He seemed healthy physically. Vision and hearing gave no evidence of contributing to school failure. Miss S was puzzled by the situation and wondered if the clue might be in Paul's life at home.

When she made an opportunity to talk with Paul one afternoon after school, enough of his home life was made apparent to disturb her. It struck her that he must have a harsh, even cruel, father. His mother seemed very ineffectual, to judge from the incidents which the boy related. He spoke somewhat haltingly, but as if he welcomed an opportunity to talk things over with a sympathetic listener.

"He looks scared," thought Miss S. She could not seem to isolate any particular incident as significant, but she did feel that his story should be investigated. She knew where he lived. She had admired the place in passing. She had met his shy, quiet mother. Anxiety was apparent in this child, and perhaps his fear was even greater than he dared express. She decided to seek expert advice in the matter.

SHE COULD give the consulting psychologist who served the school a number of facts, well aware that her information was not complete. Paul lived with his parents and a twenty-year-old brother in a comfortable little home on the outskirts of town. They were near enough for Mr. Lerner to go to work in town and for Charles, the older brother, to attend the college located downtown. It was far enough away to permit a vegetable garden and some chickens, and a wide lawn surrounded by a trim hedge.

Mr. Lerner was very proud of his home. He wanted everything shipshape all the time. The grass was always smooth and green, and the vegetables were without a single weed; the very chickens seemed better groomed than chickens generally are. The porch was inviting, with its chairs and swing seeming to stand waiting for the family to have the leisure to enjoy them. Their striped covering was pulled just so, without a wrinkle, free of dust.

It was Paul who cared for the garden, so that the rows of green always looked freshly weeded when his father came home in the evening. It was Paul who gave the chickens their water and feed, and who kept their quarters almost as immaculate as his mother kept the home. He also swept the porch daily and raked the leaves and mowed the grass. He used to count the number of things he did every day and compare his responsibilities with those assumed by Charles.

Charles cut the hedge whenever little shoots of green came up. And each spring he painted the porch furniture. When Paul pointed out that he was doing most of the work, Mr. Lerner would remind him, in his rumbling, disapproving voice, that Charles had more important things to do. Charles was the one of whom they would all one day be proud. Charles was the student; he was going to be a minister, have his own church, and be recognized far and wide as a learned and important personage. Charles needed all the time he could get to study.

"And you, Paul. How did you do in school today? Bring your reader and let me hear you," would be the inevitable end of such a conversation with his father.

THAT WAS WHY Paul didn't often complain of the work he had to do. His father was never pleased with his reading and would make him go over the material time and time again. It soon became meaningless as he stumbled through it in a monotone, outwardly compliant but inwardly despairing and rebellious.

The sessions usually ended with his father in a temper and Paul in tears. The boy soon became convinced that he was dull and slow-witted, as his father said. He wondered why he should bother to try, since his father was never pleased anyway.

"You *must* learn!" Mr. Lerner would shout at him. "To use your hands only is not good. You must study. Be like Charles. If you do not study, you will never amount to anything. What do you want to do, work with your hands all your life?"

Once Paul had ventured, "Papa, you work with your hands, don't you?" That, he found, was something not to be mentioned again. His father's temper lasted longer that day than ever before. In between his own sobs and his father's roaring, Paul gathered something about being one's own boss, not depending on the whim of an employer, earning enough money to buy shoes for sons who wore them out fast and to get a new dress for a wife who because she was only a woman thought clothes important. Paul was frightened and confused. It was easier to try to work just as his father demanded than to raise questions about doing more than his share. It was better just to listen quietly when his father was "in a state" than to try to say anything in his own defense.

He soon developed the trick of letting his thoughts wander away from the tempest. He took *himself* away, even though physically he stood with drooping head before his father. He would build for himself a

126

lurid story of being so big and strong he could whip anybody, strike out at anyone who failed to follow exactly an order he had issued. Or he would fancy a world in which only boys and women were present, never young men or older men. Everyone in his dream world was cheery and easygoing and casual. No one cared particularly if a little dust showed on a table top or if a weed peeked through the ground. Life was good in his dream world.

WHEN A HABIT of daydreaming is practiced often enough, it becomes a pattern of response any time that it seems desirable to avoid something difficult. It was therefore no wonder that Paul shifted his habit of removing himself, via a daydream, from his father's scolding and upbraiding, to removing himself via another daydream from the teasing of children on the playground, from the remonstrance of his teacher when he did an exercise at his desk incorrectly, or from her explanation of a new task which he didn't understand and felt was beyond him anyway.

"If you'd only pay attention," Miss S would say. "You can't learn if you don't listen." Paul would turn his eyes toward her. But he would not be listening even when he seemed to be. He would be lost in daydreaming.

Although Miss S's picture was incomplete, it did suggest the desirability of trying to enlist the parents' cooperation in a plan to help Paul to more adequate adjustment.

When Mr. Lerner was invited to come to school to talk with the teacher and the school psychologist about Paul's progress, he raised no objection. He greeted them with a somewhat blunt statement, "You want to tell me my Paul is not smart enough for school?" It seemed he wanted to say it first, rather than have someone else inform him of his son's failings.

There was rather pathetic relief in his expression when the teacher informed him, however, that Paul was certainly smart enough for school. Her concern, she explained, was because he was not progressing as well as he could, and she thought that if his parents and his teacher worked together they could help him. Mr. Lerner immediately became somewhat excited.

"He must be punished," he said firmly, and with rising anger told Miss S that not a week went by that he did not hear Paul read to him or that he did not criticize the way Paul was doing his school work. "That I should have such a son!" he ended. "If he cannot study medicine as I planned for him, he will have a hard life like me. His brother Charles will do better. He is smart. He will be a minister. It was a doctor I wanted for Paulie. What can I do?"

The psychologist assured him that what he must *not* do was punish his boy. They talked for a long time about the feeling of disappointment Mr. Lerner had, and his great concern lest the boy be a failure in life.

IT IS NOT always easy to convince a parent that his tactics are not helping but are actually harming his child. Here it was not a matter of a single chat, but of a series of interviews between Mr. Lerner and the psychologist. Mr. Lerner's cooperation after his first anger had died down was all that could have been desired.

He was helped to appreciate how his own feeling of insecurity had made him plan almost fiercely to help his children to a happier life. Although actually his own income was sufficient to care for his family comfortably, he felt keenly that only the professions were worth while to earn a good living. He was apparently somewhat ashamed of his own status as a skilled workman.

As his story was revealed, it was explained to him that his own father's disappointment in him when he was a youth and had not done well in academic work had left him feeling guilty all his life for having been a disappointment to his father. His efforts to draw his sons into the professional fields (their grandfather had been a chemical engineer) were his unconscious atonement for his feeling of not having met his own father's expectations.

His extreme demand for exactness, his scrupulous overattention to cleanliness and orderliness, his overemphasis on certain aspects of daily living—all were further evidence of inner personality problems. His quick anger when Paul did not meet his demands was the result of his feeling that again he would, in essence, disappoint his own father, for he had determined in his mind that only by the success of his sons could he compensate for his own early refusal to follow an academic career.

The several hours with the psychologist were well spent. It became clear as they talked that Paul's daydreaming could not be simply brushed aside as a persisting naughty trick but had to be considered as a habit pattern acquired for a purpose. He was understandably upset at his father's constant dissatisfaction and displeasure. And since no one likes to feel unsuccessful, or enjoys scolding and criticism, it was not strange or odd that Paul sought to evade such discomforts by building soothing fantasies wherein he felt capable and accepted and very secure.

"You do expect a great deal of Paul," said the psychologist, "both in schoolwork and in jobs around home and you evidently often show annoyance with him. Perhaps you expect too much."

Mr. Lerner admitted disappointment in his younger son and concern lest the boy be a failure. "I have done what I could to help him. Now I do not know what to do next." He was greatly disheartened.

But he was helped to see how inconsequential were many demands he had been overemphasizing, and how belligerent had been his attitude. He began to show his genuine interest in the boy, and placed less stress on scholastic perfection. He was able to reevaluate the entire situation. He granted the greater desirability of a happy life spent working enjoyably rather than earning a living in distasteful activity, and he conceded that simply because his older son was studiously inclined and eager for a career requiring years of academic preparation, he had no reason to think less of his younger son. Paul's talents might not lie in the same direction as Charles', but he could be helped to be as successful *as a person*, which was, after all, much more important.

THESE ARE all areas of investigation and counsel which clearly lie beyond the training and experience of the classroom teacher. They are not her province. But since the children whom she teaches are influenced by so many apparently unrelated factors, it is well for her to be alert to recognize when she would do well to call in the help of one more skilled than she in dealing with deep personality adjustment problems.

The indirect help given Paul through helping Paul's father created a happier atmosphere in the home, a happier child, and eventually, therefore, a child more successful and better adjusted in his school work. The tangled threads of a child's reactions sometimes take one far from the child himself. But they can generally be drawn back to him, to straighten the twisted thinking and distorted viewpoint back of his difficulties in living.

128

CHAPTER EIGHT

Looking

toward

adolescence

As CHILDREN enter the period of pre-adolescence our thoughts naturally turn toward the years of adolescence which lie ahead of them. Because boys and girls mature at such varying ages, we cannot say that adolescence begins or ends with any certain year. Some children mature rapidly and are ready for adulthood and its responsibilities when others the same age are still immature, still working through the adjustments of the adolescent years.

The physiological changes of the body that herald the beginning of the period are those which change the child into an adult capable of reproduction. They are gradual changes, built upon the physical and psychological development of the child which has been proceeding since birth. The young person begins to experience an intensity of certain drives and emotions which he has not known as a child, and which he will need as an adult. But with his new physical maturity he does not necessarily have the knowledge, judgment, and attitudes which should accompany the power of reproduction. By the end of adolescence the individual should have had the kind of guidance which will enable him to establish his own family unit and enter into the responsibilities of family life.

In recent years our interest in this period and our recognition of the very real strains and adjustments involved have made us highlight the adolescent years. This has tended to set them apart from the rest of the growth process. Thus we have often overdramatized and overemphasized the difficulties which our children have at this time. As a result we have caused many parents and teachers and even some adolescents themselves almost to dread these transition years. Yet they are valuable years, vital in the total developmental picture. They are part of normal growth and continuous with what has gone before. We need not fear them, but should consider carefully the rôle which the adult must play in guiding young persons who are growing through them, so that they will

be able to step with some confidence into their places in the adult world.

DURING the adolescent period, the young person faces some major tasks of which parents and teachers should be aware. The first of these is his adjustment toward the changes that are taking place in his own body—the boy's full acceptance of himself as a man, the girl's acceptance of herself as a woman, and their realization of the rôles which they will play as men and women. Growing out of this adjustment, and part of it, is the desire of the adolescent to learn about members of the opposite sex and to be able to establish normal, happy, healthy relationships with them.

The second task which concerns the adolescent is that of being accepted by others his own age, not only of the other sex but of the same sex. Boys want to be like the other boys, girls like the other girls. At this age it is the rare child who wants to be "different." The young person feels it highly important and desirable to be like the others and part of the group. We need to recognize the heartaches suffered by those who are not accepted by the others, in order to be alert to give them the help and guidance they should have.

Boys and girls must also face the task of finding a vocational interest during their adolescent years so that they will be able to plan toward establishing themselves as self-supporting, self-respecting adults. They must find their strengths and weaknesses, their interests and aptitudes, as they fit into a realistic situation, translating the daydreams of childhood into the actual possibilities of adult life.

And finally they face the task of establishing independence from their parents and identifying themselves with adults so that they may themselves be self-reliant,

adult citizens when the years of adolescence are behind them.

These are not easy tasks for our growing young people. They need the wise support and understanding of both their parents and their teachers as they try to work through the problems which are inevitable sometime between the ages of thirteen and twenty.

THE FIRST of the three tasks is perhaps the one for which thoughtful parents and teachers most often find it difficult to give the guidance they would like to offer to their boys and girls. It is not easy to give adequate sex education, but it is of vital importance because the type of sex education children receive will affect adjustment not only to sexual relationships but to all their social relationships and their total adjustment to life. For sex education is more than just the giving of certain facts about how life begins. It is the imparting of an attitude toward life itself, toward the human body, toward the creating of life,

and toward the affectional relationships which we build through the years. It is an attitude which the child absorbs as he grows. He learns it from his parents and from other adults around him as he senses and observes their attitudes toward and adjustment to the place of sex in the whole life pattern. It cannot be given just by sitting down and talking to a child or reading a book with him, or even through a course in school, helpful as these methods may be. The child learns it from babyhood onward through the many ways in which we show our feelings and attitudes and acceptance or nonacceptance of sex and of the rôle our own sex is supposed to play. He learns it as he learns how to love and be loved by other people. A happy home and the good marital adjustment of his parents are the best bases for the real sex education of the child.

Unfortunately, not all children have this background, and so the teacher and the school, the church and the community have a responsibility to see that all children are

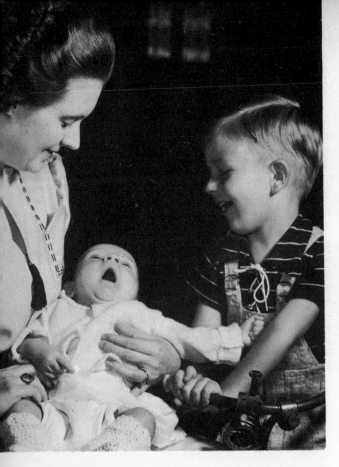

and to marry. They are part of the same life force. The successful development of those feelings which lead a young person to love and marriage are not new at that time, but have been steadily developing since his baby days. The ways in which a child learns to love and be loved are as much sex education as are the physiological facts which he should receive as part of his information about life and his relationship to the world around him.

His ability to develop a satisfactory marriage and family life begins with his early attachment to his mother as he suckles and is cuddled in her arms. It grows through the early years when the little child has very deep and real feelings for both father and mother. It continues through the stage of close friendship with youngsters of the same sex in grade-school days, and on into attachment for members of the opposite sex during adolescence. It culminates in marriage and the starting of a new family cycle.

If we are really to help boys and girls we must understand this gradual growth cycle in learning to love. The ways in which we attempt to fill their needs for certain kinds of experience at each level both in the schoolroom and in the home are a significant part of sex education. What counts is the way we answer children's questions at each level and the way we help them to understand themselves, to live successfully through each stage, and to progress normally into the next phase of development. We need to be aware of the interest and normal curiosity which all children have in this area of life and of the types of questions and situations that are likely to arise in the normal process of a child's growing up.

Children normally ask many questions about sex. These questions vary with the

helped to a fine and adequate understanding of sex. And here again it is not simply a matter of devoting specified class time to the subject. Each individual teacher is giving sex education to her boys and girls in her daily teaching through her attitudes, her comments, and her reactions to situations. It is not a question of whether teachers *should* guide children in this area, but of *how adequately they are doing it*.

WE USED to think that sexual feelings developed suddenly at puberty. We now realize that they are present in infancy and are part of the child's normal growth pattern as he passes from one phase of life to another. We cannot distinguish between those elements which tie a child in close affection to his parents and his friends, and those which later cause him to love age of the child. The same questions will be asked many times over as the child grows and wants more information. At whatever age the questions are asked they should be answered simply, honestly, and at the time they are asked, if this is at all possible. A child often learns more from the way in which something is said than from what is actually said. A good general rule is to answer just what the child asks. When he wants more he will ask for more, if he feels that you are willing to answer his questions. Too often in our eagerness to do a good job we give far more information than the child is seeking or can absorb. Too much information given too soon only bewilders and confuses.

U NTIL THE child is six or seven, simple information in answer to questions is usually the wisest course to follow. If information is presented more formally, as in a classroom setting, it should contain material on understanding the differences between boys and girls, which often need clarifying to children of these ages. It could also contain stories showing the rôles of mothers and fathers and men and women generally, so that the children are able to identify more clearly and strongly with the rôle their own sex plays in our culture. Stories about family relationships, the new baby, and other family experiences are also helpful to the little child who is learning to establish his own relationships. Pets in the classroom, especially if baby pets are born during the year, provide a valuable learning experience.

The older school-age child not only will ask questions about the differences between boys and girls, and where babies come from, but will want to go into these things in much greater detail as he listens to the radio and to the talk of adults, reads papers and magazines, and observes what is going on

about him. With the school-age child it is often a good technique to turn the question back to him in a conversational way, asking him what he thinks about it. In this way we are often able to go beyond the surface question and find out just how much the child really knows and whether he has obtained inaccurate information that is confusing him. We will then be able to correct mistaken notions or fill in the gaps in what he already knows. With the grade-school child we must also be sensitive to what is underneath the question—there may be anxiety or feelings of guilt or fear which we need to ease.

Even after children have been given the factual answers many times, they may still not fully understand and may return to try to get a clearer answer or more information as their concepts grow. If we are able to keep the channels of talk open, we shall be able to meet their needs as they reach out again and again for fuller information and greater understanding.

THE YEARS between ten and twelve are probably the best ones in which to make sure that children have the physiological knowledge which they need to understand the coming changes in their bodies. This is also the best time to provide the basic knowledge for an understanding of how life begins. By the end of the grade-school years youngsters should have basic information. It can be received during these years with much less emotionality than can be achieved when the child has become adolescent.

The information which the child of this age receives should be specific, so that he understands the physiology of the sexual organs of both sexes and the way in which they function. They should know about menstruation and nocturnal emissions. It is always preferable to give this information as part of a general course of study including

the other parts of the human body. If this is done, boys and girls will learn to think of their sexual organs simply as part of their total bodily equipment, and not something upon which to focus special attention. Their knowledge should also be clear as to the birth of babies and the rôles of both mother and father.

They should know what to anticipate both in bodily changes and in new emotional reactions and problems during the coming adolescent years. They especially need to realize that not all boys and girls mature at the same time, that girls usually mature first and for a few years are very often bigger and better developed than boys. There should be opportunities for boys and girls to talk through the problems and anxieties that may arise when they find themselves either far in advance of or far behind their friends in these years of maturing.

AMONG OUR grade-school children there will be a few who have already matured and are facing the problems of adolescence. Of these we need to be especially aware. As they become interested in members of the other sex there should be sympathetic opportunities for them to talk about their growing interest in one another, and opportunities for them to begin to work out wholesome relationships together.

During the adolescent period, if the basic information has been well given, the questions asked will more often be those which deal with feelings and emotions and with finding ways in which to get along well with each other. What kind of girls do boys like, and what kind of boys do girls like? Should we kiss good-night after a date? What about necking—is it all right? How can a girl get a date? Adolescents are interested in learning the ways of boys and girls together.

The need of each to accept his or her own

sex is heightened at the adolescent level by the physical changes which are obviously taking place. At first these may seem strange and even distressing, especially if the child has not been adequately prepared for them. The growth in weight, the development of the breasts and hips, the beginning of the menstrual flow are bewildering experiences to many growing girls and need careful interpretation and anticipation. Boys are often concerned by their changing voices, the need to shave, or their nocturnal emissions. Boys and girls need time to adjust to these changes, and help in understanding them.

In answering the questions of adolescents, it is well to remember that while the acceptance of their own sex culminates during adolescence, it has been in process since early childhood. Even when the child is very small, during the preschool years, he normally begins to try to identify himself with his own sex. The little girl takes her mother as her pattern of what a woman should be and copies her ways. The little boy watches his father and tries to walk like him and talk like him, imitating those qualities which we think of as manly.

During the grade-school years this attempt to find oneself as girl or boy continues. Girls grow close to each other as best friends or members of a secret club, and boys identify closely with each other in their special gang. Through these experiences, and by the imitation of older boys and girls whom they admire, they learn what our society expects of each sex in behavior and attitudes.

With the coming of adolescence there is usually again a close identification of the girl with her mother, or with a mother substitute in the form of a greatly admired teacher or other woman, and of the boy with his father, or his athletic coach, or some other man. There is also a heightened

interest at this time in imitating and being like the successful and admired members of their own sex in their peer group.

Most adolescent boys and girls pass through this period successfully and are able to accept themselves fully as man or woman by the time their high-school days are over. But some young people need special help in accepting their own rôle without too great a conflict.

If the child has had a conspicuously unhappy relationship with those who exemplify in his life the basic pattern of his sex, he may reject the pattern of his own sex and identify with the parent, or some other adult, of the opposite sex. If a mother has intensely resented being a woman, she may have created in her daughter a difficulty in accepting the feminine rôle. Or again, if a father who wanted a son has brought his daughter up to value manly activity and scorn "the things girls do," she may have great difficulty in making the transition to the feminine rôle as she grows older.

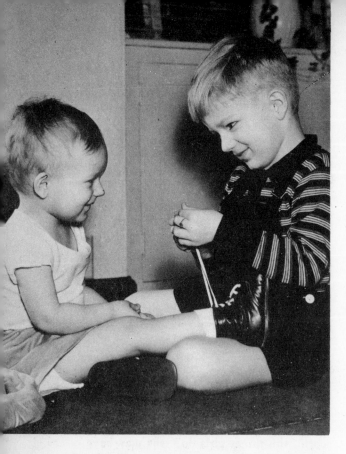

In like manner, if a mother has wished for a little daughter and has brought her son up to be too gentle and effeminate, has disliked cutting his curls and has taught him to be "her sweet little boy" and to stay away from the other boys because "they are too tough," the child may find it almost impossible to assume the masculine rôle when he grows up. We need to be aware that although children of this type are not numerous, they do exist in every school and will need particular guidance if they are to be adequately adjusted adults. Some of these children may need the expert help of the school psychologist or the community guidance clinic in order to be able to work through their problems and develop more normal, healthy attitudes.

Many parents and teachers recognize the importance of preparing children for the physiological changes of adolescence and for the emotions and feelings which will arise from these changes, yet find it extremely difficult, or even almost impossible, to talk with them about these things. In fact, many parents find the difficulty so great that they put it off from year to year until the child enters adolescence totally unprepared, or with only the haphazard and often erroneous facts and attitudes which he has picked up from his playmates, from the newspapers, the movies, the radio, the comics, or the scattered remarks and innuendos of the grown-ups. In the same way many teachers hesitate and are embarrassed or perplexed when boys and girls ask them direct questions about these things, or when situations arise which involve questions or problems of a sexual nature.

This is only a natural and expected result of the training which most present-day adults received in their own childhood. In the past, in our particular culture, questions involving the birth of children and the relationships between men and women have been considered taboo, something to be discussed only in whispers and with embarrassment. Most adults today received very inadequate information, and what they received concerned only the so-called "facts of life." These were presented as something totally apart from the rest of living, in a small compartment by themselves.

To THIS lack of adequate preparation for life and family living have been added our own varying personal experiences and adjustments, all of which color attitudes in this area. Many significant factors apply in this connection: the way in which our own parents lived together in happiness or in discord; their opinions about the relative value of a boy or a girl in the family group; the amount of affection we received as children; our parents' attitudes when a baby was born or coming; or the punishment we may have received for asking questions or for trying to find out, as all normal children do, about our bodies; our own adjustments or difficulties as we left the home circle and tried to make friends with other boys and girls, our feelings of success or of inadequacy. All these things help to determine whether it is easy or difficult for us to talk without embarrassment with boys and girls who come to us and whether we give them wholesome or distorted attitudes. It is no wonder that so few adults today can talk with natural simplicity about the beginnings of life. Sometimes both teacher and parents may need to seek help in working through their own problems, and in understanding their own attitudes, before they can be sufficiently free, comfortable, and well adjusted to be able to help a growing child.

In the list of suggested readings starting on page 185 are many books and pamphlets which the individual parent or teacher may find helpful in answering the specific questions which children ask throughout their years of growing up. The answers found in these books can be used as a guide, although each one will need to be modified to fit the need of the particular child or the particular question which has been asked. They must be colored by our own individual way of saying things, so that they will not sound cold and stilted, but will bear the ring of sincerity.

Books can be a valuable aid in giving us confidence and the right information with which to give understanding to our boys and girls. But they can only supplement. They cannot take the place of the day-to-day development of attitudes, the informal talking things over together and answering of questions as they arise in their natural setting of everyday life.

137

If the parent is too tense or embarrassed to be able to talk informally with his eight- to ten-year-old, then it is probably wiser for him to read a well-written book with the youngster; an older child can be provided with a book to read for himself. In the reading list (pages 185-188) we have indicated which books are written for parents and which are suitable for boys and girls to read. Even if a youngster is given a book to read, the parent should realize that he must still try to answer the questions that will often be stimulated by the reading. Although factual information may be quite detailed we must always remember that the child is seeking attitudes as well as facts.

Many parents turn to the teacher or the counselor for help in giving the

information which they earnestly want to pass on to their children. Thus it becomes vitally important for teachers to be prepared to give clear, simple, understanding help to parents who seek it.

During the grade-school years both home and school will be faced with specific situations which involve sex experiences. We cannot protect our children fully from playground knowledge or words or from some sexual play, which is prompted frequently by curiosity and a lack of adequate information about the bodily differences between boys and girls. There are always situations of writing on the toilet walls, and occasionally the more serious problem of sex experimentation among some of the children; or the presence of a sex offender in the neighborhood makes it necessary for us to warn the boys and girls for their protection.

How these situations are met is important in the sex education of our youngsters. If we meet them with tension, over-excitement, or disgust, with anger or an attempt to punish or shame or frighten the boys or girls involved, we have failed in our responsibility to these children. We should understand that these things are most often only a natural attempt on the part of youngsters to find out about themselves. It is best to meet curiosity and sex play not with anger and stern repression, but with the realization that these children are in need of information to satisfy their curiosity and should be helped to establish wholesome attitudes to replace those which are expressing themselves through garbled knowledge and playground-accumulated information. Often they are in need, too, of other outlets for their energy besides those that are being supplied in the regular routine by either home or school.

Even the acutely serious situation should be treated as a problem to be worked through rather than as a misdemeanor to be met with punishment. The children concerned need study and adjustment, sometimes by a trained person, if they are to be able to change their behavior. The best results are obtained when we are able to approach these situations with calmness and insight. We are then able to help the children involved instead of further entrenching the wrong attitudes toward sex which they are developing.

These grade-school years are a time not of completion, but rather of experimentation, of finding out, of learning. The developing child is trying to orient himself to the adult world about him and to his place in it. As manifestations of the sex force in life are everywhere about him, it would be a dull child indeed who did not include in the span of his curiosity an interest in the beginnings of life and the differences and relationships between men and women. He does not usually think of these things with the same emotional connotations as do adults. He wants to know. It is the adult with a deep and close personal interest in him who should give him the knowledge in the wise and realistic manner which will help him absorb it into his own life. In order to do this the relationship between the adult and the child must be warm, friendly, and accepting, not driving or condemning. We may not like what the child does. We may tell him that some things are not socially acceptable. But we must keep it clear in the child's mind that we like him in spite of what he has done. In no situation is this more important than in the meeting of sexual problems which arise on the playground or in the school building. However serious the problem, punishment is no sufficient answer. We must first look for the cause and seek to help the child toward healthy attitudes.

WHETHER the school should meet the responsibility for sex education by a formal plan of study through the years is a question which cannot be answered here. It depends to a great extent upon the attitude and readiness of the community, upon the teachers who are available, and upon the religious background of the school. There is no question but that the responsibility must be met in some adequate manner, for the readiness of our boys and girls to establish satisfactory marriage and family relationships is a matter of such vast significance that those of us who are responsible for the education of our boys and girls cannot ignore it. It would be desirable for parents to educate their children in this field, but some parents cannot do so. Thus the teacher often finds herself in a position where necessity demands that she give some guidance not only to a child, but in many cases to the parents as well. Such guidance must be given wisely and with an understanding of the feelings and inhibitions of those involved.

It is unwise to rush into this field with an enthusiasm which roughly pushes aside the taboos of the years or the sincere beliefs of the parents of the community. If the school considers a formal course of sex education to be the most effective answer to the real needs of the boys and girls of the school or of the community, it is best, first of all, to study the attitudes of the parents and find out how far they are able to accept the education of their children in this field. It is usually wise to meet first with the parents, respecting their prior interest in this area, and talk over together the needs of the young people and the plan which the school has for meeting these needs, the factual material which will be covered, and the way in which it will be presented. Once the cooperation and support of the parents have been obtained, the school can proceed upon a sound footing, with parents and teachers working together to the benefit of the children.

Such a plan of procedure enriches the course for the boys and girls whether it is given during one year or becomes a part of the total curriculum, for the parents are often able to add much by the type of support and approval which they give in the home. In addition, the materials presented in the group meetings frequently give added insight to many parents, lessen their own anxieties, clarify their attitudes, and even give them factual information which they may not have had before.

Whatever methods of approach we use, if during the years of growing up the home and school can work together to develop in boys and girls a respect for the human body, an appreciation of the rights of others, and a feeling of mutual respect for each other, we shall have given them a firm basis for their adolescent years.

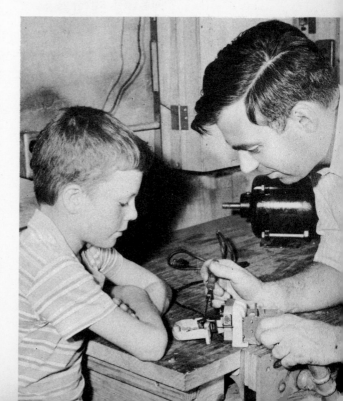

Living with your children

THESE are your children. When the door of the schoolroom opens each morning they will enter, some of them eagerly, some of them unwillingly, some of them noisily, some of them timidly. But to each one of them the experiences which they have in school will be important. A child's school experience can have either a helpful or a hindering influence upon his mental health and his adjustment to life. Parents who realize this will build desirable attitudes toward the school and will work with the teacher in every way possible to improve living and learning conditions. The teacher who realizes how profound and lasting are the effects of a child's school experiences recognizes that her chief responsibility is to understand the needs and characteristics of her children, so that she may live with them each day in a way

140

that develops confidence, trust, and co-operation. In order to help her children she will try to understand the "age pictures" for each maturity level, as well as the unique and individual pattern of development of each of her youngsters. To this latter end she will at the outset attempt to establish a close working relationship with parents, which will help her understanding and will contribute to the child's feeling of security.

A child's relationship to his teacher is of the utmost concern to him. The teacher who really wants to help her children, who thinks in terms of their happiness and their development, will make it possible for the children in her care to find security and joy in the pupil-teacher relationship during each school day. Her boys and girls will feel that she is their friend, that she likes them and is interested in the things they do. This means unbending in order to talk or play with them, laughing with them when occasion warrants, and showing sympathy when a loved pet has been lost or a knee badly skinned. Children appreciate, too, the smile or individual greeting when they come into the classroom, and they like the teacher who notices the new hair ribbon or the treasure that means so much to a child. It means the "listening ear," so that the child knows he can "tell teacher" without being reprimanded or scolded, and it means an atmosphere of friendly acceptance in which the child feels comfortable and can grow. The way in which the teacher answers questions is every bit as important as the answers she gives because of the contribution it can make toward building a child's confidence and self-respect.

THE WISE TEACHER knows when to overlook. She knows that good friends do not perpetually harp or nag or correct flaws in grammar. She knows it is human to forget sometimes, to make mistakes, to get angry, to lose one's temper, to spill or break something. Ridicule, belittling, shaming, and sarcasm, all of which tend to destroy self-respect and self-confidence, have no place in a friendly schoolroom. Once destroyed, these qualities do not easily grow back, and there is no substitute for them. A personality without them can never be healthy or live happily with other human beings.

This is why it is so dangerous to tease a child. Too often, teasing will drive him back into himself or bring about other undesirable emotional reactions. Friendly teasing in a relaxed, give-and-take spirit can be fun for everyone; it can help teach a child not to take himself too seriously and help to immunize him against the inevitable belittling and criticism that he will sooner or later encounter. But it is extremely important that adults and older children at all times avoid any teasing with intent to hurt or to shame a child. Such teasing, aimed at making the child behave more acceptably, will rarely have this effect. What it does instead is alienate the child and make him resentful and unsure of himself. Thus it lessens the very self-confidence which is so necessary to happy adjustment; even if behavior is temporarily improved, the real problem is increased instead of lessened.

Rather, a good friend builds confidence and self-respect by words of praise and appreciation, knowing that giving praise and recognition for a job well done is one of the best ways of helping children to learn. She knows that the "smarties" and those who are doing poor work are often the very ones who are starving for legitimate attention and praise. They need someone who watches for opportunities to say, "You can do it, I know," "That's fine," "How smart you were to think of that," "What a thoughtful thing to do," "That was kind of you," "Your work is very neat," "This is the best you've ever done," "You really tried on that one, didn't you?" or "What a brave person you were to do that." She must realize, however, that children are quick to detect and resent indiscriminate praise, given without sincerity and without merit. The watchful teacher will find something worthy of praise in each child, but will never distribute praise carelessly.

It is important to make an especial effort to be friendly to those children who most need it—the noisy ones, the slow ones, the belligerent ones—the very boys and girls who may seem most irritating and unlovable.[1] The understanding teacher tries to discover why these children act as they do. She makes an opportunity to get to know them, to talk with them whenever she can before school, after school, during recess. She tries to find out all she can about their homes and their backgrounds.

At the same time, of course, she does not become so absorbed in the problems of the less well-adjusted children as to overlook the fact that the better-adjusted youngsters also still need recognition for work well done and responsibility well carried.

[1]The case of Patty Morris (page 55) is illustrative of the necessity as well as the value of giving special time and study to the aggressive, obstreperous child.

Consistency in dealing with children at home and at school also helps to give them a feeling of security. They need to know what to expect—what they can count on. What they are permitted to do today must usually be comparable to what they were permitted to do yesterday, unless there is a valid reason for a change. "Yes" should mean "Yes" and "No" should mean "No." Unlimited freedom today and severe restrictions tomorrow are most confusing to children.

A classroom which is a "lived-in" room gives children security and a comfortable feeling of belonging—"This is our room." It shows that the teacher cares and is interested. Plants in the window, gay, colorful pictures, an interesting bulletin board, bright book jackets, blackboard borders of leaves or birds, or a frieze made by the children make a room more attractive. An aquarium or fish bowl, or a tub with turtles in it, will be an interesting spot. A few chairs or bookcases made perhaps from orange crates will add color if painted red or blue or green. Drapes made and block-printed or appliqued by the children always make a room livable and gay. Admittedly, it isn't always possible to establish in the classroom an ideal physical environment. Each teacher must work within the framework of her given situation. But there are many things, simple things, that any teacher can do with even the drabbest room.

PARENTS who understand the needs of children will demand schools that provide for the best possible physical health of children. They will appreciate the teacher who gives thought and care to making sure that her classroom is a place where children are physically comfortable. It may not be easy, but it is usually possible to keep the classroom at a proper temperature (68° to 70°). A pan of water near a radiator will keep the air moist. Fresh air is sometimes hard to manage, but it is essential. If drafts are inevitable when a window is raised, children may engage in some form of brisk physical exercise while the windows are raised high for a few minutes. Let the fresh air in and let that "schoolroom smell" out.

The schoolroom lighting is important. If the classroom is equipped with movable desks or tables and chairs, they should be so arranged that no one has to face the light; the daylight should come over the left shoulder of right-handed children and over the right shoulder of left-handed children. In classrooms equipped with movable desks there is no problem since these can be placed to take care of each child's need. Where desks are fixed it may be possible to bring a few movable ones which can be placed to provide proper lighting for the left-handed children. The shades should be so adjusted as to avoid any child's having to work in the glare of brilliant sunlight. If the lighting in the classroom seems inadequate on dark days when the lights must be turned on, perhaps the principal or superintendent will cooperate in obtaining a light meter. This little machine measures the intensity of light in a room. Its use frequently reveals the need for stronger bulbs for parts or all of the room.

When children are sitting, it should be possible for their feet to rest on the floor comfortably and for the lower part of their backs to rest against the backs of the seats. Everything possible should be done to see that children have chairs or desks that are properly adjusted to the user. When a classroom is equipped with "screwed-down seats" that are all the same size, blocks of wood or simple footstools as high as children need for comfort can always be secured. If the desk is uncomfortably high for the child when he is writing, an oilcloth cushion may be used to overcome the discomfort and possible spine curvature brought on by bad posture. If Mary is sitting in a seat that is too deep for her, a cushion to support her back might make a big difference in both her health and her behavior.

IT IS IMPORTANT, too, to pay attention to the "little things" in the daily routine of schoolroom living. There should be plenty

of time for getting drinks, going to the toilet, and washing the hands. If a child needs to go to the toilet or get a drink at other than the routine times, he should be permitted to do so without asking permission, as long as he goes quietly and inconspicuously. Children need to feel that they are trusted, and they should be encouraged to take care of their own needs without embarrassment or fear of scolding.

Children cannot sit still for very long at a time without becoming tired and restless. They need periods of activity and periods of rest, as well as periods of concentrated work. The kindergarten children are fortunate, for they are usually provided with cots or mats upon which to stretch out and rest. This would be of value for older children as well. Unfortunately it does not seem workable in the usual schoolroom, but there is much the teacher can do to relax and rest her children, from the opening of the windows and a bit of active exercise to the "forty winks" with head on arms for the child who needs it—even if it means time out for a minute or two from the work he is doing. What teacher has not sometimes felt that if it were possible to lie down for one minute or even just get up and stretch,

she would feel like a different person? And how often children must feel the same way! As long as it is not yet possible in all classrooms to allow much freedom to move, it is important to plan plenty of opportunities for rest and for a "stretch."

THE TEACHER who is concerned with the needs of children and with their comfort, health, and happiness, will be constantly alert to indications of sensory impairment. The child who is having difficulty in attacking new work may have poor auditory perception because of a hearing defect. Mary may have poor eyesight; she may be squinting, rubbing her eyes, or squirming about because she needs glasses.[2]

Again, perhaps there is no sensory impairment: George's poor color, Peggy's lassitude, or Jim's restlessness may mean the onset of contagion, an infected tooth, or loss of sleep.

Or there may be emotional conflict which is affecting physical condition and general adjustment. The understanding teacher will be alert not only to children's physical health needs but to their emotional and social needs as well.[3]

Children need safety valves to reduce the pressure of pent-up feelings. Many boys and girls devise their own safety valves which we see in use when they engage in "horseplay," shout, and spontaneously act out violent dramatic episodes.

But some children have had a little more than they can take in their home situations. They may be overprotected, pressed hard, held to too high standards, or upset by

---

[2]It is hard to believe that such an obvious cause of difficulty could be overlooked, yet this often happens, as was the case with Margaret (see page 93).

[3]It has been repeatedly demonstrated, as in the cases of Huntley (page 77) and Mark (page 106), that adequate physical care does not insure emotional security or well-being.

family bickerings.[4] These are the children who make life difficult at school by their disturbed behavior. And these are the children who most desperately need safe ways of letting off steam.

Some of the safety valves through which children can release their tense feelings are these:

Periods for hitting and pounding—It is amazing how angry feelings can be dispelled through the simple acts of slapping and pounding clay, banging and pounding wood and nails, and punching the punching bag in the gym or on the playground.

Dramatic experiences — experiences in which boys and girls can have the opportunity to be big and powerful, to be the mother, father, king, queen, or general and do some bossing for a change.

Opportunities for getting dirty—Perhaps nothing causes so much fussing and nagging at home as the continual admonition of parents to "keep clean." From infancy on, some children have been subjected to too much pressure about keeping themselves clean, their clothes clean, their rooms clean. They have been pushed and prodded, punished and shamed. Such children are in especial need of being allowed to get "good and dirty." Activities such as finger painting and clay modeling give boys and girls the much needed chance to get dirty in acceptable ways.

Periods for free drawing or painting—periods during which children can draw or paint just what they want in their own way. It is surprising how many feelings are revealed through drawing or painting—and show themselves in ways that are safe and acceptable.

Opportunities to write about their feelings—opportunities in which children "write what they feel" with full permission later to choose between sharing their efforts or tearing them into shreds.

All boys and girls must learn that some kinds of actions are not permissible, even though all kinds of feelings are.[5] It is wise to keep in mind that while it is necessary to stop certain kinds of undesirable actions

[4]*Several of the case studies presented throughout this volume show children whose problems were directly traceable to home situations that were overwhelming for them. Carla (page 34), Robert Blake (page 58), Huntley (page 77), Johnny (page 73), Mark (page 106), and Paul (page 125) were all helped when the problems at home were understood and ameliorated. Larry, too (page 31), was handicapped by his home situation, though in a different way: he was kept a helpless, immature child by an overprotective mother who, with the best intentions, was nevertheless satisfying her own emotional needs rather than his.*

[5]*The case of Carla (page 34) illustrates the importance of helping a child make this distinction between antagonistic feelings, for which one should feel no guilt, and actions, which one can and should control.*

such as slapping or kicking, or other behavior which is disturbing to the whole class, it is not wise to try to curtail the feelings behind them. Such feelings cannot be banished. Suppression merely makes the child hide them inside and show them in other ways. If the teacher understands this and is willing to let her children be honest about their feelings in day-by-day situations, many of them will feel enough confidence in her to talk out some of the larger troubles that lie behind their behavior.

A SENSE of successful achievement in group activity is essential to a feeling of security and to good mental health. The teacher who recognizes this avoids comparisons among boys and girls in the classroom in so far as possible. She puts less emphasis on competitive activities and more stress on cooperative ones. Also she avoids setting a premium on brainwork alone. Instead of making academic progress the sole criterion of success, she tries to create a situation wherein ability in any field of endeavor, whether it be painting, singing, rock collecting, hammering, gardening, or cleaning the closet, can be appreciated and respected. It takes all kinds of people to make the world go round; the school should be a

prime force in recognizing the need for planning well-rounded programs through which every child can experience some degree of success. Failure cannot always be avoided for any child; but it is important to balance failure with success. The child who has difficulty with his reading may perhaps be able to sing well, or take good care of the goldfish bowl. The important thing to remember is that the balance must be on the side of successful experiences if the child is to have good mental health.[6] Teachers have a responsibility in helping parents understand this important principle of child development.

A sense of personal achievement can be built through providing "interest spots" to which children can go, when required work is completed, and work at something of absorbing interest to them personally. If space is limited, there can be frequent changes in what is placed in each spot. If space permits, it is desirable to have as many different interests as possible represented. The fol-

[6]*For the many children of definitely limited intelligence it is especially important for the teacher to find avenues of expression and participation through which the child's emotional needs can be met—ways in which he can experience the satisfactions of success and recognition. The case of Edith (page 109) illustrates some of the ways a teacher can do this.*

146

lowing are a few suggestions drawn from limitless possibilities. Some of them are better suited to younger children's interests; some are for older children; some can be adapted to any age.

A corner equipped with two or three chairs and materials for playing school. According to the age of the group, these materials might include a miniature card container, with word cards for the words children know, sentence and phrase cards, arithmetic cards and materials of all sorts; books, maps, and a small globe; pictures which can be used for identification, classification, and discussion—pictures of animals, birds, trees, flowers, plants, machines, means of transportation, foods, kinds of clothing, houses and buildings of all kinds, pictures of children or adults engaging in various activities.

A table or a single desk for puzzles (jigsaw and crossword) adapted to the age group.

A game table equipped with games such as dominoes, checkers, lotto, Go Fish.

A paper-doll table or desk where children can cut out dolls, create dresses, or cut dolls and clothing from catalogues.

A spot for favorite toys. Older children might have a toy-repair corner. Girls might have materials for making doll clothes; boys might have materials for making small airplanes or boat models.

A place for science collections or hobbies.

An interest center equipped with scissors, paste, crayons, cardboard, oaktag, or manila

paper on which pictures can be arranged. The pictures may be cut from old catalogues or magazines of all kinds. Crepe paper and patterns for hats, costumes, nut cups, etc., could be put here some of the time.

A craft table where children can carve soap or wood, weave, embroider, sew quilt pieces together, or work with clay.

A spot for special holiday interests: Halloween, Valentine's Day, Thanksgiving, Christmas.

A reading table, of course.

One or more easels equipped with large sheets of paper or a roll of white wrapping paper, paints, crayon, and chalk; if easels are not available, a blackboard section may be designated for this purpose.

It is not only the "difficult" children a teacher should try to understand. She needs also to look twice at the "good" children, those who "never cause a moment's trouble." She needs to stop and study those children in her classroom who always cooperate, who drive themselves overly hard to reach for perfection, who try too hard to please, who are "model chil-

dren."[7] Are these youngsters bottling up their real feelings inside of them? Are their emotional needs being met? Do the other children like them? Have they any close friends? Are they timid or withdrawn? Often these children need far more help than the more outgoing youngster who has been labeled a "behavior problem."

The wise teacher will look for the causes of the behavior rather than merely treating the symptom—the behavior itself. Thus when difficult situations arise, when a youngster is upsetting the class, is not doing good work, or is not entering into class activities, the teacher will not solve the problem by punishing or scolding, urging or blaming. Often she may be unaware, until she looks twice, that some of the children in the classroom are desperately lonely and are not wanted by the others, either as social companions or as co-workers on class projects. These lonely boys and girls, unless given special help, may either withdraw into themselves and become shy and timid, or else try to meet the situation by being bossy and aggressive. Some may become rebellious and resentful and, as they grow older, reveal in nonsocial ways their frustration at their own social rejection and lack of friends.

Once the teacher discovers which children in the class are socially unacceptable to the others, she can plan ways of helping the youngsters in this overlooked group. Sometimes children are not liked because of personal qualities, sometimes because they are "different" from the other children: the

[7] *Again and again we see that it is the "model child" who becomes neurotic in later life. Overt manifestations of maladjustment are more annoying to teachers and parents because they are so disruptive of group discipline, but they are far healthier for the child than repression. Johnny (page 73) had presented no problem prior to his troubles in second grade, yet he had severe emotional problems and his behavior, though exemplary, was not that of a normal, happy child.*

child from a foreign home, the slow child, the handicapped child, the unusually brilliant or talented child—all these may have difficulty in being accepted by the group.[8] It is not always possible to help these children to be fully accepted by the others, but it is often possible for the teacher to lessen their aloneness.

Children unaccepted by the others must be studied individually, to discover not only their problems but also their special interests and abilities. Often their skills or abilities can be adroitly brought to the attention of the class—and thus prestige and sometimes new friendships are built for the child. Similarly, parents can be encouraged to help the child develop some skill that is admired by the group and will make the child more highly valued.

Definite responsibilities can be given to the shy, withdrawn children to help draw them into the group. Praise can be given to them as they do their quiet jobs well. Little by little, through praise and encouragement, they can be helped to greater participation and acceptance.

Sometimes a timid child can be seated near a popular and friendly one who can help him feel more a part of the group. If the less accepted children are teamed with the more popular and successful ones in group activities, they may all be drawn closer together.

THE WISE TEACHER remembers always that the child in the schoolroom is part of the group. Although she must develop an attitude of looking for the needs of each individual child, she must also think in terms of the total group situation. Sometimes one cannot meet in full the needs of a particular child without disturbing the group feeling of the class. Johnnie may need outlets for his aggressive drives—space and freedom to move, to use his energy, to be noisy and boisterous, perhaps even destructive. His teacher can be "child-minded" to the extent of giving him extra opportunities for moving around, for changing his activity often, or for letting off steam by pounding clay or hammering nails, but she cannot let his tendency toward destructiveness upset or frighten the group. Or take Betty, an overly sensitive, timid child who needs much encouragement and individual attention to give her enough security to function at all. A teacher can try as often as possible to encourage Betty, and by her own warmth and interest try to build a greater self-confidence, but she cannot give such a preponderance of her time to one difficult youngster that she leaves too narrow a margin of attention for the better-adjusted children in the group. To keep the fine balance between individual needs and group needs is no easy task.

Sometimes, through our deep interest and our eagerness to help the poorly adjusted child, we do allow the pendulum to swing so far that we neglect the needs of the other youngsters. But the morale of the whole group is of crucial importance, for if Johnnie and Betty are to adjust to the group we must keep a group for them to adjust to. If the total group situation is neglected, we lose the very basis of that security and feeling of stability within which alone it is possible to adjust the individual.

[8]*Too often we think of a gifted child only as having a tremendous advantage over others in his group, forgetting that anything which makes one different from the others, whether for better or worse, poses an adjustment problem. The story of Isabel (page 90) shows a child who, though of very superior intelligence, got off on the wrong foot in her social adjustment and developed a vicious circle of maladjustment and unwise compensation. On the other hand, in Marlene (page 88) we see a child who, despite a difficult problem, is making an excellent adjustment, with wise guidance both at home and at school.*

149

IT IS NECESSARY to recognize, too, that in some cases the problems of these children cannot be solved without an understanding and insight into the deeper underlying factors which are causing them. The teacher may be able to help by manipulating the situation in the classroom, but she cannot always cure the underlying difficulties. One of the skills which a teacher acquires as she lives and works with children, and continuously gathers and organizes her information about them is her ability to distinguish between those children whom she can help within the classroom situation and those who require the services of specialists. Like Miss L, who saw Paul's need (page 125), she will turn if possible to the school psychologist, whose

major function is the continued improvement of mental health.[9] Or when she observes evidence of physical impairment or suspects infection or malnutrition, she will consult the school nurse. She will understand and use the services of the dentist, oculist, orthopedist, and pediatrician.

If the school does not have the services of a school psychologist, the community may have a child-guidance clinic, or there may be a fully staffed reading clinic nearby, or the state may provide a traveling child-guidance service which may be available not too far away at certain times during the year. The teacher should acquaint herself with the resources of the community and state, so that she may be instrumental in bringing help to those children whose emotional maladjustment is too severe to be helped by schoolroom procedures. The more serious psychological problems of children are just as much in need of clinical and technical treatment as are serious infections or fractures.

The teacher who is interested in helping her youngsters toward physical, emotional, and mental well-being will also cooperate with the physical education personnel. Often the behavior and attitude of a child during the physical education class or on the playground will be quite different from his appearance in the classroom and will suggest

[9]*Several other kinds of problems also need the services of specialists. Elizabeth Holmes (page 122) posed problems for her home, her school, and herself simply because of a normal but early physical development of which those around her were unaware. Margaret's severe visual handicap (page 93) went unnoticed for eight years, until she finally was taken to a reading clinic. To understand and cope with Huntley's and Isabel's problems (pages 77 and 90), there was recourse to all the specialists of a child-guidance clinic. Carla (page 34) also needed the help of a professional psychologist. And in some cases, as we saw with Larry (page 31) and Paul (page 125), it is the parents who need professional help.*

aspects of his character and of the problems he is fighting which have been unsuspected by his teacher. Perhaps Jimmy's tendency to withdraw from all group activities will be found to be grounded in poor muscular co-ordination. A child who is facing severe problems at home may follow all classroom routines and procedures as directed but on the playground be a bully and a disrupter. Frequently the physical education personnel can suggest ways of working out physical and psychological problems that might not be used in other phases of the curriculum. The most important development in physical education during the last twenty years has been the growing realization that physical activities affect the entire personalities of pupils and not alone their muscles, circulation, respiration, and other bodily functions. Because of this, the program of physical education in the elementary school today is placing special emphasis on recreational interests and skills and on the social training children receive as they learn to play with each other—to choose and respect leaders, to obey the rules, and to give and take in friendly competition. And a child who cannot do good academic work may be helped to compensate in physical activity and find in it the sense of successful achievement which every child needs.

HAPPY CHILDREN require the cooperation of home and school because everything that happens throughout the day—whether at home, at school, in the neighborhood or the larger community—affects total behavior. If what children see and hear and experience and learn outside the school is in conflict with what is being done in school, progress will be hampered. Every teacher needs to be familiar with the disciplines, traditions, customs, taboos, and attitudes of the community in general and especially of the homes of the children in her class.[10]

The home, even more than the school and the classroom, is the workshop in which the child's personality is being shaped. The personalities of a child's parents will make up, to a large extent, the emotional atmosphere in which he lives.[11] Hence it is absolutely essential for a teacher to have the fullest possible information regarding the personalities of the members of the household in which the child lives.

It is frequently impossible for the teacher to change materially an undesirable home environment. Yet, by her knowledge of the home conditions that surround the personalities of her children, she can do much to give them the help and support they need. Perhaps children are subjected to the influence of many relatives in a home and to all the conflicts of "in-laws." Perhaps the household is divided, or divorce has created a problem. One or the other of the parents may be physically handicapped—deaf, blind, or trying to direct the household from a wheel chair or an invalid's bed. The disturbances brought about by war casualties of all kinds—inadequate housing, long illness, economic pressures—are significant

[10]*In the case of Patty Morris (page 55) the child was especially well adjusted at home, and highly regarded by all there. Her problems arose only when she was confronted with the school situation, in which she met for the first time a completely new set of social and ethical standards. Had Miss M remained unaware of this fact, she could never have helped Patty.*
[11]*Huntley (page 77), Johnny (page 73), and Mark (page 106) suffered emotional insecurity as a result of the parents' difficulties. In Mark's and Johnny's cases a fairly stable, secure home base was eventually established; in Huntley's the original insecurity was aggravated by the subsequent abnormal family group, where the harsh and eccentric grandmother, the aloof aunt, and the rejecting father made a happy adjustment impossible for the boy.*

151

factors.[12] Knowledge of a child's home life cannot help but make a difference in a teacher's attitude, the limits of her patience, and the techniques she will find useful in handling problems that arise.

Many health and personality problems may never develop if through the year parents can meet with the teacher to discuss the needs and characteristics of the boys and girls in her classroom. Through such meetings parents can gain a knowledge of the guidance program which has been planned or is being developed, and the teacher will gain insight into child-parent relationships and home conditions that will enable her. to guide her children more wisely. This is one of the best means a teacher has for studying her children to get complete and accurate pictures of them and of their difficulties and points of view. The various case studies presented throughout this volume have been selected to show many types of problems in which the teacher's study of a child will lead her outside her classroom to talks with the parents.

PARENTS, like children, teachers, and everyone else, appreciate recognition. Their children are usually precious to them, and anything good a teacher may have to say about a child gives pleasure to them. Conversely, a negative remark is just as surely interpreted by the parents as a reflection on them and will arouse the same defensive feelings that a teacher experiences when the principal or another teacher takes one of her pupils to task. Some parents will take out their defensive feelings on the child while others will defend the child at the teacher's expense.

There are many ways in which a teacher can help parents feel comfortable and at ease. One teacher who has established an excellent working relationship with parents started out by listing every good thing she could think of about each child in her classroom. Starting with a few parents scattered throughout the district, she sent penny post cards. On one she wrote:

Dear Mr. and Mrs.———————,
Dorothy did something today which made me realize you must be wise parents. When someone made an unkind remark about Charlie's inability to draw, she spoke up and said, "Don't forget Charlie's the best one in the room in science." Dorothy is always thoughtful of others and quick to come to the rescue when anyone is in trouble. Won't you come and visit us someday? I am so eager to meet you.

Sincerely,

On another card she wrote:

Dear Mr. and Mrs.———————,
Were you as proud of Joseph as I was when you saw the "Pet" booklet he had made? He is such a hard worker. I wish you would come and visit us someday soon. You'll enjoy watching Joseph at work.

Sincerely,

As the news got about that the teacher had written so-and-so and said such nice things about Dorothy or Joseph or Bill, other parents began to wonder if they would get a card and an invitation to come to school. Needless to say, when any problem arose parents were eager and willing to work with the teacher because they felt secure in the knowledge that she was personally interested in each child and was herself ready to work with the parents.

---

[12]*Wartime family separations were the start of the problems of both Larry (page 31) and Robert (page 58), though in both cases other factors were involved, too. Mrs. Drake's own emotional immaturity might have made her an overindulgent and overprotective mother under any circumstances. In Robert Blake's case the early years of being constantly on the move and always in the way were followed by a thoroughly discouraging home in which the boy was made to feel that he never could possibly do anything right.*

In connection with individual parent-teacher conferences, teachers often think only of children with problems. One teacher invited for a conference the parents of a popular child who was making excellent adjustments. Their faces beamed when she said, "I have observed Raymond for more than a month. He makes friends easily, the children like him, I like him. He is kind and thoughtful, and courteous in spite of his quick temper. He is one of the happiest, most cheerful children in the room. Could you tell me some of the procedures you have used with him? I'd like your recipe." If Raymond ever does get into trouble with that quick temper of his, his teacher will have no difficulty in getting parent cooperation. Or if, as sometimes happens, Raymond begins to change disturbingly as he enters a new phase of growth, there will probably be less reluctance on the parents' part to talk it over and enlist the teacher's help.

Such expressions of genuine interest in a child place the home and the school in a friendly, working relationship where the prestige of neither is at stake when unpleasant things must be said. Parents, too, have a responsibility in this two-way relationship. If the best cooperation is to be achieved, parents should invite and welcome the teacher into the home.

The keynote of a cooperative relationship is not the professional training of the teacher, nor her understanding of learning processes or even of child psychology, but her willingness to seek and understand the reasons behind certain behavior. What does the parent think the problem is? Has he any idea as to how the problem arose? What action has the home taken? How does the parent think the child has interpreted this action? What does the parent think the school should do? What can school and home do together? Thoughtful discussion

between teacher and parents may seem to make little headway, but the conclusions reached are likely to succeed where a plan of attack dictated by the teacher alone usually fails.[13]

THE IMPORTANCE and benefit of a complete and detailed progress report to parents can hardly be overstressed. A report such as Jimmy's (page 52) gives a perspective on both progress and problem areas from which parents and teachers can then plan intelligently. Thus each child can be helped to grow in his own best way.

It is well worth the time it takes to keep short anecdotal records of the individual children. Some teachers keep a daily diary while others prefer to jot observations on slips of paper to file in folders for each child. Records should be both brief and objective. What has happened is more important than the observer's reaction to it.

As a teacher's collection of anecdotes increases, she will find it fascinating to trace the growth of various children in such diverse matters as, for example, social adjustment or learning to follow directions. These records may help her decide when a conference with parents might be helpful. In some schools anecdotal records entirely replace formal grade cards; in others, anecdotes are used as a basis for making progress reports to parents. Needless to say, one advantage of the anecdotal form is the opportunity it offers to suggest a child's strong points as well as his weak points,

---

[13]*In most of the case studies presented throughout this book, the teacher was able to enlist the cooperation and help of the parents. Tackling the problem together, they were able to make real progress. Where the parents were not so cooperative much less could be done. Huntley (page 77) finally had to be put in a foster home. Larry's mother (page 31), hostile at first, was won over by the teacher, as were Johnny's mother (page 73) and Paul's father (page 125).*

and to accentuate progress in relation to his own record rather than through comparison with his classmates.

SOME teachers have an earnest desire to create a "climate" in their schoolroom that will promote mental health, but find themselves unable to do so, or realize that they are falling too far short of the goal. Teachers are people, too. Each one brings to the classroom not only her knowledge and training, but her personality as well. Just as the personality of the parents helps to create the home environment in which a child must live, so the personality of the teacher determines in great part the environment of the schoolroom.

Sometimes a teacher finds herself unable to be relaxed and patient, warm and kindly with her children even though she desires to do so. She may be under strain and tension herself. She may have home problems and worries which crowd into her mind during the school day in spite of her attempts to forget them and think only of the children. Or she may feel insecure because of inexperience or lack of adequate training. She may be afraid that her class will get out of hand, that she will not be a good disciplinarian, and that the supervisor will walk in at a crucial and difficult moment.

It is natural for some teachers to be worried, strained, and anxious as a result of past experiences or a present difficult situation. It is important, however, that every teacher be aware of how deeply her own personality and her own anxieties can affect the children under her care. If her problem or her anxiety is not something which she knows will pass, but results in a pattern of behavior which prevents her from achieving a happy, calm atmosphere in her classroom, if her irritabilities run away with her, then she should seek help and try to reach an

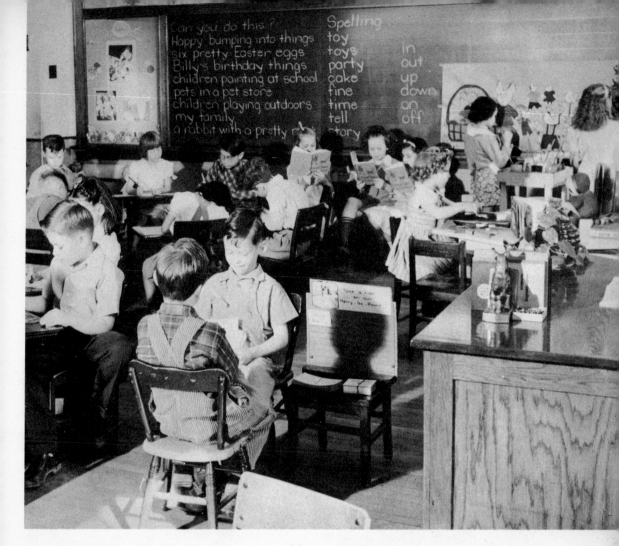

adjustment which will make life more comfortable both for herself and for the youngsters in her class.

I**T IS NOT** easy for the busy, overworked teacher of thirty or forty children to think of each child as an individual and study his needs. There may be times when the pressure is so great that it becomes impossible for her to do so. But it is her basic attitude toward the children which is of prime importance. Even though she may be under the strain of an overlarge class, the youngsters quickly sense whether she is a friendly person who likes them and wants to know and help them, or whether she is thinking more in terms of subject matter, techniques, reports, and routines. Even in a crowded class the teacher can give the youngsters the feeling that she likes them and likes being there with them. If she can keep the "climate" of her room relaxed and happy as she moves among her children in a friendly, understanding way, they in turn will respond to her. Such a teacher can do much for the mental health and the total adjustment of her children. Even if she makes mistakes, even though it may not be possible to do as much as she would like to do for each child, they will feel her kindliness toward them and will be able to grow as they should.

CHAPTER TEN

A plan for action

THE PRIMARY purpose of the foregoing chapters has been to help teachers and parents toward a better understanding in developing rich and happy relationships with children.

Over and above these relationships, however, there remains for the school and for the home another important task—that of unfolding directly to boys and girls themselves a series of carefully planned learning experiences, through which they can become acquainted with workable techniques for solving personal problems and for improving human relationships. They should become acquainted with sensible methods of caring for the body, based on satisfying information about the body and how it works; they should be helped to understand the important facts about their own physical growth and taught how to deal with worries and tensions common at each stage of development; and finally they should be motivated to assume personal responsibility for their own safety and for the safety of others.

Learning experiences such as these are an essential part of growing up. We all want to teach our children how to live. We cannot teach them directly, but we can help them discover how for themselves.

Some of the learning experiences suggested above—those pertaining to safety and physical health—have long been a recognized part of the school curriculum and home training. But there has been neither understanding nor agreement as to just how the broader field of general personal development should be treated or where it might be fitted into an already crowded curriculum. Recently, however, we are meeting with increasing frequency such statements as the following, from the newly adopted constitution of the World Health Organization: "Health is a state of complete physical, mental, and social well-being, and not merely the absence of disease or infirmity."

Widespread acceptance of this new, broader concept of health both by education and by the National Congress of Parents and Teachers opens the way for a truly significant program in which both home and school have an important part. To the typical teaching of safety, physical health, and hygiene can be added materials and experiences that will aid in promoting good mental health, and help boys and girls to understand why people feel and think and act as they do. There can be added learning experiences concerning how human beings are alike, how they differ, how no one is alone or unique in his problems or emotional reactions. Included, too, should be experiences through which children learn that reasonable standards of behavior, rather than perfection, constitute legitimate goals, that unpleasant situations must be met squarely rather than evaded, and that there are learnable techniques for solving our

own personal problems as well as for getting along well with other people.

Specifically, what concepts shall we teach? This, naturally, is an important question for both parent and teacher, which until recently has been only partially answered.

On pages 166-178 are detailed suggestions as to the basic type of understanding which can be developed at each age level from five to eleven. In this program the needs and abilities of children at each stage of development have been determining factors in the selection and placement of the learning experiences to be presented. And all concepts have been grouped under the main headings of physical health, mental health, social health, and safety and first aid. It is a program that makes a detailed and frontal attack on the problem of helping children discover how to live—to live healthfully, safely, and in harmony with themselves and others.

How can we most effectively teach these concepts? Obviously the dynamic and often crucial concepts of this new program for physical and emotional health and safety should be presented to children in the most interesting and appealing manner possible. Both at home and in the classroom, the materials most sure to arouse children's interest will be those which present close parallels and tie-ins with children's own experiences and problems.

Parents and teachers who are deeply concerned with helping children achieve physical, mental, and social well-being will seek out every aid that text materials can give. In selecting materials they will keep in mind such criteria as the following.

What kind of motivation is employed? Is it in harmony with what we know about children of the age for which the book is intended? Does it portray the kinds of be-

157

havior normal for children at this stage? Does it set reasonable, attainable standards for this age level? Does it describe typical growth patterns; e.g., the period of plateau in height and weight gains common among young preadolescents, followed by the height and weight spurts that appear sometime during preadolescence or early adolescence? Are the child characters real? Do they behave in childlike ways? Do they have problems, face difficulties, and sometimes get into trouble as normal children do? Do they exhibit emotional reactions common to all human beings—feelings of anger, excitement, worry, jealousy, and all the rest? Are they shown learning how to deal with everyday problems of living—problems of coping with emotions, facing disappointment, meeting failure?

Can children read and understand the content? Are the ideas and concepts right for the maturity level of the children? Is the text material easier than the basic reading texts for this level? Can the children enjoy and think about what they are reading without being burdened by overdifficult text material? Materials that are too difficult will not contribute to the sense of success and achievement so essential to healthy personality development.

Is the content inclusive? Does it include material on physical health, mental health and personality development, social health, safety and first aid? Does it help children understand their feelings, their emotions, and the effect of emotions on body functioning? Is there material which helps children acquire skills and techniques for healthy personality adjustments, for making and keeping friends, for establishing satisfying human relationships?

Is the information contained accurate and up to date? The acceptance of a broader definition of health demands *new* material.

Are the problems related to the everyday living of children for whom the book is intended? Are they current problems at this particular stage of development?

Once materials and concepts have been decided upon, there still remains the problem of developing the most effective

158

method for establishing desirable habits of action and thought based on these concepts. Lecturing or the mere recounting of essential information are not the methods best calculated to make boys and girls eager and active learners in this vital field of understanding. As Arthur Steinhaus so ably put it in his booklet *More Firepower in Health Education,* "Feeling is equal to knowledge in the learning process." Without feeling, the concepts remain entirely academic, without the power to influence thought or action. Thus the challenge for teachers and parents is to become skillful in evoking feeling to the end that more knowledge will be translated into ways of living.

At home it will be to a considerable extent a matter of utilizing experiences as they come up, resorting to text materials mostly to supplement or amplify the family discussions that result from real-life situations and problems. In the classroom there will of necessity be a greater reliance on instructional materials as a starting point and springboard to the learning experience. Because it is so essential to approach such a group study of problems in personal develop-

ment in a personalized manner that immediately arouses interest and recalls to the children their own similar problems and feelings, a method combining case studies with group discussion will be found highly effective.

With this method, each story or "case-study" incident in the text is first read and enjoyed for its own sake. The story may concern Jack, who has trouble remembering to wash before eating; Jane, who fails a test; Sue, who is jealous when her brother gets a new pair of shoes; Kenneth, who fears his impending visit to the dentist; Sally, who rebels at trying out a new kind of food; or Elizabeth, who is hesitant about attending a party.

After silent reading of the story as a whole or in page-by-page fashion, boys and girls talk about the problems and behavior of the characters. From there the discussion can quite naturally lead into consideration of the children's own parallel experiences, observations, and feelings. With younger children this discussion can eventually be rounded out to include setting up goals for everyday living that boys and girls them-

selves deem reasonable and attainable. For older children the discussion can usually be enriched and "brought to a head" by means of additional pages of pictures and explanatory material furnished in the text itself.

ACTUALLY this group discussion is a simple technique. It consists merely of bringing a group together for the purpose of considering and understanding some particular problem of everyday living. In so far as possible, an attempt should be made to encourage the same informal give-and-take of ideas as when a small group of friends talk together in the living room at home. Although the classroom may be crowded, there are ways of creating an informal setting. Movable desks can be drawn closer together and pulled into a semicircular group. If desks are fastened to the floor, friends may sit together in the front part of the room. Sitting on the floor may be the answer in some situations. If the teacher draws up her own chair, there will be generated a friendly, pleasant feeling that cannot so easily be gained if she sits at her desk or stands more formally before the class.

Of course, as in all other undertakings, facility in participating in group discussions

increases with practice. At first the teacher may have to make strenuous efforts to keep the conversation moving along. She may have to cite incidents from her own experience and ask direct questions freely. In these early stages of learning to do group thinking and talking, questions and comments such as the following will often serve to keep the conversational ball rolling: "Does anybody disagree with John? Helen, what makes you think that? Is there any way you can prove your point? I see that you want to make a point, Joe, but let's hear from Ray first. He hasn't spoken yet today. Let's see if you can dictate to me some ways of changing unpleasant feelings to more pleasant ones. Thelma, what is one way that I might record here on the blackboard? I see only one of you has a comment to make right now. So I'll ask the question again and wait a moment, for I know some of the rest of you will have something to say, too."

Later, as boys and girls become more fluent and more eager to talk, the problem may be that of keeping to the main theme under discussion. Often a pertinent question or two will serve to bring the discussion back to the main idea if children have become too involved in irrelevant points. However, when children occasionally get side-tracked on a truly vital issue, it is usually well to explore that point briefly before returning to the main theme.

Sometimes in frank group discussions the teacher may become a little concerned about the feelings expressed. George, perhaps, will state, "Say, sometimes I've felt just like Ellen did. I've wished I didn't have a little brother because he's a pest and a tag-along." Explosive and negative feelings frankly expressed often trouble adults, but the teacher will do well to remember the advice of Dr. Lawrence K. Frank, who says: "Children need to read specially selected stories which . . . provide releases for their fears and worries and which give them the reassurance that only the emotional experiences of certain stories can provide. They need safe ways in which they can 'blow their tops,' such as telling their own stories, beginning, 'Once I felt that way when . . .' or 'Once I got mad like that when. . . .' "

Naturally, letting children get such release is only the first step in making them feel better about a situation. Thus frank expressions of feelings can later be supplemented by consideration of positive steps that might need to be taken; e.g., facing a situation squarely, doing something constructive about it if possible, trying to accept it with some equanimity if nothing can be done, turning one's attention to other activities instead of brooding about the disagreeable situation. Teacher's notes or a teacher's guidebook to accompany the pupils' materials can be invaluable sources in suggesting how children can best be helped to cope with their emotions.

Informal group discussion, properly carried out, can do much to foster the personality development of individual members of the group and at the same time promote their understanding of their relationship to one another. This method of teaching emphasizes the importance of the individual, for it assumes that each member has something to contribute. It helps children understand themselves as individuals and as members of a group. By projecting themselves into the stories on which the discussion is based, by listening to the opinions of others, by examining their own lives, and by the teacher's guidance, children are helped to gain insight and skill in handling their own problems.

A child can analyze his problems far more clearly through such discussions than he possibly can by himself. Thus he reaches a better understanding of the issues involved in his problems. The knowledge that others have the same problems gives each child security because he comes to realize that he is not "different" but is very like his fellow human beings. As it becomes plain that no one is perfect, most children will find it easier to talk about fears, worries, and difficulties of their own. And when these difficulties can be brought out into the open, there is less danger that children will grow dependent upon daydreams, illness, alibis, or bullying to hide their real feelings.

As boys and girls progress in the art of group discussion, they speak more and more freely and with diminishing self-consciousness. The alert teacher is thereby given opportunity to learn more about the ideas, hopes, ambitions, and personal problems of each child than she might in individual conferences, even assuming she had time in her crowded day for such conferences. And not the least of the values of group discussion is its contribution to creating a happy, wholesome, sympathetic relationship between children and teacher which will permeate all their daily activities.

161

It has already been pointed out that group discussion is most effectively motivated by reading about the experiences of someone who has a problem common to the group. For example, the story might concern a boy who, by his posture and the way he walks, reveals to others his feeling of discouragement or unhappiness. Following the reading of such a story the teacher might initiate the discussion by giving children an opportunity to demonstrate how one may walk when discouraged, happy, uncertain, and angry, leading into a more general discussion of the many ways in which individuals reflect how they feel.

Then she might continue the discussion with "Because how we feel is so imporant to the way we look, perhaps we should think together of the important things that help keep us happy." After telling the children that our physical needs for adequate food, shelter, and clothing are, of course, essential to well-being, she might ask, "What other needs do we have?"

In response pupils might say, "We need someone to like us"; "We need friends to play with"; "We need to get along well at school"; "We need to know how to make a living someday," etc. After the children have contributed their ideas, the teacher might remark, "These important needs that you boys and girls have suggested can really be grouped under three main heads. I will put these on the board, and we will classify your suggestions under them."

1. Need for love and affection
2. Need for success and accomplishment
3. Need for belonging to a group and having friends

Then the children's previous suggestions could be fitted in under these three headings.

This discussion could lead naturally to a consideration of what happens when someone is not having one or more of these needs adequately met. Here again the concept could best be developed through actual examples such as the following, after each of which the teacher would ask, "What need of this child is unsatisfied?"

Jerry went slouching out of the room, the very picture of unhappiness. In his hand he carried a crumpled arithmetic paper—ten problems on it and all ten wrong!

Henry was in the fifth grade, but he couldn't do any of the fifth-grade work very well. There was one thing Henry could do, though. He could cause a disturbance, and he often did. He threw erasers when the teacher wasn't looking, pulled the pigtails of the girl who sat in front of him, and sometimes put his feet in the aisle to trip those who passed by.

Annabelle began coming right home from school and spending her time reading books. "Annabelle," her mother would say, "why aren't you out playing? You used to spend all your time with Joyce and Mary, and now you never seem to be with them."

"They are silly—and mean, too," Annabelle answered. "I don't want to have anything to do with them or any of the other girls, either. It's more fun to stay home and read."

It wasn't until weeks later that Annabelle's mother learned what had happened. Joyce and Mary and a few other girls had formed a club, and they hadn't invited Annabelle to join.

In conclusion, the teacher would emphasize that all of us, when one or more of our basic needs are not met, tend to show the lack in one way or another. We may be unhappy and show it in our appearance, as Jerry did. We may tease or annoy others, as Henry did. Or we may draw away from people and spend too much time by ourselves, as Annabelle did. The teacher might then go a step further and say, "It has been said that all our behavior is *caused*. What might cause a boy to be a show-off?" (Need for more affection or need for more success) "What might cause a girl to steal money from her mother's purse to treat classmates to sodas?" (Need for friends)

162

Pupils' interest in how posture reflects the emotions might be furthered by having them make a bulletin-board display of pictures of persons whose postures give clues as to how they feel at the moment. The comic strips offer a fertile field for pictures of this kind, as do various advertisements. If the pictures showed enough of the situation causing the posture, there could be subsequent discussion, too, about the needs the characters were trying to satisfy.

AFTER SUCH a discussion the teacher would want to examine as far as possible the children's lives at home and at school to see if their basic emotional needs for love and affection, for some measure of success, and for belonging to a group, having friends, etc., were being met.

There are many ways in which a teacher can directly contribute much toward satisfying these important emotional needs of the children in her classroom. They will require a little extra time and thought but the results are richly rewarding. In particular, the teacher can take steps to aid the friendless, lonely child whose need for belonging is far from being fulfilled. The busy teacher of a large class cannot always rely on direct observation to locate the desperately lonely children—the ones who are not desired by other pupils either as social companions or as co-workers. But she can administer from time to time a simple friendship test or quiz such as the following, to determine quickly the few children in the class who are socially unacceptable to their classmates. She can explain to the children that she wants to know who their friends are in order to make committee assignments and the like.

"Who Would It Be?"
(Answer with the names of your classmates)

1. If your mother said you could invite a friend for dinner and the movies on Friday, who would it be?
2. If this child couldn't come, whom would you ask?
3. Whom would you choose first to be on your team in a relay race?
4. Suppose you needed someone to help you with your arithmetic and the teacher told you to ask a classmate, who would it be?
5. If you were choosing someone to work on a science exhibit with you, who would it be?
6. Write the name of the boy you think gets along best with his classmates.
7. Write the name of the girl you think gets along best with her classmates.

The result of this quiz may be easily tabulated in such a way as to show at a glance where the existing friendships are, as well as which students have no class ties at all. The children who have received no votes at all are the children who must be given help. Many of those who later are emotionally unstable or who become delinquent were, during their school years, members of the socially unacceptable group.

163

VALUABLE as it is, group discussion both within the family and at school should be supplemented by as many other vital aids to learning as possible.

There should be family trips and class excursions to afford opportunities to study things at first hand. Excursions to find and study safety signs in the neighborhood, to observe the work in a neighborhood dairy or dairy farm, to inspect the city sewage plant, to notice health warnings in public places, to see provisions for cleanliness in a modern food store or factory—all these are prime sources of enrichment for concepts under consideration. Usually these trips are doubly valuable as follow-up excursions after text material and class discussion have built an understanding of what to look for. These trips will then lead to further discussion with far greater feeling and active interest.

Experiments are a valuable aid to learning. Whenever possible, the facts presented should be tested for their accuracy and reasonableness. Little children can try washing their hands in cold water alone, in cold water and soap, and in warm water and soap and judge for themselves the most efficient way. Older children can dip fingers in bowls of water and blow on them, noting for themselves how much more readily wet skin is chilled. Still older children can take their own pulses to note how the individual pulses vary after exercise.

As frequently as possible, boys and girls should have a chance to profit from the excellent films which are available. *Parents' Magazine* contains a very helpful family guide to current movies, in which films are rated for suitability and interest for different age levels. In recent years many fine educational films have been made for children—films about care and structure of the teeth, how disease germs are spread, how a city protects its food and water supplies, why a balanced diet is essential, and so on. (Sources for obtaining films of this kind are listed on page 188 of this book.)

BY CAREFUL study of radio program listings, parents and teachers will often find some excellent broadcasts to recommend to children. Some teachers actually assign these and later use them as subjects for class discussions. Boys and girls can have their horizons greatly widened by well-planned broadcasts about safety, modern advances in medicine, and health heroes. And even the advertising "plugs" can be turned to good account if children are challenged to "see if these statements about laxatives square with what has just been learned about the digestive system" or to "tell why there is no need for people to rush out and buy vitamins just because an announcer suggests it."

Dramatizations of social behavior—the courteous thing to do and say—have long been helpful means of giving boys and girls the social "know-how" they all crave sooner or later. Little children also find satisfaction in dramatizing things they can't actually do. And all boys and girls find release in occasionally entering into an imaginary world where they can be as powerful as kings and queens, as obnoxious as the villain, as magnanimous as the fairy godmother.

Creative expression is a basic need. Often important ideas are aptly reemphasized, tactfully stressed, or artistically illustrated by means of cartoons, paintings, drawings, posters, soap carvings, or the like. Frequent opportunities should be given for children to use these means of enriching concepts under discussion. Such opportunities add life and richness to the classroom; they also make it possible for varied talents to be revealed and appreciated. Thus a tendency to place too much premium on "book learning" alone can be avoided.

The contribution that children's literature can make in the field of human relations and personal problems should not be overlooked. For example, the timid, somewhat resentful middle child who at home has neither the privileges of the older child nor the advantages of the younger may well profit from reading *The Middle Sister* by Miriam E. Mason. The physically handicapped child cannot help but find renewed courage and optimism after reading such books as *Old Con and Patrick* by Ruth Sawyer and *Triumph Clear* by L. L. Beim. Because of the significant rôle which the "right book at the right time" may play in the lives of children, parents and teachers should be prepared to recommend some of the many books that may help a child to see his own problems and personality traits objectively— and thus come to understand them better and deal with them more effectively.

T HERE IS a certain release of tension that comes from sitting down and "writing out" one's feelings. Many of us know from experience how much it helps to react to some unpleasantness by writing a blistering letter of protest or complaint. And then usually, once the letter is written, we feel so much better that we tear it up and go on to more fruitful occupations.

Children, too, need an opportunity to release tensions through writing and can be encouraged to do so both at home and at school. Occasionally the teacher should provide opportunities for them to write about "My Biggest Worry," "My Most Annoying Problem at Home," etc. Often, if children are later willing to share their writings by reading them aloud, valuable discussion can result. They will see the similarity of their problems, and suggestions can be offered

about helpful ways of meeting or cooperating with the situation. However, boys and girls should be made to feel perfectly free to say how their writings are handled—they may mark them "Confidential," for the teacher alone, or they may even throw them away once completed. In this latter event, it should be remembered that the time spent in writing has not been wasted. Many problems become clarified or less worrisome to the child merely through the process of telling or writing about them.

Again it should be emphasized that the habits of action and thought based on the concepts developed can become an integral part of a child's life only when the school and the home work together. The school can undo the good work of parents or the good work done in school can be negated if the child has no opportunity to practice in his home the habits of action and thought initiated at school.

Concepts which can be developed at each age to help build mental, social, and physical health.

for **5** and **6** year olds

Mental health—*Understanding the way we think, feel, and act.*

Appreciating the desirability of assuming responsibility in so far as possible for dressing, taking care of toys and clothing, etc.

Realizing that discomfort and dissatisfaction often result from disregarding body needs.

Appreciating the values of being cheerful and co-operative in matters of daily routine.

Learning to make the best of disappointments or unfortunate happenings.

Understanding some of the causes for disturbing dreams, and realizing that such dreams are not real and should not be so considered.

Learning to cultivate a sense of humor.

Understanding that dawdling may inconvenience others—and may result in the missing of some enjoyable activity.

Learning to employ intelligent self-analysis—to know the limits of one's own abilities, and to set attainable standards.

Understanding that all of us at times exhibit such emotions as anger, fear, hate, jealousy and that no one is alone in experiencing them.

Learning ways of satisfying our basic emotional needs for love, success, belonging, approval.

Learning to face reality—to admit a difficult situation and then see what can be done about it.

Learning how to release emotional tensions.

Social health—*Harmonious relationships with others.*

Learning that helping others can be satisfying.

Realizing that satisfaction can come to older children through being considerate and thoughtful of younger children in play activities.

Learning to show appreciation in various ways.

Learning to put oneself in another's place and to consider his needs and his feelings.

Learning the essentials of being a courteous guest, a courteous host, and a courteous co-worker.

Appreciating that cooperation is an essential factor in getting along harmoniously with others.

Appreciating the values of sharing.

Physical health—*Learning about our bodies and how to care for them.*

CLEANLINESS AND GROOMING

Understanding that soap and hot water are needed to wash the hands after play, before eating, and after going to the toilet.

Realizing that it is all right to get play clothes dirty; but that there are times when "good" clothes should be kept as clean as possible.

Learning to use correctly and to give proper care to comb, brush, nail file, and other toilet articles.

Appreciating the desirability of being clean and looking one's best on appropriate occasions.

CARE OF THE TEETH

Using the toothbrush correctly.

Understanding the need for brushing teeth every day, especially after meals.

Learning why regular visits to the dentist are important.

Avoiding biting on hard objects.

Understanding how diet may affect the teeth.

CARE OF THE EYES, EARS, NOSE

Taking care to read in adequate light.

Learning to avoid shadows and glare.

Understanding the reason for blowing the nose gently.

CLOTHING

Appreciating the desirability of being dressed appropriately for work and play.

Appreciating the values of clean clothing.

SLEEP AND REST

Understanding that sleep is an essential part of our physical routine and an important factor in growth.

Learning that children of six need eleven to twelve hours of sleep each night—and that adequate sleep keeps children rested and refreshed.

Realizing that failure to get rest at proper times may result in inability to appreciate enjoyable activities later.

Understanding that all children, big and little, need rest during the day.

SUNSHINE, FRESH AIR, AND EXERCISE

Understanding both the good and the bad effect of sunshine.

Appreciating the need for adequate protection from the sun.

Realizing that sunshine, fresh air, and exercise are all necessary for good health; and that every child needs at least one to two hours of outdoor play daily.

Appreciating that children's growing bodies need many opportunities each day for exercising.

Understanding that although exercise is good for us, play should not crowd out other important aspects of the daily routine.

FOOD AND NUTRITION

Understanding that food contributes to body growth.

Gaining a willingness to try new foods in diet; appreciating that often unfamiliar foods are good, once they are tried.

Understanding that milk is a healthful food.

Appreciating the need for well-balanced breakfasts.

Gaining a simple understanding of foods that make a healthful lunch.

Understanding the proper place of desserts.

Learning that sweets eaten before a meal are likely to take away the appetite.

Avoiding putting unknown substances in the mouth.

Learning that depending on Mother for after-school and playtime snacks is better than getting into the candy-store habit.

CARE AND PREVENTION OF DISEASE

Appreciating the importance of using a handkerchief when coughing or sneezing.

Learning that the best place for anyone with a cold is at home; appreciating that in so far as possible others should stay away from a person with a cold.

Understanding that clean hands may be a factor in helping avoid the spread of germs.

Realizing that the sick-a-bed child can have fun, too—there are pleasant ways of passing the time during convalescence.

Understanding the importance of observing quarantine signs.

Safety and first aid—Learning to live safely.

Understanding the meaning of traffic signals.

Learning the safe way to cross an unguarded corner.

Understanding that even in emergencies traffic signals and precautions should be heeded.

Appreciating the need for avoiding undue recklessness and exhibitionism in play.

Realizing that it is not safe to play with animals that are not really pets.

Realizing that older children should take some responsibility for protecting younger children.

Appreciating that cooperation in play may prevent accidents and injuries.

Appreciating the importance of seeking attention for even minor cuts and abrasions.

Learning safety precautions at home.

Learning safety precautions at play.

Learning safety precautions with fire.

Appreciating the need for safety in vehicles.

Learning not to accept rides with strangers.

for 7 year olds

Mental health—Understanding the way we think, feel, and act.

Learning to employ intelligent self-analysis—to know the extent of one's abilities, to learn to set attainable standards.

Appreciating the fact that individuals differ and that each of us has strengths and weaknesses.

Learning to cultivate a sense of humor.

Learning ways of satisfying basic emotional needs— needs for love, success, belonging, and approval.

Understanding that all of us at times exhibit such emotions as anger, excitement, anxiety, fear, and jealousy.

Learning how to release emotional tensions.

Understanding that there is a relationship between our emotions and the way our body works.

Learning to face reality.

Realizing that everyone makes mistakes but that we can learn from our mistakes.

Appreciating the desirability of assuming responsibility in so far as possible for dressing, taking care of toys and other possessions, etc.

Realizing that dawdling and lack of punctuality can inconvenience others.

Understanding that it often helps to tell grown-ups about dreams or other fears that are disturbing.

Realizing that being left-handed doesn't mean being "different" and that children should use whichever hand is most natural for them.

Learning to make the best of a disappointment.

Understanding that sharing and taking turns result in more fun for everyone.

Appreciating that an illness or other misfortune isn't nearly so bad if we try to be cheerful.

Realizing that being thoughtful of others brings happy feelings to all concerned.

Appreciating that perseverance is needed to acquire any new skill.

Social health—*Harmonious relationships with others.*

Appreciating the importance of trying to realize why people feel and act as they do.

Realizing that we all have faults—and that understanding and forgiveness are more effective than criticism in helping a friend overcome weakness.

Realizing that cooperation is a valuable asset in learning to get along well with others.

Learning to be courteous.

Appreciating the need for showing consideration for younger children.

Learning that bossiness and too frequent volunteering of advice can be annoying to others.

Appreciating that independence is desirable but that sometimes it pays to heed the advice of others.

Realizing that doing things for others cements family relationships.

Understanding that big brothers and sisters do have interests and friends of their own—and that it isn't fair to "tag along" all the time.

Realizing that we shouldn't try to have our own way all the time.

Realizing that disagreement need not mean a quarrel.

Appreciating the importance of keeping a secret.

Learning some valuable techniques in making and keeping friends (sharing, giving in now and then, taking turns, showing friendliness, accepting unpleasant behavior of others).

Understanding that the best of chums need other friends, too.

Physical health—*Learning about our bodies and how to care for them.*

CLEANLINESS AND GROOMING

Realizing why it is important to wash hands before meals, after play, after using the toilet.

Appreciating the desirability of systematic procedure for personal care in the morning and at night.

CARE OF THE TEETH

Learning to use a toothbrush correctly.

Understanding the importance of brushing the teeth after meals and before going to bed.

Learning why regular visits to a dentist are important.

CARE OF THE EYES, EARS, NOSE

Appreciating the importance of proper care of the eyes (reading in a good light).

Learning to use a handkerchief properly—including blowing the nose gently.

CLOTHING

Realizing the necessity for having clothes suited to the occasion and weather as well as to the individual who wears them.

Understanding why it is desirable to remove wet clothes after coming into the house (to avoid chilling the body).

Appreciating that it is all right for play clothes to get dirty.

Realizing that in severe weather special provisions must be made for protective clothing.

SLEEP AND REST

Understanding that sleep is an important factor in growth.

Understanding that seven-year-olds require about eleven to twelve hours of sleep each night.

Appreciating that the best place to get a good night's rest is in a comfortable bed.

Understanding what some of the causes of disturbing dreams may be; e.g., too-late bedtime hours, exciting radio programs, indigestible evening snacks, etc.

Appreciating the need for rest periods to alternate with periods of strenuous activity.

SUNSHINE, FRESH AIR, AND EXERCISE

Appreciating that wholesome outdoor play is essential to health and happiness—and that two to three hours of outdoor play each day is desirable.

Understanding that outdoor play and exercise help stimulate the appetite.

Realizing that physical exercise is a factor in developing stronger, more vigorous human beings.

FOOD AND NUTRITION

Understanding that food serves as an energy fuel and as a growth factor.

Realizing that food should be eaten slowly and chewed thoroughly.

Understanding that it's natural for healthy, growing children to have good appetites.

Realizing that not everything that grows is a food;

learning to avoid putting strange plants in the mouth.

Appreciating the need for everyone to eat one green and one yellow vegetable every day.

Learning the value of fruit in the diet.

Considering what constitutes a good breakfast, a good lunch, and a desirable type of between-meal snack.

Appreciating that hunger often leads to irritability.

Appreciating the effect of pleasant emotions on digestion—avoiding quarrels at mealtimes.

CARE AND PREVENTION OF DISEASE

Appreciating the importance of sunshine, outdoor play, sleep, and good food in preventing illness.

Understanding the importance of vaccination and immunization.

Understanding the best procedure to use in caring for colds and in avoiding the spread of cold germs.

Appreciating the rôle of clean hands in helping avoid the spread of germs.

Realizing that the quarantine sign and quarantine regulations must be respected.

Understanding that after a long illness one must take things easy and not overdo.

Safety and first aid—*Learning to live safely.*

Learning that safe riding in vehicles includes keeping hands and head inside the vehicle, avoiding "horseplay" in the car, etc.

Learning that some plants are harmful, and that it is unwise to pick or eat unfamiliar things.

Learning that caution in playing with strange animals is necessary.

Appreciating the values of learning to swim—and of exercising caution in the water.

Learning essential precautions at home.

Learning to exercise proper precautions in play activities.

Learning to observe traffic regulations.

for 8 *year olds*

Mental health—*Understanding the way we think, feel, and act.*

Developing healthy attitudes toward the body and its functions.

Learning ways of satisfying basic emotional needs for love, success, belonging, approval.

Developing healthy attitudes toward one's own feelings.

Understanding that everyone at times experiences such human emotion as anger, fear, anxiety, jealousy—learning ways of coping with unpleasant feelings.

Realizing that there is a relationship between physical and mental health.

Learning to employ intelligent self-analysis—to determine one's strengths and weaknesses, to set attainable goals.

Learning to cultivate a sense of humor.

Learning to release emotional tensions.

Learning to face reality: physical handicaps.

Appreciating the causes and "cures" for dawdling.

Learning that individual differences in people are natural and help make life more interesting.

Understanding that elaborate equipment is not necessary to having a good time—a little ingenuity can provide a lot of fun.

Understanding that being left-handed is by no means a handicap—at times it has advantages.

Realizing that in a crisis it's important to be able to keep calm and ascertain the essential facts.

Realizing that it's fun to do things for others—and that planning for the pleasure of others often yields unexpected pleasure to the planner.

Social health—*Harmonious relationships with others.*

Trying to understand why others feel and act as they do.

Developing the ability to put yourself in another person's place.

Realizing the desirability of sharing ideas and possessions with others.

Learning to show consideration for younger children.

Learning ways of showing appreciation—by deeds as well as words.

Learning to respect the privacy of others.

Appreciating the need for learning to cooperate with others.

Learning some valuable techniques in making and keeping friends (showing friendliness, avoiding over-bossiness, giving in now and then to the needs and desires of others).

Learning to be courteous: as a host, as a guest.

Realizing that there is always room for new friends —and new friends can be as satisfying as old ones

Physical health—Learning about our bodies and how to care for them.

CLEANLINESS AND GROOMING

Appreciating the importance of establishing systematic personal care morning and night.

Understanding the need for washing hands before meals, after play, and after going to the toilet.

Appreciating the need for washing hands before handling food.

Realizing the need for taking baths and washing hair at regular intervals.

Understanding when clothes should be kept clean and when it is all right to get them dirty.

Appreciating the importance of keeping clothes neat and presentable.

Learning to take proper care of hair brush, comb, and other personal articles.

CARE OF THE TEETH

Maintaining a wholesome attitude toward the dentist—realizing the need of periodic check-ups.

Understanding how to brush teeth correctly (brush up on the lower teeth, brush down on the upper teeth, brush chewing surfaces of back teeth).

Realizing that teeth should be brushed after meals and before going to bed.

Understanding the value of proper diet in building strong teeth.

CARE OF THE EYES, EARS, NOSE

Understanding what constitutes good light when reading.

Developing a wholesome attitude toward glasses—understanding necessary safety precautions with glasses during playtimes.

Observing proper precautions when something is in the eye.

Understanding the need to report any illness or unfamiliar symptom in connection with the ears, eyes, nose, or throat.

CLOTHING

Knowing the value of clothing as a protection.

Realizing the need for removing heavy or wet clothing when indoors.

Understanding why wet clothing should not be worn outdoors.

Understanding the need for adapting clothing to the situation or activity.

Selecting clothes (and shoes) that are well-fitting and becoming to the wearer; interpreting "feet pictures" as taken by the X-ray machine.

Gaining knowledge of available ways to help anticipate weather and resulting clothing needs.

SLEEP AND REST

Realizing that sleep is an important factor in growth.

Understanding the sleep requirements of eight- and nine-year-olds (eleven hours per night).

Observing good sleeping habits—avoidance of over-excitement just before bedtime, value of fresh air, understanding of need for seeking comfortable sleeping positions.

Realizing the need for rest periods during the day, especially after violent exercise and after meals.

SUNSHINE, FRESH AIR, AND EXERCISE

Realizing that outdoor play is essential.

Knowing the need for adequate protection from sun, wind, and cold temperatures.

Understanding that physical exercise, sunshine, and fresh air are all factors in developing strong, vigorous human beings.

Learning to avoid overdoing—to alternate quiet activities with violent ones.

Realizing the value of a quiet period after eating.

Understanding the desirability of good standing, sitting, and sleeping posture.

FOOD AND NUTRITION

Understanding the function of food as a source of energy fuel and as a growth factor.

Learning what constitutes a balanced meal.

Understanding that milk is essential to health and growth—and that most children need 3-4 glasses per day.

Learning the specific values of fruits; vegetables; meat, fish, and eggs; milk and milk dishes.

Knowing the value of regularity in eating habits.

Learning to observe good eating habits.

Understanding that sweets eaten before meals may decrease the appetite.

Appreciating the need for refraining from condemning a new food before trying it.

Realizing why growing boys and girls should avoid tea and coffee (contributes no food value and too often substitutes for milk as a beverage).

Appreciating the need for avoiding overeating.

Understanding what constitutes a healthful snack.

CARE AND PREVENTION OF DISEASE

Building an elementary understanding of germs and how they are spread.

Understanding the values of vaccination.

Keeping things out of the mouth—avoidance of sharing whistles, balloons, etc.

Washing hands before eating, washing fruits before

eating, washing hands before preparing foods, washing hands after going to toilet.

Learning the need for maintaining healthful room temperature.

Realizing one's personal responsibility for helping prevent disease—for carrying a handkerchief and using it properly, for staying home while sick, etc.

Knowing the value of proper clothing in helping keep the body from being chilled.

Knowing the need for fresh air, sunshine, wholesome outdoor play, and good food.

Learning to care for colds properly—using handkerchief properly, blowing nose gently, staying home and in bed with a cold, keeping away from others, taking fruit drinks, etc.

Using handkerchiefs to cover a cough or sneeze.

Observing quarantine signs.

Observing wholesome attitudes toward doctors and nurses and the work they do.

STRUCTURE AND FUNCTION OF THE BODY

Understanding some of the causes for poor posture —inadequate diet; poorly fitting shoes; inadequate sleep, rest, or exercise; unhappy feelings.

Understanding the effect of emotions on digestion.

Understanding some of the factors that help contribute to strong bones and teeth.

Understanding that there is no exact weight or height for any child at a given age (too much stress should not be placed on gaining weight as some children become overanxious when they do not make anticipated weight gains).

Safety and first aid—*Learning to live safely.*

Learning to play safely: keeping off streets during play, avoiding foolhardiness and making unsafe dares, avoiding reckless play with toys, selecting safe places for play, using proper precautions with playground equipment.

Learning to take safety precautions at home; helping safeguard younger children at home.

Learning to take safety precautions in the car or in public conveyances.

Understanding the meaning of traffic signals.

Understanding necessary safety precautions when walking on a highway, i.e., keeping to the left side of the road.

Learning necessary safety precautions with fire, matches, etc.

Learning to take safety precautions with strange foods and medicines.

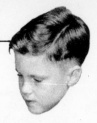

for 9 year olds

Mental health— *Understanding the way we think, feel, and act.*

Learning to accept helpful criticisms and profit by them.

Realizing that having material possessions is not everything in life—they are less important for happiness than friendships and good health.

Realizing that clean, neat houses have a relaxing effect on us, and that children should—within reason—share in the work of the home.

Understanding that we are happier when we accept our difficulties and "take them in our stride."

Learning to face reality—facing handicaps, facing unpleasant situations such as having to wear braces on the teeth, realizing that taking preventive measures early is better than suffering more serious consequences later.

Appreciating the joy to be found in other people's pleasures as well as in our own.

Appreciating that giving of oneself helps the giver.

Losing or avoiding the misconception that doctors and nurses are fearsome persons and realizing that they are likable people whose main object is to keep us strong and well.

Understanding that it's natural and desirable for boys and girls to seek increasing independence in such matters as selecting their own clothes— with this independence, however, must come a growing awareness of the need for buying wisely.

Realizing that times of suspense and waiting pass more quickly if you are busy.

Learning ways of satisfying the basic emotional needs for love, success, belonging, and approval.

Developing healthy attitudes toward one's feelings.

Understanding that fear, anger, jealousy, despair, and the like are common to us all—learning to cope with these feelings.

Learning how to release emotional tensions.

Learning that there is a relationship between physical and mental health.

Learning ways of working for happy feelings.

Learning to cultivate a sense of humor.

Learning intelligent self-analysis — admitting strengths and weaknesses, setting attainable goals.

Appreciating the values of hobbies and relaxation.

Accepting individual differences as natural and desirable.

Realizing that dawdling may be annoying and may inconvenience others.

Social health—*Harmonious relationships with others.*

Learning to understand some of the reasons why people feel and act as they do.

Learning to put yourself in another's place.

Appreciating the need to respect others' privacy.

Learning some valuable techniques in getting along with others.

Realizing the values of sharing.

Learning ways of showing appreciation.

Learning to be a courteous host and guest, to make strangers feel at home, to perform necessary introductions, to make friendly conversation.

Learning some useful techniques in keeping a conversation moving along; e.g., asking a question now and then.

Learning some techniques of making and keeping friends.

Realizing that people appreciate friendliness and a nonprobing interest in them and their problems.

Appreciating the importance to others of giving them friendly encouragement now and then.

Realizing that even though a person has a physical handicap, he still needs to feel he "belongs."

Understanding that people who have been ill for a long time are apt to become irritable or depressed.

Realizing that it is unfair to make snap judgments about others on the basis of color, clothes, religion, or the like—without ever having made the attempt to know them as individuals.

Physical health—*Learning about our bodies and how to care for them.*

CLEANLINESS AND GROOMING

Appreciating the importance of establishing systematic personal care morning and night.

Understanding why frequent bathing is essential.

Understanding the importance of washing hands before eating, before handling food, and after using the toilet.

Realizing the need for frequent changes in clothing, especially underclothing.

Appreciating the desirability of keeping hair brushed or combed.

Learning to care for fingernails properly.

Realizing the importance of regular toilet habits.

Appreciating the types of modern equipment that aid in cleanliness.

CARE OF THE TEETH

Understanding how to brush teeth (brush up on the lower teeth, brush down on the upper teeth, brush chewing surfaces of the back teeth).

Realizing why it is important to brush teeth after meals and before going to bed.

Learning the make-up of the teeth (crown, neck, root, enamel) and the importance of preserving the enamel.

Appreciating the importance of the baby teeth and the need for taking care of them—learning to distinguish between baby teeth and the sixth-year molars.

Understanding some of the reasons why second teeth come in crooked.

Realizing why it is important that second teeth be given good care.

Understanding the function of the different kinds of teeth (some cut, some cut and tear, some grind).

Understanding the dangers of biting hard objects.

Appreciating the function of braces in helping to straighten the teeth.

Learning why regular visits to the dentist are important.

CARE OF THE EYES, EARS, NOSE

Gaining a simple understanding of the different parts of the eye and of how these parts function.

Learning what constitutes good light for reading.

Understanding that usually we hold a book about 14-16 inches from the eyes and that great variations from this may indicate the need for having the eyes examined.

Learning what to do if a particle gets into the eye.

Gaining a simple understanding of the different parts of the ear and how they function.

Learning ways to keep the eyes and ears safe from injury.

Learning to blow the nose very gently to avoid forcing mucus up the Eustachian tube into the middle ear.

CLOTHING

Appreciating the need for selecting clothes to suit the weather.

Understanding why woolen clothing keeps us warm, why cotton clothing helps keep us cool, and why it is not wise to sit around in damp clothing.

Learning a few basic points about what makes clothing becoming to us; e.g., the fit, the color.

Appreciating the need for buying clothes wisely.

SLEEP AND REST

Understanding that children between nine and eleven need about eleven hours of sleep.

Realizing that adequate sleep provides energy for the next day's work and play.

Appreciating the fact that sleep gives bones and muscles their best chances for growth.

Learning that one of the effects of too little sleep is irritability.

Understanding some of the factors that often interfere with getting enough sleep.

SUNSHINE, FRESH AIR, AND EXERCISE

Appreciating the importance of sunshine, fresh air, and exercise in building strong bodies.

Realizing that growing boys and girls need two or three hours of outdoor play each day if possible.

Understanding that outdoor play should be chosen rather than indoor play whenever the weather permits.

Understanding that exercise helps build strong muscles.

Appreciating the fact that exercise builds coordination and more efficient motion.

Appreciating the need for interspersing vigorous activity with quiet play.

Understanding why it is desirable to "take it easy" for a while after eating.

FOOD AND NUTRITION

Learning the basic daily food requirements (the Basic Seven).

Gaining knowledge of what constitutes a well-balanced breakfast, lunch, and dinner.

Understanding that good nutrition is a vital factor in building resistance to disease, in contributing to good posture, in building strong bodies.

Learning about daily milk requirements.

Understanding that different foods do different things for the body.

Learning the importance of drinking when thirsty.

Developing awareness of vitamins, especially the contribution of Vitamin D in winter months.

Learning why growing boys and girls should avoid tea and coffee.

Understanding why alcoholic drinks should be avoided by boys and girls.

Understanding ways to help food digest.

CARE AND PREVENTION OF DISEASE

Understanding what germs are and how they are spread.

Appreciating the importance of avoiding unclean stores, restaurants, and washrooms.

Learning how to care for a cold.

Realizing that there are ways of helping prevent colds; e.g., avoiding those suffering with colds, avoiding chilling the body, eating properly.

Appreciating the importance of keeping homes clean—especially places where food is stored.

Learning the proper treatment of cuts.

Understanding the importance of quarantine, of vaccination, and of immunization.

Realizing the importance of proper ventilation in home and school.

COMMUNITY SAFEGUARDS TO HEALTH

Realizing that ill-kept yards are a menace to health, a potential source of breeding for mice and rats, and an eyesore to the community.

Developing awareness of and appreciation for the kinds of work that a local health department performs in the community.

Understanding of ways by which water in swimming pools and bathing beaches is kept as pure as possible; e.g., by use of filters, by chlorination.

Understanding the measures a community takes to control communicable disease.

Appreciating each individual's responsibility for helping keep the community safe and healthy.

STRUCTURE AND FUNCTION OF THE BODY

Developing a wholesome appreciation for the wonders of the human body and for its many protective functions.

Developing a simple understanding of the various functions of the skeleton.

Understanding, in a simple way, the basic functions of the heart, lungs, stomach, liver, intestines, kidneys, and bladder.

Developing an understanding of "how we look inside"—the outside layer of skin, hair, and nails; the layers of fat; the muscles; the skeleton; and the essential body organs.

Understanding what constitutes normal body temperature and noting ways the body has of maintaining this temperature (perspiration, shivering).

Realizing the importance of elimination of waste; learning about body organs that aid in elimination.

Developing an awareness of the importance of good sitting and standing position and of the factors that contribute to good posture.

Considering the values of keeping height and weight charts over a period of time, coupled with the understanding that weight gains do not always occur regularly, that there is no exact weight that is normal for all boys or girls of a particular height and age.

Understanding the value of regular habits in connection with eating, sleeping, and elimination.

Appreciating the importance of periodic physical examinations and dental examinations.

Safety and first aid— *Learning to live safely.*

Learning safety precautions in connection with fire.

Learning safety precautions at play.

Learning safety precautions at school.

Appreciating safety precautions to be observed at home.

Understanding essential safety precautions to observe when riding on vehicles.

Learning a few simple principles of first aid.

for 10 *year olds*

Mental health— *Understanding the way we think, feel, and act.*

Learning ways of satisfying the basic human needs for love, success, belonging, approval.

Learning to understand what may lie back of the way others are acting.

Learning to put yourself in another's place.

Realizing that all of us, while alike in some ways, differ in many others.

Understanding that we all experience such emotions as anger, fear, jealousy, etc.

Learning to regard the human body in a wholesome way rather than as something not to be talked about or investigated very much.

Developing an awareness that some accidents don't "just happen" but are the result of personal problems or conflicts.

Realizing that all of us at times have problems and difficulties. Usually the best and most helpful thing to do is to face our problems squarely instead of "running away" from them.

Realizing that growth from childhood to preadolescence inevitably involves bodily changes such as growth of hair on boys' faces, deepening of boys' voices, growth of breasts in girls, and widening of girls' hips.

Learning that happy feelings are as essential as are sleep and rest, exercise, fresh air, and good food in helping develop strong, healthy bodies.

Appreciating the importance of our feelings in helping the body to do its work.

Learning some of the ways of consciously working for the happy feelings: (1) by talking over difficulties with a sympathetic grown person; (2) by working for fundamental satisfactions which bring happiness; (3) by remembering that few people do everything well, and that if you can't do one thing well, there is something else you can do better than others can do it; (4) by "letting off steam" through writing about the upset feelings, or through drawing, dramatization, or using a punching bag.

Developing an awareness that there is distinct harm in keeping feelings "bottled up" inside us —and an awareness of how suppressed feelings may sometimes come out disguised in other ways; e.g., in teasing, bullying, headaches.

Social health— *Harmonious relationship with others.*

Learning to understand why others think and feel and act as they do—looking for the causes and motives underlying surface behavior.

Learning to put yourself in another's place.

Learning some valuable techniques in making and keeping friends.

Appreciating the value of sharing.

Learning to be courteous: as a guest, as a host, at the table.

Realizing that cooperation is essential for harmonious relations with others.

Realizing that we can disagree with others without having to quarrel.

Physical health— *Learning about our bodies and how to care for them.*

CLEANLINESS AND GROOMING

Learning how to give care for hair, skin, and nails.

Understanding how to care for articles used in personal grooming; e.g., hair brush, comb.

Appreciating the need for frequent washing of hands and for taking baths often (baths help us relax, help remove perspiration odors, remove dirt and germs from the skin, and help improve our personal appearance).

Appreciating the desirability of looking clean and neat and being appropriately dressed.

Appreciating the need for adopting a hair style that is becoming—and not necessarily the "latest thing" in styles (an item of interest to girls only).

CARE OF THE TEETH

Learning the different kinds of teeth (incisors, cuspids, bicuspids, molars), the function of each kind, and the need for each in proper mastication.

Learning the make-up of a tooth (root, neck, crown, enamel) and how a tooth looks inside.

Learning about the proper way to brush the teeth.

Appreciating the need for visiting a dentist often, and especially for having a dentist care for small cavities before decay spreads.

Understanding why brushing teeth after meals and before going to bed is essential.

Appreciating the influence of diet in building healthy teeth.

Appreciating the fact that teeth aid digestion, improve appearance, and aid speech.

CARE OF THE EYES, EARS, NOSE

Appreciating the function of the eyes and ears as safety devices and as important means of keeping us in touch with the world in which we live.

Developing a simple understanding of the different parts of the eye and ear and of how they function.

Considering the protective functions of the different parts of the eye and ear.

Reviewing proper care of the eyes and ears.

Understanding that many eye and ear injuries result from careless play.

Understanding the advantages of wearing glasses if needed.

CLOTHING

Appreciating the need for clean clothing, especially underclothing and socks or stockings.

Appreciating the need for being dressed appropriately for the weather and for the occasion.

Learning how to select shoes that are well-fitting.

SLEEP AND REST

Understanding that overtired muscles do not function as well as rested ones.

Realizing that plenty of sleep is one factor that aids in building strong muscles.

Appreciating that sleep plays an important part in contributing to good posture.

Learning that rest after eating promotes digestion.

Realizing that interspersing rest periods with periods of strenuous activity and getting plenty of sleep are ways of helping take care of the heart.

Learning that ten-year-olds need about 10 hours of sleep each night.

SUNSHINE, FRESH AIR, AND EXERCISE

Understanding that ten-year-olds need two to three hours of outdoor play and exercise each day.

Realizing that muscles need to be used continually to keep them functioning at their best.

Appreciating that exercise helps build strong muscles and helps make the muscles more skillful.

Realizing the need for not exercising too long or too hard at one time.

Appreciating the fact that during the summer the body manufactures Vitamin D if exposed to plenty of sunlight.

FOOD AND NUTRITION

Learning how proteins, minerals, vitamins, fats, and carbohydrates help the body.

Understanding and becoming thoroughly familiar with the Basic Seven Food Groups.

Appreciating that pleasant surroundings and attractive methods of serving food have a definite effect on the appetite.

Appreciating that good table manners are important because, among other things, their use makes the meal more pleasant for all concerned.

Realizing that our feelings can have a profound effect on promoting or hindering the digestion.

Learning some of the causes for poor appetite and for overeating (poor appetite may be caused by eating between meals, by upset emotions; overeating is quite likely to have as its cause unhappiness and poor adjustment at home or school.

Reviewing the kinds of foods that constitute desirable between-meal snacks.

Realizing the importance for cleanliness and safety of proper handling and storing of food.

CARE AND PREVENTION OF DISEASE

Learning the proper way to care for a cold—and ways of helping prevent the spread of colds.

Appreciating the importance of vaccination and immunization.

Developing an awareness of some common means by which germs are spread; i.e., by the use of carelessly washed eating utensils, by workers with unclean hands, and by the use of unclean storage places for food.

Learning the correct way to wash dishes, glasses, and silverware to kill disease-spreading germs.

Learning the dangers of spoiled food and some of the causes of food spoilage.

Learning to prevent the spread of infection, through using one's own towel and washcloth, through blowing the nose gently to avoid sending mucus into the middle ear, by caring for burns, cuts, and splinters properly.

COMMUNITY SAFEGUARDS TO HEALTH

Understanding some of the functions of the local health department in helping make a community safer and more healthful.

Learning the provisions for sanitation that should be made in homes, restaurants, food stores.

Appreciating the work of health heroes of the past —Dr. William Beaumont, Dr. William Harvey, Dr. René Laënnec.

STRUCTURE AND FUNCTION OF THE BODY

Developing a wholesome appreciation for the human body and its many amazing functions.

Understanding the make-up of a tooth, the different kinds of teeth and their functions, the appearance of a tooth on the inside.

Developing an understanding of the various parts of the eye and the ear and how they help us.

Learning about the work of the digestive organs.

Learning about the body's circulatory system.

Understanding the work of the organs involved in elimination of wastes.

Learning the make-up and functions of the body's skeleton—bones, joints, ligaments, tendons.

Understanding how the body grows—body cells, function of the endocrine glands, effect of general health on body growth.

Learning some of the many protective functions of the body.

Learning about the body's respiratory system.

Gaining an over-all view of the body's make-up—hair, skin, nails; layers of fat, layers of muscle, skeleton, internal organs.

Understanding in a simple way the work of the body's glands—salivary, sweat, oil, endocrine.

Learning about the voice box (larynx) and its function.

Appreciating individual differences in body build, height, and weight.

Learning the effect of emotion on body functioning.

Appreciating that general health, happy feelings, adequate diet, sleep, exercise, and properly fitting shoes are important factors in good posture.

Safety and first aid—*Learning to live safely.*

Considering the common skin injuries, ways such injuries can be prevented, and first-aid treatment.

Learning basic procedures to follow in the event of bad sprains or broken bones.

Reviewing the need to avoid eye and ear injuries.

Reviewing the individual's part in avoiding accidents at home, at school, on the playground, in vehicles.

Reviewing important traffic regulations.

for 11 year olds

Mental health—*Understanding the way we think, feel, and act.*

Learning to stop and consider what makes us do the things we do and feel as we do, when everything seems to be going wrong; learning satisfactory ways of coping with difficult feelings. We can often do something to change what we don't like. Just "letting off steam" by being cross, irritable, or sulky relieves tensions for a little while but it is better to find more worthwhile ways of changing unpleasant feelings to pleasant ones.

Understanding that the way we feel—excited, angry, worried, relaxed, or happy—influences body functioning; e.g., blushing, sweating palms, or "butterflies in the stomach"; fear of some school subject may cause stomach ache.

Realizing that happy feelings are as important to good health as good food, exercise, sleep, etc.

Appreciating that if a situation cannot be changed we must try to accept it.

Learning ways to resolve the upset feelings created by feeling discriminated against in the family; i.e., (1) accepting the idea that "the fairest plan in a family is to have each help according to his age and ability"; (2) seeing the advantages and the disadvantages of one's special place in the family; (3) "doing one's best" and not becoming unhappy by comparing oneself with others in the family.

Realizing that telling someone what is bothering you helps get rid of unhappy feelings.

Understanding that such feelings as jealousy, hate, and anger are common to all human beings.

Realizing that if feelings are buried deep inside they may come out later in such disguised behavior as

176

teasing, bullying, bragging, and bossing; appreciating that such behavior should make you stop and think "What is making me act this way?"

Learning that once you understand and admit your feelings it is easier to do something about them.

Appreciating that life is often more interesting to those who have hobbies.

Learning how to handle disappointments, e.g., the best way of meeting disappointment is to accept it and see if you can't make other plans or find some other way of having a pleasant time.

Learning that growth during preadolescence may be irregular and that it is nothing to worry about, e.g., one's feet may grow very rapidly, but other parts of the body will catch up sooner or later.

Realizing that we all have difficulties or weaknesses or handicaps of one sort or another which we must learn to face.

Understanding that the first step in handling a difficulty is to admit it, then see if anything can be done about it and above all setting goals that are reasonable for oneself.

Learning how to make the best of any difficult or unpleasant situation.

Learning how to meet failure when it comes and how to profit by the experience.

Social health—*Harmonious relationships with others.*

Understanding that we are all born with different capacities and that our experiences have made us still more different; that this is why not all of us respond the same way to a given situation.

Realizing that there is always a good reason for what individuals do and we should not judge a person to be "mean" or "queer" when he does something we do not like or understand.

Appreciating that regardless of personal desires, there are times when it is only fair to be a good sport and do one's share in a group project.

Realizing that we feel more comfortable in social situations when we know what to do or say.

Appreciating that in social situations it helps to think less of oneself and more about others.

Understanding that we should try to find out why we are ill at ease in a social situation and then see if we can correct the causes.

Appreciating the importance of "giving in" now and then to the needs and wishes of others.

Realizing that while it is natural and normal for boys and girls to do what others are doing, there are times when good sense must prevail over the desire to conform.

Appreciating that every individual should share in the responsibility of making the community a pleasanter place to live.

Physical health—*Learning about our bodies and how to care for them.*

CLEANLINESS AND GROOMING

Learning what constitutes good grooming.

Learning how to care for one's hair.

Appreciating that the knowledge that one looks "right" for any occasion can be very satisfying.

CARE OF THE TEETH

Learning how the teeth grow.

Learning what causes tooth decay, what happens when teeth decay; learning how to keep the teeth and gums healthy.

Appreciating the need for periodic visits to the dentist and daily care of the teeth.

Understanding why giving proper care to the teeth is important to health.

Appreciating how diet affects teeth.

Appreciating the values of strong, healthy teeth.

CARE OF THE EYES, EARS, NOSE

Learning that the five senses are hearing, seeing, smelling, tasting, and feeling.

Appreciating the importance of seeing and hearing to school work and to enjoyment of living.

Reviewing knowledge of the structure and functioning of the ears and eyes.

Reviewing care of the ears, eyes, and nose, and of ways to prevent the spread of eye diseases.

Developing an awareness of the signs of eyestrain and of the need for consulting a doctor if these signs are present often.

POSTURE

Appreciating that achieving good posture involves properly fitting shoes, plenty of sleep and rest, an adequate daily diet, and happy feelings, and sufficient exercise.

CLOTHING

Understanding that the feet of rapidly growing preadolescents need shoes carefully fitted.

Learning that well-fitting shoes help the feet.

SLEEP AND REST

Understanding that taking short periods now and then to relax may increase personal efficiency.

Realizing that a little relaxing after a meal aids digestion.

177

Appreciating that sleep and rest play an important part in contributing to good posture.

Learning that eleven-year-olds need about ten hours of sleep each night.

Understanding how sleep and rest help growth.

SUNSHINE, FRESH AIR, AND EXERCISE

Understanding that eleven-year-olds need at least two hours of outdoor play each day.

Reviewing understandings about the part exercise plays in helping build strong muscles and in keeping them functioning at their best.

Realizing the need for not exercising too long or too hard at one time.

FOOD AND NUTRITION

Reviewing the need for carbohydrates, fats, proteins, vitamins, and minerals and how they help the body.

Understanding that there are basic daily foods that we all need to keep us strong, healthy, and relatively safe from disease.

Understanding the effect of emotions on digestion.

Appreciating that cheerful feelings promote good digestion.

Appreciating that food attractively served and eaten in pleasant surroundings has a beneficial effect on the appetite and on digestion.

Understanding the reasons for avoiding tea, coffee, alcohol, and tobacco.

Appreciating the importance of cleanliness in handling foods.

CARE AND PREVENTION OF DISEASE

Understanding that the best treatment for a cold is plenty of sleep, rest in bed, and lots of fruit drinks.

Learning how germs are spread and the precautions which prevent their spread.

Appreciating the importance of keeping away from others to prevent the spread of colds.

Realizing the importance of observing quarantines and how quarantine prevents the spread of disease.

Appreciating how important cleanliness is in the preventing of disease.

COMMUNITY SAFEGUARDS FOR HEALTH

Understanding the main duties of the local health department.

Realizing how the community safeguards health by supplying pure drinking water.

Learning how the community takes care of sewage disposal.

Learning how the community provides for disposing of garbage and rubbish.

Realizing the danger of flies and rats as carriers of typhoid fever, intestinal disease, tuberculosis, and the plague.

Learning how to fight flies and rats.

Realizing how the community safeguards health through the local health department's regular inspections of food stores, bakeries, food factories, and eating places.

Learning how milk is cared for to safeguard health.

Appreciating the contribution to our health made by health heroes of the past—Anton van Leeuwenhoek, Edward Jenner, Louis Pasteur, Joseph Lister, Robert Koch, and Walter Reed.

Appreciating the individual's responsibility for contributing to the health of his community.

STRUCTURE AND FUNCTION OF THE BODY

Increasing appreciation for the human body and the amazing way in which all parts of the body function and cooperate.

Reviewing the structure and functioning of the teeth, the eyes and ears, the digestive organs, the circulatory system, and the muscles.

Learning the make-up and functioning of the autonomic and the central nervous systems.

Understanding the work of the body's glands—especially adrenal and sweat.

Learning the growth patterns of preadolescents.

Appreciating individual differences in body build, height, and weight.

Safety and first aid—*Learning to live safely.*

PERSONAL SAFETY

Learning that one should never touch electrical equipment with wet hands.

Learning basic safety precautions to observe when on a hike.

Appreciating the need for correcting conditions which cause accidents at home.

Reviewing ways of avoiding eye and ear accidents.

Learning when and how to give first aid in the event of minor injuries or ills such as nosebleed, pimples, cinder in the eye, insect bites, frostbite, and poison ivy, oak and sumac.

COMMUNITY SAFETY

Participating in a survey of safety precautions the school takes to protect its pupils.

Learning how the community protects our safety.

Appreciating that each individual must take responsibility for making the community safer.

For discussion

A liberal use of the supplementary materials recommended on pages 185-188 will broaden and enrich your understanding of the principles and concepts developed in this book, and will consequently be of great help in the formulating of thoughtful answers to the questions and typical case-study problems below.

CHAPTER ONE *Children are not small adults*

1. When Bobby was two and a half years old his father bought him an electric train and settled down to teach Bobby to run it. When, after many tries, Bobby finally broke the screw which controlled the switch, his father became angry. Bobby threw a temper tantrum, kicked the train, and twisted the tracks. The expensive toy was ruined and Bobby, kicking and screaming, was soundly spanked. Where did the trouble lie?

2. Mrs. Dawson, whose son is fifteen, complains bitterly at his lack of initiative and independence. Her husband insists it is all her fault because she has always babied the child, made all decisions for him, and kept him "tied to her apron strings." What could both parents have done to prevent the present situation? What should be done now?

3. There are three children in the Wells family. Jimmy is six, Jerry three, and June eight. Their parents pride themselves on the fact that they treat each child just like the others. Is this a good thing? Why or why not?

4. Joe's parents felt that he was a failure at everything. When he was two he could not feed himself without spilling his food and occasionally smearing food over his face. At four he was unable to dress himself satisfactorily even though his mother had been working with him for two years. He couldn't put his erector set together at five although his father showed him again and again. Because his birthday fell in January, he started first grade when he was five and a half. He failed in his reading and his writing continued to be illegible. He became one of the most troublesome children in the room and soon refused even to try. His parents were discouraged and his teacher at her wits' end. Where does the trouble lie? What can his teacher do?

5. Growth may be retarded in different ways. Give an example of how growth may be retarded because

of each of the following: physical care, failure to recognize readiness for learning, too high standards, competition, lack of harmony.

6. Carol was very bright. At four she could read as well as her brother who was in first grade. When she started to school she was soon placed in second grade. She was only eleven when she entered high school. Her mother is worried now because she does not enter into the social life of the other high-school girls. What would have been a better plan with Carol?

7. How do you teach a child caution without fear about real dangers like fire, railroad tracks, and so on?

8. Mrs. Harms wants Don to be as perfect a child as possible; therefore she watches and guides almost every move he makes. In the same earnest tone of admonition, she tells him to pull up his socks, not to touch the gas jet, to say "Thank you," and to share his toys. What is wrong here?

9. The neighbors all contend that Mrs. Martin's children behave badly much of the time and even Mrs. Martin agrees with them. "It's natural for children to quarrel and not to like to be clean or to eat what they should. I just make them eat what they're given and obey when they're spoken to and I don't listen to their complaints," she explains. Their next-door neighbor says, "Letting them get it out of their systems may be good, but those children certainly express a lot of rebellion. If they were happier at home, I can't believe there would be so much ill feeling among them." What do you think these children have and have not in their home situation that accounts for their bickering, complaining, and hostility?

10. Mrs. Lewis says: "I tell Jean that I will always love her whatever she does, but that if she loves me she will do as I ask her to." Do you think this is a good basis on which to develop desirable behavior? What is lacking?

CHAPTER TWO *Five is a comfortable age*

1. What reasons would you give to your Board of Education to convince them of the desirability of kindergarten experiences for five-year-olds?

2. Discuss some situations in which children of the same family should be encouraged to play together. Discuss others in which they should not be expected to do so. What effect do age and sex differences have upon this question?

3. One day five-year-old Anne was left behind

when her mother had planned to take her shopping. Anne's mother kept telling her that the taxi would come in ten minutes, then five, then that it was waiting and costing money. But Anne continued to dawdle and was reluctant to leave her play. Yet when she was left behind with her grandmother, she wept and called her mother "mean." Do you think she will behave differently next time? What change in tactics would you suggest?

4. Jack, who is five, has never liked his little sister and is intensely jealous of her. Recently he has discovered that he can completely crush her with scornful words alone. Should he be allowed to express his feelings as freely as he likes? How would you set about correcting the cause of the conflicts?

5. If you know a five-year-old, spend some time observing his free play alone or with other children. Note particularly any play that seems to you to have special significance in terms of his emotional life. For example, Sue plays she is sick and persuades other children to cover her, take her pulse and her temperature, give her medicine and chocolate candy. Jane on the other hand likes to be the nurse and is constantly dosing her dolls. Jimmy likes to play he is the father and takes delight in making the others step around, threatening them with a strap if they don't "mind." Jessie is always straightening up and seems unhappy and bothered when anything is out of place. What might these play activities reveal about each of these children?

6. What toys and play equipment would you recommend for a five-year-old boy or girl? What kind of toys would you discourage anyone from buying for this age?

7. How would you prepare a child for the coming of a new baby brother or sister? How should the mother's going to the hospital be handled? the homecoming? Discuss a number of practical ways in which parents can protect the older child from a feeling of displacement in the weeks following the baby's arrival. How can parents show their children that they love each one for himself?

8. Suggest ways in which the kindergarten teacher can help the shy, timid child who is slow to enter into group activities and also the aggressive, self-centered child who takes what he wants, or keeps what he has, by force.

9. What kinds of experiences can parents and teachers give the five-year-old that will contribute to his readiness for reading? to his ability to take his place in a group and work and play with other children? Should a five-year-old be taught to read?

Discuss and give reasons for your answer.

10. What are some of the evidences of maladjustment caused by overprotection and indulgence by one or both parents? If you know a child who evidences maladjustment caused by overprotection how would you help the parent overcome the harm that has been done? What else might Larry Drake's teacher have done? (See pages 31-33)

11. In what ways can the younger child be helped to understand that the older child also has rights that must be considered?

12. Discuss ways in which the older children can be given a feeling of status and importance to help them in their adjustment to a younger child in the family.

CHAPTER THREE *When they are six*

1. How would you answer the mother who says: "I can't imagine what has happened to Bobby these last few months. Ever since he started first grade he has been like a different child. Last year he had the sweetest nature, you couldn't ask for a better child. Now he seems possessed, never still a minute, loving me one minute and striking at me the next. He doesn't seem to know what he wants. He's driving me crazy."

2. Six-year-old Alice picked up a pencil lying in the aisle. It was a long red pencil, just what she had always wanted—so she hid it in her desk. When the owner discovered her loss she was much disturbed and the ensuing search revealed the culprit. How would you handle this situation?

3. Mary Lou, who is six, told her class at school a long story of the prize fight she had attended the night before, giving a blow-by-blow description. The teacher knew it would have been impossible for the child to have attended and called the parents to tell them of Mary Lou's falsehood. Her parents were horrified at the "lie," punished her severely, and made dire threats as to the consequences if she ever should lie again. What would you have done if you had been the teacher? the parents?

4. Bobby's father is very proud of his young six-year-old son. One day he asked Bobby to show a guest how well he could throw and catch a ball. Bobby refused, and in the clash of wills which followed, his father punished him by tossing the new football into the furnace. Discuss the cause of Bobby's refusal and the punishment.

5. Would you recommend or discourage the following procedures for six-year-olds?—why?

(a) Participating in rehearsed plays or programs.

(b) Giving them responsibilities such as making simple purchases at the store or washing dishes.

(c) Following an orderly program in day-to-day activity in the classroom.

(d) Insistence on their dressing themselves.

(e) A grading or marking system for first grade.

(f) Asking them to choose one of two new coats.

6. Taking into consideration that activity is an outstanding trait of the six-year-old, what type of play would you encourage—how would you incorporate this desire for activity in teaching the six-year-old to read?

7. List the characteristics which Patty displayed that indicated normal six-year-old behavior. Had she come from a home with a different economic background, what explanation might have been found for her aggressive behavior?

8. What might Robert Blake's mother have done to give him the needed sense of security even though she was constantly taking him from one place to another in order to be with his father?

9. What other kinds of maladjustment have you observed in children whose lives were influenced by conditions during the war years?

CHAPTER FOUR *Slowly and steadily ahead*

1. Compare and contrast physical developments and activities of the six-year-old and seven-year-old.

2. What type of stories would you recommend for the seven-year-old to read?

3. How much supervision do you believe a parent should exercise over the movies a seven-year-old attends? over the radio programs he listens to? What is the school's responsibility?

4. In what ways would you expect the competitive drive and developing sensitivity of the seven-year-old to manifest themselves?

5. What is the significance of Dr. Gesell's calling this the "eraser age"?

6. After reading this chapter, what responsibilities around the home and at school would you think could be carried by a seven-year-old?

7. What do the frequent dreamy, inactive periods in the seven-year-old's day tell you about him?

8. Although (or perhaps *because*) seven is a responsive age—one in which the child is especially anxious to please—what possible pitfalls must an adult who is guiding the child be especially aware of?

9. What does the frequent tattling of the seven-year-old indicate to you about his development?

10. What reasons other than those given in Huntley's case might justify taking a child out of his home and placing him in a new environment?

11. Why does fear of losing his mother's love disturb a child so seriously? Discuss some of the far-reaching effects of a feeling of rejection. What can a mother do to help her child get over feeling uneasy in her absence? How can children be taught to accept necessary disappointments and deprivations?

12. Mrs. D often tells her friends, "David is selfish. He refuses to share his toys, always wants, and if possible takes, the biggest piece. He has no consideration for others." His father, who thinks David should be forced to share, says, "He has always been selfish and he's got to get over it." How would you counsel these parents?

CHAPTER FIVE *Eight is an eager year*

1. What are some of the points to be considered in a good health program for children of this age? How can these points be presented in order to gain the cooperation of the child?

2. How would you utilize the "gang" interest constructively?

3. Plan a good after-school program for eight-year-olds.

4. How can an adult-organized group supplement the informal "gang" or "club"?

5. How can the hobby of "collecting" be encouraged? What are its values?

6. How can the eight-year-old be helped to a better use of his allowance without too much adult interference or control?

7. Suggest ways we can help the eight-year-old to take responsibility without putting on too much pressure or nagging at him.

8. How can we help the eight-year-old to accept criticism when it is necessary?

9. When the feeling toward the "enemy" gets out of bounds, how can the adult give interpretation and redirection?

10. Discuss reasons why the possession of a high I.Q. may not bring either success or happiness in life. How does emotional stability or instability affect an individual's ability to use his intelligence effectively? What rôle does character play?

11. What physical handicaps might explain a child's failure in school? What are some emotional problems which might be the cause of failure?

12. Anything which sets a child or a group of children apart as "different" creates an adjustment problem. Not all such children are as fortunate as Marlene, who reflects the careful guidance in her home. How would you go about helping a child of another race or nationality to accept differences in color or culture and become an accepted member of a group?

How would you help a child whose "difference" was the result of always having had a governess or tutor and who must now adjust to public school? A refugee child who had known the horror of war and displacement? A child who is hard of hearing? A child who is rejected because he is dirty and uses filthy language? A prodigy who is bored by the class work and rejected by other children?

CHAPTER SIX *The mature child*

1. What are some of the skills which nine-year-old children appreciate and admire in one another? Which of these can parents and teacher help to develop at this age level?

2. How would you encourage an interest in reading in the child of nine who is not up to his reading level? How can parents and teacher cooperate in helping the child to enjoy reading?

3. What kinds of trips can be planned in your community to interest the nine-year-old?

4. Suggest ways in which we can build on the nine-year-old's interest in his own country. How can we help him understand the real meaning of patriotism?

5. What means would you use to develop character in the nine-year-old through actual situations and experiences?

6. In what situations might it be safe to allow a nine-year-old to learn good judgment by experience?

7. Suggest ways to help the left-out child to become better accepted by other children.

8. How would you go about helping a nine-year-old to be more tolerant and accepting of those children who are "different"?

9. What is the rôle of the adult in relation to nine-year-old children?

10. Where there is a reading difficulty how can home and school keep the child from feeling discouraged and ashamed of his failure?

11. Think of the slow-learning children you know and suggest ways you might help them to become useful, happy members of their group.

12. It has been said that crime is but another name for need or an aspect of a desire. Discuss the needs which were not fulfilled in Lee's case.

13. George is the despair of his parents. His hands are always dirty, his hair tousled, and his clothes untidy. He never has time for careful grooming and his slouching posture is becoming habitual. He resents the eternal nagging of his mother and the sternness of his father. Lately he has been seen with a gang of "roughnecks" who look as he does. How would you advise his parents if they asked your help?

CHAPTER SEVEN *The preadolescents*

1. Sandra, at age eleven, is inches shorter than her classmates. Recently she has been seeking the companionship of younger children or coming home immediately after school to busy herself in a book. How would you help her meet her problem?

2. One member of a neighborhood gang of boys carried his mischievous pranks to the point of destruction of a valuable statue on the lawn of a wealthy resident. Harry Jones knew who had done the damage but refused to tell even when threatened with severe punishment. How would you handle this situation?

3. Mr. Maxwell was an excellent executive. He wanted to run his family as efficiently as he ran his business. Each child was given specific responsibilities and held to completion of the tasks regardless of circumstance. When the father went away on a business trip, he left orders for every member of the family. Mrs. Maxwell began, long before he was due home, to try to jack the children up to complete the work he had left for them. It was pathetic to see the children's strained faces on the day he returned.

When the oldest son was eleven he repeatedly tried to run away from home, in spite of the severe punishment meted out each time he rebelled against his father's authority. Finally when he attempted to shoot himself, his father sought help from a guidance clinic. How would you have helped this father? What might the mother have done at an earlier time?

4. List some evidences of the onset of adolescence in girls and in boys.

5. How would you help a mother who is disturbed because her daughter no longer seems to value the suggestions and opinions which always have been readily accepted in the past?

6. Julia's mother feels that an eleven-year-old girl is too young to stay out until eleven o'clock. She goes after Julia at ten. When told that the result of this will be that soon her daughter will not be invited to parties, she said, "I know it, but I think that might be just as well." How would you counsel this mother?

7. What would you do to turn the destructive antics of a gang of ten- and eleven-year-olds into constructive channels?

CHAPTER EIGHT *Looking toward adolescence*

1. As you recall the manner in which you received your own sex information, would you say it created in you a desirable or undesirable attitude toward the subject? Do you experience a feeling of embarrassment in connection with the discussion of this chapter? Try to explain to yourself the reasons for your own reactions to a discussion of this subject.

2. How would you answer a child of three who asked "Where do babies come from?" A child of six who asks "Where was I before I was born? When is the baby born?" A child of ten who asks "How can you tell if the baby is a boy or girl?"

3. How would you protect a child of seven for whom you felt responsible if you knew a sex pervert was abroad in your vicinity?

4. When should children be told the truth about sex? Who should do the telling? What preparation if any should there be? What attitude should be displayed?

5. According to his father, Paul at ten had never asked a single question about sex. What are some of the reasons that might explain this statement?

6. If questions have been dodged or wrong attitudes allowed to develop in early childhood, how can teacher or parent overcome the harm done?

7. In your opinion what responsibility for sex education does the school have? the home? the church?

8. How would you use the books on this subject recommended as suitable for children?

9. What attitude would you like a child of your own to have toward his body, its functions, and the reproduction of human beings?

CHAPTER NINE *Living with your children*

1. Even the best of parents or teachers make mistakes. It is the overall relationship that is most important. Describe the kind of "climate" in the home and in the school that is good for the child's social and emotional development.

2. Describe concrete ways in which parent-child and parent-teacher-child relationships affect children's physical, mental, and social well-being.

3. Why is it always wise to check first with a physician to see whether bodily ailments or behavior symptoms may possibly be due to physical causes? Give several examples of physical ailments that appear to have their sources in emotional or mental attitudes. Give several examples of the opposite—that is, mental or behavior symptoms that are caused by physical illnesses.

4. Why is the emotional atmosphere in the home and the school of vital importance to a child's healthy growth and development?

5. Some people think that the parents' rôle in homework is to aid the child in the task which the teacher has assigned. Some believe that it is important to urge the child to do better work, to keep him at the job and see that it is done perfectly. Others consider that parents should help by providing the child with many kinds of experiences that will give him a broader background for schoolroom learning. These experiences include reading to him if he is just beginning, taking him to see interesting things in his community, and encouraging him to observe his surroundings closely. What do *you* think the parents' part in homework should be?

6. Ruth doesn't like to read and refuses to do her schoolwork if it means reading. What points should her parents discuss with her teacher? With the school's guidance specialist? With the principal?

7. How would you go about finding out whether a child was having difficulty with his school work because he didn't know how to read well enough or because he was bored and didn't care to put forth the effort?

8. Joyce Crew is very fond of her teacher and would like her mother to invite Miss Lee to dinner. Mrs. Crew feels she doesn't know Miss Lee very well and that the teacher would construe such an invitation as "apple polishing." What do you think about Mrs. Crew's attitude?

9. What is your community doing to meet the after-school needs of children in the elementary grades? What is your P.T.A. doing to help?

10. Think back to your own elementary school

days. What system of reporting did your school use? Compare it with the system used by schools you know today. Discuss some of the recent improvements in reporting children's progress. What combinations of old and new methods seem to have merit? How valuable is the interview between parent and teacher? Should it, in your opinion, be an indispensable accompaniment to the Progress Report? Why or why not?

11. What are the reasons why some parents may be dissatisfied with letters and conferences in lieu of grades?

12. What are the things most parents want report cards to tell?

13. "The child's Progress Report ought to provide for two-way communication. Parents have as much to tell teachers about their children as teachers have to tell parents." Why is this statement so important? What are the educational principles that underlie it? How would you go about providing for two-way communication?

14. Which of these items should a parent be able to find out from his child's Progress Report? His progress in terms of his own capacities and abilities; progress in terms of achievements of his group; progress in terms of the particular society in which he lives.

15. Just as we all need feelings of security, so we all need feelings of adequacy. What can parents do to help a child feel adequate?

16. What are some situations and relationships that wound children's feelings?

17. We all agree that a child should know he is loved and accepted by his parents and teachers. But in what specific ways does this knowledge prepare him for the hard realities of the world?

18. "One of the most important tasks of parenthood is to help the child live at peace with himself, as well as with others. He must eventually be able to accept himself and to be the kind of person he can accept." Discuss the meaning of this statement. What parental attitudes and practices can assist each child in achieving these goals?

19. As you look back on your own childhood, what do you recall hurt your feelings most? How long did it take the hurt to wear off?

CHAPTER TEN *A plan for action*

1. How do you think the acceptance of the definition of health given in this chapter would affect the total elementary curriculum?

2. As a teacher, how would you enlist the co-operation of the parents whose child showed evidences of malnutrition?

3. As a parent, how would you enlist the aid of the school if you were having difficulty in getting your child to eat properly?

4. Why do you think training in safety is included in the plan for action?

5. Why is it necessary to provide learning experiences every year which develop concepts and attitudes about personal hygiene? about ways of meeting disappointment and failure and ways of working for happy feelings? about putting yourself in the other person's place?

6. There are two major types of maladjustment. Some children, in their efforts to conform, develop inner conflicts which may ultimately result in mental illness. Others resist the social requirements and may make adjustments which are at odds with society, becoming "behavior problems" at school and sometimes juvenile delinquents and criminals later. Which type was Johnny? (page 73) Patty? (page 55) Think of "model children" you know, and compare their method of adjusting with that of nonconforming children you know.

7. If you trace the development of concepts relating to growth throughout the years you will note an increasing relationship between physical growth, and mental and social well-being. Why is this?

8. Do you think it possible to carry out a plan of action of the kind outlined here without a basic knowledge of the growth patterns of all normal children?

9. How does the group discussion of common problems make possible a better knowledge of individual children's needs? How would you record and use such knowledge of a child's need for friends?

10. What is your opinion as to the value of good basic texts as an aid to the carrying out of this plan of action?

11. As a parent or teacher, how would you improve the plan outlined? What would you omit? What would you add? What new learnings would you include for twelve- and thirteen-year-olds? For adolescents?

12. How would you use films in such a plan? Stories of fiction in which characters meet various kinds of human problems?

13. As a parent or as a teacher, what steps could you take to put such a plan into action in your own particular situation?

For further study

BOOKS FOR TEACHERS, PARENTS, AND CHILDREN

ALDRICH, CHARLES A. and MARY M. *Babies Are Human Beings*. New York: Macmillan, 1938. An informal study of the progressive growth changes of children from infancy, noting the influences of social controls over the young child.

————. *Feeding Our Old-Fashioned Children*. New York: Macmillan, 1941. An interesting discussion of the relationship between facts of nutrition and the personality and behavior of children.

AMERICAN ASSOCIATION OF SCHOOL ADMINISTRATORS. *Education for Family Life*. Nineteenth Yearbook. Washington, D.C.: The Association is a department of the National Education Association, 1941.

————. *Health Education*. Washington, D.C.: National Education Association, 1941. A statement of the administrator's rôle in a school program of health education. Includes a discussion of the functions and preparation of school health personnel.

AMERICAN COUNCIL ON EDUCATION. *Helping Teachers Understand Children*. Washington, D.C.: American Council on Education, 1948. Procedures for studying child behavior. Many detailed observations and case studies.

AVERILL, LAWRENCE A. *The Psychology of the Elementary School Child*. New York: Longmans, Green, 1949. Anyone who reads this book will quickly be disabused of the idea that there is a single standard for all children, that they are very much alike or will all respond equally to the same instruction.

BACMEISTER, RHODA W. *Growing Together*. New York: D. Appleton-Century, 1947. A series of chapters dealing with problems of the care and management of children at various periods of their growth and development and as they are affected by the growth and development of a family life itself. Some of the material was first published in *Parents' Magazine*.

BAKER, HARRY JAY. *Introduction to Exceptional Children*. New York: Macmillan, 1944. For teachers who expect to specialize in some field of exceptional children, this book is designed to give an overall view of the entire field. Intended also as a reference book for school administrators, supervisors, principals, teachers in service, and others who deal with exceptional children. The large scope of the book makes it impossible to give full discussion of many topics.

BARUCH, DOROTHY. *Parents and Children Go to School*. Chicago: Scott, Foresman, 1939. The director of the preschool and parent-education department, Broadoaks, School of Education, Whittier College, California, gives an intimate, detailed account of its activities. The school has worked out a coordination of mental hygiene with nursery, kindergarten, and parent education.

————. *Parents Can Be People*. New York: D. Appleton-Century, 1944. A discussion of the reactions, conflicts, and attitudes of parents and children, from prenatal impressions through many of the perplexing problems of babyhood and childhood.

BARUCH, DOROTHY W., and REISS, OSCAR, M.D. *My Body and How It Works*. New York: Harper, 1934. A frank 12-page discussion of reproduction and the functioning of the reproductive organs—included as a phase of the total bodily physiology. Written in simple, understandable language and endorsed by numerous specialists and educators.

BAUER, W. W. *Stop Annoying Your Children*. Indianapolis: Bobbs-Merrill, 1947. Interesting, informal presentation of the everyday problems involved in living with children. Advice on how to bring up children, based on the principle that, perhaps, many of the problems to be faced are due to the faults of the parents and not the children.

BELL, EVELYN S., and FARAGON, ELIZABETH. *The New Baby*. Philadelphia: Lippincott, 1938. A photographic book for children aged three to five, on the mother's part in reproduction. Emphasis on cooperative family relationships. Will help parents begin the sex education of their children properly.

BIBBY, CYRIL. *How Life Is Handed On*. Emerson Books, Inc., 1947. An excellent book to put in the hands of preadolescents who are seeking to understand the problems of sex. A clear scientific treatment handled with skill and finesse. The story of reproduction in animals and humans, including information on courtship, mating, birth, and family life. Written in too elementary a style for children much above the seventh grade.

BIBER, BARBARA; MURPHY, LOIS B.; WOODCOCK, LOUISE P.; and BLACK, IRMA S. *Child Life in School: A Study of a Seven-Year-Old Group*. New York: Dutton, 1942. For teachers, parents, and social workers who believe that adults need to be listeners and learners themselves where children are concerned, this is an interesting and important text.

BRECKENRIDGE, MARIAN E., and VINCENT, ELIZABETH L. *Child Development*, 2nd ed. Philadelphia: Saunders, 1949. The primary task of this book is to trace the physical and psychological growth of children through the school years.

CHILD STUDY ASSOCIATION OF AMERICA. *Parents' Questions*. Rev. ed. New York: Harper, 1947. A collection of questions frequently asked by parents, with straightforward, helpful answers.

DAVIS, W. ALLISON, and HAVIGHURST, ROBERT J. *Father of the Man*. Boston: Houghton Mifflin, 1947. A scientific study of the effects of cultural environment on personality development. Very readable and illuminating. A "must" for those who seek to understand all the children of all the people.

D'EVELYN, KATHERINE E. *Individual Parent-Teacher Conferences*. New York: Teachers College, Columbia University, 1945. Reports of actual parent-teacher conferences, with analyses of the discussions.

DESCHWEINITZ, KARL. *Growing Up.*, 2nd ed. New York: Macmillan, 1935. Good, clear explanation of the process of being born and growing up; serves as a guide for elementary health and sex instruction.

FAEGRE, MARION L. *Your Own Story*. Minneapolis: Minnesota State Department of Health, 1943. Human reproduction explained in an "honest, simple, friendly" way. Includes a section for parents on the needs for and methods in sex education. To be read to small children.

FINE, BENJAMIN. *Our Children Are Cheated*. New York: Holt, 1947. Discussion of the status of American education, school housing, teachers and teaching, and the effect our neglect of education is having on American children.

GESELL, ARNOLD, and ILG, FRANCES L. *Infant and Child in the Culture of Today*. New York: Harper, 1943. A careful and detailed study of development in early childhood; emphasizes the influence of present social patterns on the behavior of children.

———. *The Child from Five to Ten*. New York: Harper, 1946. A companion volume for *Infant and Child in the Culture of Today*; contains a rich fund of information about the personality growth of children in the important years from five to ten.

GRUENBERG, SIDONIE M. *We, the Parents.*, Rev. ed. New York: Harper, 1948. The author has taken into account what scientists and practical experience—and even the war—have taught us about child development and children's needs and people's worries.

HECK, ARCH OLIVER. *Education of Exceptional Children*. New York: McGraw-Hill, 1940. Perhaps more comprehensive and thorough than any previously written book treating the field of special education.

HUNT, L. W. *The Child in the Home*. Prentice-Hall, 1939. Home and family-life series; deals with nutrition, child care, and hygiene.

HYMES, JAMES L., JR. *A Pound of Prevention*. New York: Mental Hygiene Committee, 1947. This small pamphlet presents a picture of the "war babies"—their problems and how to help them.

ISAACS, SUSAN. *The Children We Teach*. New York: Robert Brunner, 1932. Although written primarily for teachers, this book contains much that will be helpful for parents of children in the grades. Dr. Isaacs is writing for English audiences, but children are the same on both sides of the ocean. Her emphasis on individual differences is valuable and clearly discussed. Although published in 1932, this book is still recommended.

JERSILD, ARTHUR T. *Child Psychology*, 3rd ed. New York: Prentice-Hall, 1947. A discussion of the emotions of children; implications for education.

JOINT COMMITTEE ON HEALTH PROBLEMS IN EDUCATION, NEA AND AMA. *Health Education*. 4th ed., 1948. A comprehensive study of health education by a large committee of doctors, teachers, and related experts of the NEA and the AMA.

KELIHER, ALICE. *Life and Growth*. New York: D. Appleton-Century, 1938. An explanation of how one becomes an adult and how nature has provided for the reproduction and continuance of human life. A good book for adolescents.

LEVINE, MILTON I., and SELIGMANN, JEAN H. *The Wonder of Life*. New York: Simon & Schuster,

1940. For preadolescent and adolescent children. Simply written. Deals with fertilization, embryological development, birth, child care, multiple births, and heredity. Illustrated with drawings and photographs.

MacMURRAY, JOHN. *Reason and Emotion*. New York: D. Appleton-Century, 1938. Lectures on emotional education, personality, creative expression, and religion.

NATIONAL EDUCATION ASSOCIATION, DEPARTMENT OF SUPERVISORS AND DIRECTORS OF INSTRUCTION. *Mental Health in the Classroom*. Thirteenth Yearbook. Washington, D.C.: National Education Association, 1940.

NATIONAL EDUCATION ASSOCIATION AND AMERICAN MEDICAL ASSOCIATION, JOINT COMMITTEE ON HEALTH PROBLEMS IN EDUCATION. *Mental Hygiene in the Classroom*. Washington, D.C.: National Education Association, 1939. A booklet containing case studies and an analysis of common classroom situations, with suggestions for handling them.

PATRI, ANGELO. *How to Help Your Child Grow Up*. Chicago: Rand McNally, 1948. An extremely practical and understanding treatment of how to help children realize their highest potentialities in today's world.

PATTY, WILLARD W. *Teaching Health and Safety in Elementary Grades*. New York: Prentice-Hall, 1940.

PLANT, J. S. *Personality and the Cultural Pattern*. New York: Commonwealth Fund, 1937. Analyzes our culture with its effects on growing young people. Author considers the individual and his environment as interacting aspects of a single unity.

PRESTON, GEORGE. *The Substance of Mental Health*. New York: Rinehart, 1943. A small but invaluable book for those who are seeking a workable understanding of what is involved in mental health.

PRYOR, HELEN BRENTON. *As the Child Grows*. New York: Silver, Burdett, 1943. Develops the scientific basis of children's individual differences simply and clearly; gives many practical suggestions for handling the problems peculiar to the child at each stage of development. Good charts of normal weight for different body builds.

RENNIE, THOMAS A. C., and WOODWARD, LUTHER E. *Mental Health in Modern Society*. New York: Commonwealth Fund, 1948. A comprehensive treatment of this important subject for both parents and teachers.

ROGERS, JAMES F. *What Every Teacher Should Know about the Physical Conditions of Her Pupils*. Pamphlet 68, U.S. Office of Education. Washington, D.C.: U.S. Government Printing Office, 1945.

SHACTER, HELEN. *How Personalities Grow*. Bloomington, Illinois: McKnight and McKnight, 1949. How personalities grow and change and develop as individuals of all ages attempt to satisfy their social and emotional needs.

SPOCK, BENJAMIN. *Pocket Book of Baby and Child Care*. New York: Pocket Books, Inc., 1936. A handbook for parents and teachers; treats the basic problem of guiding child growth from birth to adulthood.

STRAIN, FRANCES B. *Being Born.* New York: D. Apple-ton-Century, 1937. The beginnings of life explained for young children. Excellent.

STRANG, RUTH. *Reporting to Parents.* New York: Teachers College, Columbia University, 1945. A helpful pamphlet setting forth specific procedures for reporting school progress, with criteria for evaluating and suggestions for new report forms.

TRAVIS, LEE EDWARD, and BARUCH, DOROTHY W. *Personal Problems of Everyday Life.* New York: D. Appleton-Century, 1941. Dealing with everyday mental and emotional ills, this volume serves as a first step toward understanding our own troubles.

WALLACE, EDYTHE THOMAS. *Pointers for Parents.* Oklahoma City: Crosby, 1946. Everyday problems which parents encounter in living with their children. *Do This—Not This* cartoons which set forth the problems are accompanied with explanations for behavior and suggestions for dealing with it.

WASHBURN, RUTH WENDELL. *Children Have Their Reasons.* New York: D. Appleton-Century, 1942. This book was written to emphasize and reëmphasize the fact that it is insight, not formulas or techniques or ready-made methods, that makes for the successful training of children.

WEILL, BLANCHE. *Through Children's Eyes.* New York: Island Press, 1940. True stories by a consultant psychologist which illustrate the child's conception of an adult world and show parents and educators the importance of understanding his viewpoint.

WHITMAN, HOWARD. *Let's Tell the Truth about Sex.* New York: Pellegrini, 1948. Gives parents an entire plan of education, step by step, starting with the very young child on through adolescence—when to start, what to say, and how to say it. Answers to the most common questions of children of different ages are carefully phrased according to age of the child.

WITTY, PAUL A., and SKINNER, CHARLES E. (eds.) *Mental Hygiene in Modern Education.* New York: Farrar and Rinehart, 1939. Trends in the fields of mental hygiene and child development are covered by 17 contributors. Among these are directors of psychoeducational clinics, consultants of guidance centers, university teachers, and others engaged in research in child growth.

WOLF, ANNA W. M. *Parents' Manual.* New York: Simon & Schuster, 1941. There are very few definite *do's* and *don'ts* in this book, but it is full of examples and suggestions which embody the fruits of years of experience with children.

YOUNG, P. T. *Motivation of Behavior.* New York: Wiley, 1936. Presents problems of motivation and their relation to personality development.

ZELIGS, ROSE. *Glimpses into Child Life.* New York: William Morrow, 1942. A comprehensive treatment of the twelve-year-old with many suggestions for studying and guiding the child of this age.

MAGAZINES

Child-Study—Child Study Association, 221 W. 57th Street, New York, New York

Childhood Education—Association for Childhood Education, 1201 16th Street, N. W., Washington, D.C.

Hygeia—American Medical Assn., 535 N. Dearborn Street, Chicago, Illinois

Parents' Magazine—The Parents Institute, 52 Vanderbilt Ave., New York, New York

National Parent-Teacher—600 S. Michigan Boulevard, Chicago, Illinois

PAMPHLETS

The following list of pamphlets can be ordered from the Association for Family Living, 28 E. Jackson Street, Chicago 4, Illinois.

1004 *Discipline Through Affection*—Aline B. Auerbach

1005 *Fundamental Needs of the Child, The*—Lawrence K. Frank

1010 *Jealousy and Rivalry in Children*—Child Study Assn. of America

1012 *Learning to Love*—Marie W. Piers and Edith G. Neiser

1013 *Making the Most of the Child's Heredity*—Alma H. Jones

1020 *Does Punishment Work?*—Gladys Gardner Jenkins

1023 *Character Begins at Home*—Gladys Gardner Jenkins

1116 *Should a Child Talk Back?*—Gladys Gardner Jenkins

1141 *Being a Good Parent*—James L. Hymes, Jr.

1202 *Discipline*—Ralph Ojemann

1205 *Kind of Parents Teachers Like, The*—Irvin C. Poley

1206 *Preadolescents—What Makes Them Tick?*—Fritz Redl

1253 *The Exceptional Child*—George D. Stoddard (Discusses the dull, the bright, and the specially talented children)

1257 *When a Child Learns Slowly*—Elsie H. Martens (For the retarded child)

1401 *Growing Up in the World Today*—Emily O. Clapp (For the adolescent)

1404 *Sex—the Life Force*—Irma Phorylles (For the adolescent)

1405 *Technique of Sex Information, The*—Fritz Redl

1406 *Understanding Sex*—Lester A. Kirkendall (For the adolescent)

1407 *When Children Ask about Sex*—Child Study Assn. of America

1410 *How to Tell Your Children about Sex*—James L. Hymes, Jr.

1904 *Facts Speak for Sex Education, The*—Lester A. Kirkendall and Mark Fleitzer

1919 *Ways and Means of Reaching Parents*—Jean Schick Grossman

The following pamphlets can be ordered at addresses listed:

From Hand to Mouth—Community Health Series, U.S. Government Printing Office, Washington, D.C.

SHACTER, HELEN. *Getting Along with Others.* Chicago: Science Research Associates, 1949. Addressed to young adolescents, this pamphlet gives suggestions for getting along with one's parents and other adults as well as the peer group.

THORMAN, GEORGE. *Toward Mental Health*. Public Affairs Pamphlet, No. 120. Public Affairs Committee, Inc., 22 E. 38th Street, New York 16, New York

Child Development

Children Learning by Experience. British Information Service, 30 Rockefeller Plaza, New York. The unrehearsed action of children as they really are.

Yale Films of Child Development, Encyclopaedia Britannica Films, Inc. Taken at Yale Classes of Child Development in Collaboration with Dr. Arnold Gesell. Has accompanying Guide.

Community Health

How to Prevent Disease—contamination of water and milk supplies. Bray Studios, Inc.

Keep 'Em Out—Economic damage and health hazards caused by rats. American Medical Assn.

Kids Must Eat—promoting better nutrition among America's 30 million school children. U.S. Department of Agriculture.

Milk—milk production under hygienic control, from dairy farm to consumer. United World Films, Inc.

Mosquito—life cycle of the mosquito and methods of combating it. Encyclopaedia Britannica Films, Inc.

Sanitation and the Rural Home—safe water supply in city and country. National Motion Picture Co.

Vandals of the Night—methods of rat control in rural and urban areas. Visual Education Service.

Water, Friend or Enemy—how water can be a true friend. Institute of Inter-American Affairs.

Emotional Development

Mealtime Can Be a Happy Time—effects of disposition on digestion. Wisconsin State Board of Health.

This Is Robert—a study of personality growth in a preschool child. Audio-Visual Aids Library, State College, Pa.

Problem Children—two preadolescent boys, one an aggressive "show-off" and the other a shy introvert. Ohio State Division of Mental Health and Ohio State University.

The Feeling of Hostility—a case history of Clare from childhood to early maturity in an atmosphere of frustration. Clare achieves "success" as her adjustments take the form of striving for academic and professional accomplishment, but the film poses the problem of evaluating the adequacy of her adjustment. National Film Board of Canada.

Physical Health and Growth

Breathing—structure, function, and care of lungs. Encyclopaedia Britannica Films, Inc.

By Experience I Learn—case study of child from nine to eighteen months featuring growth stages—especially good for adult groups. University of Wisconsin, Bureau of Visual Instruction.

Food and Growth—animal experiments illustrating results of food deficiencies, stressing milk. Encyclopaedia Britannica Films, Inc.

I Never Catch a Cold—preventing and treating the common cold. Coronet Instructional Films, Inc.

It Doesn't Hurt—results of improper care of teeth and instructions on correct methods. Coronet.

Posture Habits—body structure and importance of good posture. Coronet.

Your Children's Ears, Your Children's Eyes, Your Children's Teeth—structure, function, care. British Information Services.

Your Ears, Your Eyes, Your Teeth—structure, function, care. Young America Films, Inc.

Reproduction

Human Growth—factual presentation of reproduction. Good for classes from seventh grade on. University of Oregon.

Safety

Crimes of Carelessness—fire damage and means of prevention. National Board of Fire Underwriters.

Let's Be Safe at Home—preventative measures for home accidents. Portafilms.

You and Your Bicycle. Progressive Pictures.

ADDRESSES OF FILM SOURCES

American Medical Association, Committee on Medical Motion Pictures, 535 N. Dearborn Street, Chicago 10, Illinois.

Bray Studios, Inc., 729 Seventh St., New York 19, New York.

British Information Services, 39 S. LaSalle St., Chicago, Illinois.

Coronet Instructional Films, Inc., 65 E. South Water St., Chicago 1, Illinois.

Encyclopaedia Britannica Films, Inc., 20 N. Wacker Drive, Chicago 6, Illinois.

Institute of Inter-American Affairs, 499 Pennsylvania Ave., N. W., Washington 25, D.C.

National Board of Fire Underwriters, Bureau of Communication Research, 13 E. 37th St., New York 16, New York.

National Film Board of Canada, 84 E. Randolph St., Chicago 1, Illinois.

National Motion Picture Company, West Main St., Mooresville, Indiana.

Portafilms, P. O. Box 752, Glendale, California.

Progressive Pictures, 6351 Thornhill Drive, Oakland, California.

United World Films, Inc., RCA Bldg., 30 Rockefeller Center, New York 20, New York.

University of Oregon Medical School, Division of Social Hygiene Education, Portland, Oregon.

U.S. Department of Agriculture, Office of Motion Pictures, Washington 25, D.C.

Visual Education Service, Michigan Department of Health, Lansing 4, Michigan.

Wisconsin State Board of Health, State Office Bldg., Madison 2, Wisconsin.

Young America Films, Inc., 183 41st St., New York 17, New York.

Index

Docility, hiding maladjustment, 73-77, 126-127

Dramatic play, as safety valve, 144, 145; at five, 23; at six, 47; at seven, 65; at eight, 85

Drawing, as safety valve, 145

Dreams, following too exciting radio programs or movies, 66, 85

Dull child, ways teacher can help, 109-111, 146

Eagerness, at seven, 65; at eight, 81; to learn at six, 48

Ears, concepts relating to, 166, 168, 170, 172, 175, 177

Eight-year-olds, 80-95; awareness of individual differences by, 87; concepts for health and personal development for, 169-171; dentition of, 81; interests of, 82-87; muscular coordination of, 82; need of, for mother's support, 80-81; physical development of, 81-82. See End Sheet

Eleven-year-olds, concepts for health and personal development for, 176-178

Emotional adjustment, affected by overweight, 91; improved by teacher-parent cooperation, 58-61, 140-141, 151-154; in preadolescence, 116-117, 118-119; not always on par with mental or physical, 41

Emotional needs, 144-146; met on playground, 151

Emotions, learning to cope with, 158, 161

Encouragement, as factor in adjustment, 92; importance of at six, 48-49; need for, at seven, 68

"Enemy" at eight, 83

Environmental factors, 12-13, 55-56, 58

Eraser age, 69

Excursions, to enrich learning, 164

Exercise, concepts relating to, 167, 168, 170, 173, 175, 178

Expectations, too high, 10, 15, 16, 34-37, 50, 58-61, 125-128

Experiments, to enrich learning, 164

Eyes, concepts relating to, 166, 168, 170, 172, 175, 177; readiness of, for close work, 20, 81, 97

Eye-hand coordination, at five, 20; at six, 40; at seven, 62; at eight, 81; at nine, 97

Eye-rubbing in seven-year-olds, 62

Fairness, at nine, 100

Fairy tales, interest in at five, 22; at seven, 65; at eight, 85; at nine, 99

Far-sightedness, 20, 40, 95

Fatigue, at five, 21; at seven, 63; at ten, 116

Favoritism, effect of, 92

Fearfulness, in girl with reading disability, 95; in emotionally disturbed child, 125; overcome by wise guidance, 60-61

Feelings, danger from suppressing, 145-146; learning to deal with, 158; relation of, to learning, 159; safety valves for, 144-145

Fighting, for rights, 66

Finger-painting, as safety valve, 145

First aid, concepts relating to, 168

Five-year-olds, 18-37; concepts for health and personal development for, 166-167; conformity of, 26; food preferences of, 24-25; individuality of, 18; interests of, 20-26; language development of, 23-24; physical development of, 19-20. See End Sheet

Food, concepts relating to, 167, 168-169, 170, 173, 175, 178; preferences at five, 24-25

Food intake, and emotional cravings, 92; in preadolescence, 123-124

Foster-home placement, 79

Four-year-old. See End Sheet

Fresh air, concepts relating to, 167, 168, 170, 173, 175, 178

Friendship quiz, 163

Function and structure of body, concepts relating to, 171, 173-174, 176, 178

Games, fondness for at eight, 82-83, 84; at nine, 98, 105; at ten, 118; interest spot for, 147

Gangs, at eight, 84; at nine, 98, 102; at ten, 114, 117, 135; redirection of undesirable, 102

Gesell, 14, 26, 69

Getting dirty, as safety valve, 145

Give-and-take, in the classroom, 33, 141; in group discussion, 160; on playground, 151

Grooming, concepts relating to, 167

Group activities, importance of, at five, 23; at six, 47; at eight, 84-85; at nine, 98, 102-103; for insecure child, 32-33, 61

Group discussion, developing skill in, 160; for personal development, 159-163; values of, 161

Growth, affected by environmental factors, 14-16; at each age, 19-20, 40-41, 44-45, 62-63, 81, 96-97, 112-114, 115-116; needs and patterns, 10-17, 112-116, 119, 158; of girls ahead of boys, 19, 97, 112; uneven, 13, 41, 120, 134

Guidance center, 77-79, 90-92, 150

Guilt, in model child, 75-76; for feelings, 145-146

Handedness, 20; in twins, 71-72

Handicapped, child, 88-89, 149; parents, 151

Hands, use of, at five, 21; at six, 43-44; at seven, 64; at nine, 97, 104

Health, broader definition of, 157; concepts contributing toward mental, 166, 167-168, 169, 171-172, 174, 176-177; concepts contributing toward physical, 166-167, 168-169, 170-171, 172-174, 174-176, 177-178; concepts contributing toward social, 166, 168, 169, 172, 174, 177; materials for teaching, 157-158; needs in classroom, 142-144; records, 93

Height, in preadolescence 115, 124, 158

Hitting, as a safety valve, 145

Hobbies, at eight, 85-86; at nine, 104-105; interest spot for, 147

Hostility, as result of new baby, 35-37

Identification, at six, 48-49; at eight, 84; with adult in early adolescence, 135

Independence, at five, 24-26, 34; at six, 46; at seven, 68, 70; at nine, 99, 100-101; at ten, 114, 117; in early adolescence, 130-131; need for, 15-16, 130-131

Individualistic play, at six, 47

Individuality, 6; at five, 18; at nine, 99

Innate factors, 11-13, 17, 58

Insecurity, effects of, 58-60, 77-79, 106-108, 125-128

Interest group helpful at ten, 117-119; interest spots in classroom, 146-148

|

PHYSICAL DEVELOPMENT

Growth still slow and steady; arms lengthening, hands growing larger.

Eyes ready for both near and far vision; near-sightedness may develop this year.

Permanent teeth continuing to appear.

Large muscles still developing, small muscles better developed too.

Poor posture may develop during this year.

CHARACTERISTIC REACTIONS

Often careless, noisy, argumentative, but alert, friendly, interested in people.

More dependent on Mother again, less so on teacher; sensitive to criticism.

New awareness of individual differences.

Eager, more enthusiasm than wisdom; higher accident rate.

Gangs beginning; best friends of same sex.

Allegiance to peer group instead of to the adult in case of conflict.

Greater capacity for self-evaluation.

Much spontaneous dramatization; also ready for simple classroom dramatics.

Understanding of time and use of money.

Responsive to group activities, both spontaneous and adult-supervised.

Fond of team games, comics, radio, adventure stories, collections of all kinds.

SPECIAL NEEDS

Much praise and encouragement from adults.

Must still be reminded of his responsibilities.

Wise guidance and channeling of his interests and enthusiasms, rather than domination or overcritical standards.

A best friend.

Experience of "belonging" to peer group; opportunity to identify with others of same age and sex.

Adult-supervised groups also; planned after-school activities.

Exercise of both large and small muscles.

PHYSICAL DEVELOPMENT

Slow, steady growth continues; girls forge further ahead, some children reach the plateau preceding growth spurt of pre-adolescence.

Lungs and digestive and circulatory systems almost mature; heart especially subject to strain.

Teeth may need straightening; first and second bicuspids appearing.

Eye-hand coordination good; hands ready for crafts and shop work.

Eyes almost adult size; ready for near work with less strain.

CHARACTERISTIC REACTIONS

Decisive, responsible, dependable, reasonable, strong sense of right and wrong.

Individual differences distinct and clear; abilities apparent.

Capable of prolonged interest; often makes plans and goes ahead on his own.

Gangs strong and of one sex only, of short duration and changing membership.

Perfectionistic; wants to do well, but loses interest if discouraged or pressured.

Interested less in fairy tales and fantasy, more in his community and country and in other countries and peoples.

Loyalty to his country and pride in it.

Much time spent in talk and discussion; often outspoken and critical of adults.

Much arguing over fairness in games.

Wide discrepancies in reading ability.

SPECIAL NEEDS

Active rough and tumble play.

Friends and membership in a group.

Training in skills, but without pressure.

Reasonable explanations; no talking down to him; definite responsibility.

Frank answers to questions about the coming physiological changes.